Post-Contemporary Interventions    Series Editors: Stanley Fish and Fredric Jameson

DUKE UNIVERSITY PRESS   Durham and London 1992

# TEXT

The

Genealogy

of an

Antidisciplinary

Object

*

John Mowitt

© 1992 Duke University Press

All rights reserved

Printed in the United States of America

on acid-free paper ∞

Library of Congress Cataloging-

in-Publication Data appear on the

last printed page of this book.

\*   **For Nine**

# ✳ Contents

# * Acknowledgments

As I write these words the fate of one of the two departments at the University of Minnesota with which I am affiliated hangs in the balance. As my colleagues and I have struggled to salvage our department, we have persistently been challenged to justify the need to exist as an institutionally organized collectivity. I can think of no better justification than the existence of this book—a book which bears testimony on every page to the dialogic vitality of the community within which it arose. It is thus fitting that in acknowledging those who have contributed to the emergence of this book I begin by identifying my colleagues (past and present) in Humanities and Comparative Studies in Discourse and Society: John Archer, Réda Bensmaïa, Lisette Josephides, Richard Leppert, Bruce Lincoln, George Lipsitz, Susan MacClary, Jochen Schulte-Sasse, Gary Thomas and Hernán Vidal.

I would also like to acknowledge the financial support of the Graduate School at the University of Minnesota which, through two successive "grants-in-aid" (1987 and 1988), enabled me and my research assistant to gather the archival materials (books, magazines, journals, films, musical scores, and photographs) that went into the preparation of the book. Without this material "infrastructure" it would obviously never have come together. In this regard I owe specific thanks to Editions Albatros (p. 157) and Harcourt, Brace and Jovanovich (pp. 198–99) for kindly permitting me to reproduce photographically materials from their publications in this volume.

This is also the proper context for extending my gratitude to Michael Metcalf of the Western European Area Studies Program at the University of Minnesota and Rob Kroes of the Institute of American Studies at the University of Amsterdam who, through the Amsterdam Exchange, gave me the opportunity to present the early stages of my research to the students and faculty at the University of Amsterdam in September 1987. This book is certainly better than it would have been without their interventions. Also, I want to thank Ellen Messer-Davidow and David Shumway who invited me to present a portion of my research at the GRIP conference convened in Minneapolis during the spring 1989, where the animated character of our discussions helped to define the argument of the book.

As with all such projects certain special people have played often unanticipated but crucial roles and their contributions deserve separate acknowledgment. Thus, I want to thank John Brenkman for "putting the idea in my head"; Keith Cohen for diagnosing my acute synaesthesia; David Hayman for sharing with me his network of intellectual contacts in Paris; Marty Roth for his warm and unfailing enthusiasm throughout; Jonathan Arac, David Bathrick, Paul Bové, and Mark Poster for their meticulous and provocative engagements with the book in typescript. And, of course, very special acknowledgments are due to the *many* graduate students whose attentive participation in my seminars forced me to think harder and more carefully than I otherwise would have. Their contribution is too fundamental to risk overlooking any of their names.

Lastly, I want to acknowledge the people at Duke University Press— Reynolds Smith, Emily Young, and especially Jean Brady—all of whom have greatly facilitated the anguishing labor of bringing this book into print. As a result of our many interactions I think I have, at last, actually begun to read what I write—a task considerably more difficult than it might otherwise seem.

# ✳ Introduction: The Two Texts

**I**

This is a book about the text (*le texte*). As such, it is something of a paradox for, as we shall see, the text has been theorized as the mode of symbolic production whose enabling conditions mark the closure of the sociotechnological era of the book.[1] Rather than conclude, however, that this book ought to be written quickly—so as to squeak past the millennial turnstile—it seems much more prudent to exploit the tactical options latent within this paradox. Obviously, either the text's relation to the book has been inadequately theorized (you are, after all, holding a book about the text in your hands), or, and this is the angle that will be played out in what follows, the text's theorization is unfinished—hence the prolongation of the era of the book. But what can this mean? In what sense can a theory be either finished or unfinished?

In Karl Marx's second thesis on Feuerbach we are invited to consider the moment of truth as the point at which theory is finished. Characteristically, this moment arises for Marx when a theory is "proven," as he says, in practice, that is, when class analysis is rendered "true" through the proletarian seizure of power. What remains attractive about this proposition, in spite of all the caution we have learned to observe when brandishing about terms like "truth" and "power," is that it refuses to separate theory from history without thereby conflating the two. The project of this book reflects an acknowledgment of this refusal which I elaborate—not by seeking its truth in a now indefinitely forestalled proletarian revolution, but by engaging the theoretical discourse on textuality in a manner designed to accentuate its historical character.

On the one hand, this implies that the history of the text must, to some extent, be fabricated—and by that I mean both written and *made* up. In failing to do so we risk sacrificing all the power historical discourse has to estrange us from that which is most familiar, namely, the apparent fixity of the present. On the other hand, in fabricating this history I, in effect, force theoretical discourse, and specifically the various theories of textuality, to become a site for the conflictual formation of a collective memory. Since, I would argue, what we believe to have happened to us bears concretely on what we are prepared to do with ourselves both now and in the future, the formation of such a memory is inseparable from historical, and ultimately political, practice. Thus, as the present theoretical status of the text is historicized, the notion of the text is disclosed to be a tool whose critical reappropriation is meant to alter the way both academic and nonacademic intellectuals engage the conditions of their practice. Perhaps an alteration of this scale may indeed hasten the closure of the era of the book.

If I speak then of "finishing" the theorization of the text, I do so in full awareness that I am necessarily proposing to fabricate history both past and present. My aim here is not to lay the text to rest, to consign it to oblivion, but rather to make its emergence some twenty-five years ago worthwhile. If the realization of such an aim turns out to require that a certain reading of the text be abandoned, then it will be necessary to clarify how such a reading has functioned institutionally to compromise the emergence of a more productive notion of textuality. By the same token, regardless of how effective this task of clarification turns out to be, my effort to finish theorizing the text will in no way suspend discussion of it. Instead, this project seeks to shift the orientation of what discussion there has been, precisely in order to spare us the energy of repeating old arguments. Thus, before going any further, it is necessary to delineate precisely which text is at issue here.[2] Once this is clarified, it will be possible to elaborate further the general aims of this project, particularly as these engage the issue of the relation between theoretical practice and cultural history.

**II**

As my chapter title implies, the task of delineation will not be an easy one, for the very notion of textuality upon which I propose to focus is one that is structured by an irreducible ambivalence. This ambivalence cannot simply be described, it must be engaged. By that I mean, its role in the determination of the "definition" of textuality cannot be separated from what makes the text worth struggling over in the present. Given then, that this ambivalence demands our attention, let us move to discover exactly how it figures within the notion of the text at issue here, namely, the semiological (as opposed to either the philological or phenomenological) text. Thankfully, this text has actually been "defined." As such, it would no doubt be prudent to initiate the task proposed here with a reading of Oswald Ducrot's and Tzvetan Todorov's *Encyclopedic Dictionary of the Sciences of Language* wherein the text figures as an entry.[3]

Printed in 1972 by the very publishing house that had long been sponsoring research on the text, this encyclopedia immediately assumed its place within a French tradition of materializing and thus instituting intellectual innovation that Robert Darnton, in his superb book on *L'Encyclopédie*, dates from the mid-eighteenth century with what he calls the "embodiment of the Enlightenment."[4] The recognition of this tradition that occurred in the French reception of the *Dictionary* took a peculiar, though perhaps predictable (given the intellectual context), form. Jean-René Ladmiral, writing in the respected *Quinzaine Littéraire*, titled his review of the *Dictionary* "Le vocabulaire de la linguistique."[5] Upon reading the review one realizes that its title is an allusion to Jean Laplanche's and Jean-Baptiste Pontalis's extremely influential *Vocabulary of Psychoanalysis*, a book which Ladmiral argues brings to a close, at least at the methodological level, the sort of tradition delineated by Darnton. This book is invoked in the review because Ladmiral is concerned to show that Ducrot and Todorov fall short of the *Vocabulary*, despite the fact that their object, the science of linguistics, should have permitted them to avoid doing so. What is striking about Ladmiral's reading of the *Dictionary* is that, while he is right to underscore the interesting form of self-reflexivity that develops within the book, he curiously fails to consider the relation within it between certain of its entries and the structure of the book as a whole, divided as it is between its body and the appendix. Significantly, since the methodological critique of linguistics as a closed referential system is key to Ladmiral's admiration of Laplanche's and Pontalis's book, he chooses not to discuss the fact that "the text" actually appears twice (it is the only entry to do so)—once in the body and again in the appendix. In the second entry (that of the appendix) the text is explicitly aligned with a theoretical outdistancing of linguistics. What we thus have in the very structure of the book is an attempt to organize and thereby bound a difference that, as we shall see, belongs fundamentally to textuality. Needless to say this attempt fails, yet it fails in ways that illuminate what is indeed at stake in the semiological text. In a peculiar way, the *Dictionary* could be said to *stage* the text better than it actually *defines* it.

As I have said, the *Dictionary* contains two entries on "the text." Aside from the complications this poses at the level of ordinary consultation (given that no distinction is made at the orthographical level, one might well be left with the problem of trying to decide which is the relevant entry for his or her purposes), the "definition" offered at the initial entry only minimally conforms to what we might take to be a commonsensical (i.e., philological) notion of a text. To some extent, of course, this has to do with the specialized nature of the *Dictionary*, but this is a small consolation once we realize that it is only in a book such as this that we are likely to find any sort of information on the text whose controversial status drove us to the *Dictionary* in the first place. This initial difficulty is complicated as soon as we start reading *either* entry since it turns out that, in accordance with standard lexicographical procedure, they refer to one another. This produces more than a moment's hesitation, because once again it becomes difficult to shake the impression that the text is not, after all, defined in one entry or the other and, instead, is to be understood as somehow suspended between the two—hence my evocation of the book's staging of the concept. Perhaps this is why Ladmiral chose to overlook this peculiarity of the book? Nevertheless, as we shall soon see, it is only by consulting the second definition and reading it up against the first that this moment of indecision takes on its significance for the concept of textuality. As a consequence, let us trace how the first, "standard" (at least from the standpoint of linguistics) meaning of the text hollows out a semantic domain that requires the supplemental appendix.

Ducrot and Todorov begin their first entry by indicating how the concept of the text responds to a triple deficiency. Linguistics, rhetoric, and stylistics have each in their own way inadequately sought to theorize the *unit* generated by one's use of an abstract system such as language. Or, put in a perhaps more familiar terminology, these three approaches have each failed to account for the specificity of the expressive vehicle. Into this "gap" ("*un vide*" as they call it) the authors wedge the text. As such, the text is to be understood as a derivative or secondary system characterized by the properties of autonomy and closure. It is secondary in the sense that the text depends for its formal features on a preexisting system, namely, the language constituting its repository of signs. And it is closed or autonomous in the sense that the text embodies a particular configuration of the primary system that, while conditioned by that system, nevertheless marks it with a pragmatic instance irreducible to the system. The text is, like an actual utterance, an event in the history of the system. To this extent, Ducrot's and Todorov's definition reformulates in linguistic categories the substance of the philological notion of textuality. What these accounts share is precisely this notion of closure, or materially defined limits, and in fact, though Ducrot and Todorov do not say as much, one could plausibly argue that it is the very tradition of textual criticism that is pressuring them to posit "the text" as the appropriate term for what could conceivably have gone by other names. As if to obscure this fact (after all, novelty must refuse to compromise), their discussion segues directly into a lengthy consideration of narrative where the preoccupations of philology seem utterly out of place.

Ducrot and Todorov pursue a double strategy in their treatment of narrative. On the one hand, they use it to illustrate and thus concretize their discussion of the text. To this end, they emphasize how the characteristic closure of the text derives from an analyst's reduction of an utterance (say, a folktale) to a set of rather simple grammatical propositions that constitute the relations among the subjects and objects of the utterance. The text is thus defined as the finite system of codes coordinating the various propositions activated by the core set of narrative materials. On the other hand, and this is made clear in the examples they offer, Ducrot and Todorov use their discussion of narrative to problematize the very category of narrative. That is to say, by showing how narrative effects (including, of course, "reading pleasure") are subject to the functioning of a specifically *textual* system, they are contributing to the general demystification of narrative art that was launched considerably earlier by the Russian Formalists. If one follows only the first leg of this double strategy, it becomes easy to read the text of linguistics as merely a customized version of the philological text. However, acknowledging the existence of both legs allows one to see how the text is also being used to situate literary narrative in a broader framework—one that utterly compromises its formal integrity. As one might have anticipated, it is precisely at this ambivalent juncture that the otherwise standard linguistic account of the text is interrupted by another text—the text of semiology.

The double strategy sketched above leads to the following dilemma. If the critique of narrative depends upon a demonstration of its derivation from a system, and this system (i.e., the analytically generated text) is revealed to be an appendage of language understood linguistically, then what is the status of the linguistic account of language once we grant that an acknowledgment of the *limits* of this account was the point of departure for the discovery of the textual system in the first place? It would appear that conceptualizing the text, even in narrowly linguistic terms, confronts linguistic science with the task of rethinking its own account of language. Without such a rethinking, the gain sought by situating narrative within language might well be sacrificed to a perfectly traditional account of literary art based on an Humboldtian model of language.[6] It is precisely in order to avoid such a possibility that Ducrot and Todorov insist upon the importance of the semiological inflection of linguistics which, instead of protecting them from a rethinking of language, requires it. However, more than simply provoking such a rethinking, semiology in France during the early seventies had made sufficient institutional headway to effect a profound transformation of the way language was conceptualized, and it is precisely this change that Ducrot and Todorov attempt to acknowledge in their appendix to the *Dictionary*. There, under the general heading of "Towards a Critique of the Sign," is where we find the text which is, apparently, not one, but which is, nonetheless, the one I am interested in.

Earlier I indicated that the two entries on the text refer to one another. The consequences of this for the integrity of the first entry have now been detailed, so let us turn to a description of this dynamic at work within the second entry, keeping in abeyance just a bit longer the task of specifying the general significance of the semiological text.

The second entry on the text is written, presumably in acknowledgment of its irreducibly interdisciplinary character, by the philosophically trained editor François Wahl who organizes his definition of the term around the notion of "productivity." This term, which was introduced into critical debates by Julia Kristeva (cf., part two), can be understood, at least initially, to operate within the conceptual field opened by the *Dictionary* as a means to rethink the notion of creativity. If we return briefly to the first entry and recall that the text was defined there as the finite set of codes actualized in a particular unit of narrative, then its relation to creativity is not difficult to understand, since one of the enduring habits of European cultural criticism has been its tendency to connect actualization and subjectivity. What the science of linguistics thus appears to be compensating for in its recognition of the text is a problem central to the phenomenological meditation on the text, namely, to what extent does the text stand in for the agency of utterance altogether? However, lest we assume that the parallel implicitly established by the notion of productivity between the specificity of a text and the more traditional unity of the author in fact reduces the former to the latter, it is worth remembering that the text (even in its standard linguistic sense) requires the sort of reconceptualization of language that raises serious questions about the coherence of the author as a model of literary agency. Consequently, rather than abandoning the question of agency altogether, the theorists referred to by Wahl (all of whom, at the time, were affiliated with the quarterly, *Tel Quel*) develop another way of designating the instance of actualization, namely, as productivity.

However, as one might expect, productivity sublates the notion of creativity by outdistancing it on both ends. On the one hand, it "de-instrumentalizes" language by implicating it in the structural formation of the human subject. Thus, the actualization of language is no longer seen as an instance of intentional expression through the *instrument* of language, but rather as an instance of cultural formation where human beings are subjected to language's codes and modes of operation. Though often confused with a denial of subjectivity (in the sense of a "free" will), this notion of cultural formation instead resituates the conditions of this freedom in the structural instabilities of the fissured (i.e., post-Freudian) subject. The gain, of course, is that one can preserve the element of play at stake in the notion of a free will, while not reducing language to a mere instrument manipulated by an impossibly sovereign subject.

On the other hand, the appeal to the notion of productivity "de-transcendentalizes" language both by underscoring the way actualized units redraw the boundaries of what can be ascribed to its domain and by indicating that the domain of language is, as I have already suggested, internally riven by forces (i.e., labor and desire) that are not subsummable within it. Implicit here, of course, is the idea that actualization cuts both ways, that is, that when a language system precipitates into a text (in the so-called standard linguistic sense) the system itself is fissured by a practical configuration which ruins its transcendental coherence. What is nevertheless preserved here about the closure of the text, insofar as it is capable of so affecting language, is a commitment to the integrity, and ultimately the power, of the phenomenal instance of actualization— a commitment that semiology shares with philology without embracing the latter's investment in tradition and the original voices that animate it. By the same token, if actualization also participates in the subjection of human agency, then the closure of the text can only be understood as a mutable effect of a social configuration that embraces language and its various actualizations, and not as an ontologically grounded formal property. In short, the closure of the text is coordinated with the socially constructed perception of its limits. Productivity, as an aspect of textuality, thus permits one to maintain the notion of a systemic conditioning of aesthetic, as well as ordinary, experience without either reifying language as an instrument or sacrificing human agency to the mechanics of subjection. It enables one to situate the phenomenological drama of "expression" within a sociohistorical configuration that reaches into the depths of human agency while nevertheless remaining unsettled.

Though much remains to be specified concerning the text's status as a mode of productivity, certain summary observations are in order at this juncture. Beyond the notion of the text as a logical configuration or system, the second text, if you will, is characterized by the emphasis it places on the *conditions* that enable the text to serve in the restricted linguistic capacity given priority in the first entry. As such, the second entry underscores the limits of the text as a unit or event of actualization, both by disclosing the presuppositions about language that support such a notion and by establishing the irreducible character of the processes exterior to language as a system that nevertheless take place within language as a means of communication. This "inner exterior" of language is the complex topography of actualization—a phenomenon evoked by Wahl in many ways, perhaps most notably in his persistent recourse to the figure of "gaps" ("*écarts*") introduced into the discourse of linguistic science by the textual sense of productivity. Understandable either in the sense of conceptual shortcomings or in the sense of structural absenses (cf., Iser), these gaps function within the *Dictionary* to motivate the referential spiral of lexicography.

Let us quickly trace the configuration of these gaps. As we have seen, the first entry on the text authorizes itself by identifying a gap within linguistics that can be filled by the subsequently elaborated notion of the text. The argument of this entry turns on a critique of linguistics—a critique which has generated, among other things, a competing notion of the text. Instead of imploding upon itself, the entry displaces this latter notion, shoring up its own authority by promising, in the name of lexicographical comprehensiveness, to address the competing notion of the text in an appendix. The second entry on the text opens by referring to the promisory rhetoric of the first, and then it gingerly (one could hardly find a more self-consciously articulated "definition") proceeds to indicate all the various ways in which the text as productivity executes the critique of linguistics by introducing an array of gaps (i.e., the subject fissured by language, the language system fissured by actualization, etc.) within it.

Upon reading both entries, one is struck by the fact that it is the effect upon linguistics of the "critique of the sign" presented in the second entry that actually founds the move authorizing the first entry, that is, the move to introduce the text into the gap or deficiency discovered within linguistic science. Moreover, and this is why the significance of the difficult relation between the entries is only legible from the vantage point of the second entry, the text (understood as productivity) designates the *general* state of affairs that prompts the first entry, if not the entire *Dictionary* project. In other words, it is what is at stake in the issues explicitly raised by the second entry that in fact provokes the encyclopedic gesture and thus serves as the historical motivation for both definitions.

Now, if we grant Darnton's political reading of the tradition inaugurated by *L'Encyclopédie*, then even if Ducrot's and Todorov's project participates in its closure, it would not be imprudent to conclude that their dictionary was also written at a time of crisis, precisely in order to seize the opportunities made available within such a moment. A hypothesis like this might well explain why the referential spiral between the two entries on the text is fraught with such acute metalexicographical tension. Of course, what is implied by such an hypothesis is that the *Dictionary*, as an institutional embodiment structured in the manner I have detailed, is a symptom of the very struggle this book is seeking to participate in. In fact, one might even go so far as to say that the *Dictionary* shows acute signs of appendicitis, that is, its body and the science of linguistics that oversees it, are being attacked by an organ that is at once necessary to their constitution and expendable: the second text.

Obviously, the editors always could have proceeded otherwise, and as a consequence their strategic choice is interesting. Rather than brazenly delete the text entry altogether, a displacement is effected which involves generating two texts: one which signals the necessity of a critique of linguistics it does not execute and another whose very existence constitutes such a critique. Even if one chooses to emphasize the generosity of Editions du Seuil in offering a group of relatively young intellectuals a legitimate forum for their activities (and this was an important gesture indeed), it is difficult to ignore the fact of the appendix which, by virtue of its generic character, cannot fail to pose the problem of supplementation, thus underscoring both the arbitrary and the obligatory character of its inclusion.[7] Consequently, I do not think that the tensions identified in the *Dictionary* can be rendered benign by appealing to the idea of a crass promotional strategy on the part of its publisher despite the friendship between Wahl and Barthes. These tensions would appear to have a great deal more to do with the challenge posed to the "institution" of the dictionary by the very concept of the text. As underscored above, the text is a contested terrain, and those who address it necessarily assume political positions in order to do so. The accent on productivity within the notion of the semiological text raises issues which are undeniably threatening, not only to competing notions of the text, but even to the institutions fostering research upon it. Nevertheless, the urgent questions have yet to be posed, much less answered: what is the character of this threat?, what is at stake in entering the struggle over a "definition" of textuality? To broach a response to these questions and thereby begin to clarify what the attempt to "finish" the theorization of the semiological text might involve, it is necessary to address those who have interpreted the ambivalence it embodies as a threat to political criticism as such. After all, there is no point in setting aside the philological or phenomenological models of textuality for an alternative that has conceivably renounced the critical moment of criticism.

## III

This book then is about the semiological text. It is the one that emerges during the mid-sixties and early seventies around the *Tel Quel* group in Paris. As we shall see, this text is also the one that has not only prompted the production of an encyclopedic dictionary, but more importantly, it has provoked the return to the referent (be it historical, social, or autobiographical) that defines much contemporary critical theory. In fact, it is the text's relation to this latter issue that bears most urgently on the question of whether its historicization is worth the effort. I take the return to the referent to be a positive development—as long as the referent is now understood in light of the questions raised about its epistemological status by semiology. To the extent that the text has indeed provoked this return, current critical opinion has tended to assume that the text has done so by default, that is, by fostering conditions under which such a return becomes desperately necessary.[8] Though there may well be a more positive sense in which the text has prompted this return, it remains to be formulated. In order to create a context wherein such a formulation might take on its greatest acuity, it is necessary to consider a reading of the text that powerfully identifies what within its theorization has led to the state of affairs this book is attempting to engage.

The reading of textuality that merits such consideration is Fredric Jameson's "The Ideology of the Text."[9] Initially written in 1975 and revised in 1986, this essay brilliantly and lucidly lays out what converts the threat posed by the text from a progressive to a conservative one. My aim here is not to refute this reading, but rather to exploit it as a way to identify what might be elaborated differently within the theory of textuality. This, of course, amounts to saying that, despite its perspicacity, Jameson's reading need not lead us to abandon the text. In fact, as we will see, the angle of his evaluation gives rise to a perspective that allows one to raise questions about Jameson's own reading—questions which, whether they are answered satisfactorily or not, invite us to develop textuality's relation to precisely those things which are often deemed antithetical to it.

The analysis that unfolds in "The Ideology of the Text" situates textuality in relation to two important contexts. The first of these involves the context of literary study, specifically the enduring debate over realism and modernism within this discipline. The second involves the context of social history, specifically the question of whether and how one is to link the intellectual superstructure to the material base of society. Ultimately, the literary context is subordinated to the sociohistorical context, but Jameson takes the distinction between the two seriously enough that, in fact, he devotes most of his energy to comprehending how textuality fits into the realism/modernism debate. Unlike other Marxist critics, Jameson insists that "monopoly capitalism" (as he likes to call it) has produced a relation between the base and the superstructure that encourages one to locate "real" social conflicts in the superstructure.

Let us then examine what happens to textuality as it is positioned in relation to these two contexts. Jameson opens his essay in a manner that resonates strongly with the phenomenological preoccupations of Ricoeur—textuality is presented as a methodological innovation that challenges the human sciences to abandon the epistemology of positivism. Though Jameson pointedly denies the theoretical pertinence of phenomenology, he unequivocally affirms the text's status as a hermeneutical object. Then, in a gesture which simultaneously underscores and undercuts the text's interdisciplinary character, Jameson moves to focus his essay on the text's status within literary study where, as he says, the model of the text is at once the "least metaphorical" and therefore the "most problematic" (p. 19). It is at this point that we encounter the realism versus modernism debate.

As a Marxist, Jameson's understanding of this debate is deeply informed by the quarrel over Expressionism that transpired among Georg Lukàcs, Ernst Bloch, Bertolt Brecht, and others in the late 1930s. In fact, Jameson has been so taken by this articulation of the debate that even in his more recent attempts to theorize postmodernism the latter keeps threatening to disappear back into modernism. In any case, as concerns textuality, this debate is used to associate it with modernism—an association which, while not compromising in itself, nevertheless places special responsibilities on those who make it. Through a cunning reading of Barthes's reading of the "realist" Honoré Balzac (*S/Z*) and Jonathan Culler's reading of the "modernist" Gustave Flaubert (*The Uses of Uncertainty*), Jameson is able to justify this association. Specifically, by showing how Barthes's notion of "textual codes" reduces realism to a linguistic effect, Jameson criticizes textuality for embracing the modernist refusal of referentiality. What is deemed troubling about such a refusal is that it reduces the rich field of connotation to nothing more than an index of effects, and, most importantly, it obstructs even the most modest attempt to historicize the text—whether this be carried out in the traditions of comparative stylistics or Marxist historiography. This in itself is a damning claim, but in order to render this a definitive blow, Jameson moves to associate the obstruction of historical reflection to the sociohistorical context of monopoly capitalism.

As the theory of textuality (insofar as it is embodied in the works of Barthes and Culler) is maneuvered into this context, Jameson indicates to what extent its preoccupations match those of an atomized society, whose fragmented subgroups and the resultant multiplicity of sociocultural "codes" inflect its art in a manner consistent with the economic imperatives of consumerism. On this account, textuality is nothing but an intellectual expression of what Jameson later calls "the cultural logic" of the latest phase of capitalism. Thus, the critique of Barthes's rejection of referentiality is nuanced so that the very preoccupation with "codes" is seen as an unconscious reflection of a referent (consumer society) that cannot therefore be opposed from within the textual perspective. The point is not that textuality is simply ideological (Jameson accepts Marx's and Engel's discussion of ideology as the struggle for hegemony in the realm of ideas), but that in its putative bracketing of history (*the* referent), textuality cannot help but affirm those social changes which condition its emergence. The model of the text is therefore problematic because it is incapable of either generating or sustaining a *critical* ideology. Here we have the deepest aspect of Jameson's concerns about modernism and, for that matter, postmodernism. Obviously, insofar as textuality can be affiliated with modernism in this way, then it too can be reduced to sheer, that is capitalist, ideology.

Entering the conflict over textuality requires that one not be struck dumb by such criticism. By the same token, the desire to prolong this conflict, to finish the theorization of the text, is rendered meaningless if this criticism is simply denied. After all, precious little is gained by refusing the challenge of a sociohistorical perspective in the name of a more epistemologically rigorous retreat into formalism, whether literary or philosophical. If the theory of the text is worth historicizing it is because it stands to gain something from the refusal of a separation between theory and history. And what is to be gained is not merely access to arenas which have, on my reading, suffered from the text's absence (one thinks of the comparative insularity of the social sciences discussed by both Ricoeur and Jameson), but more importantly, finishing the text's theorization may facilitate the project denied to textuality by Jameson whose own theoretical framework has, at times, promised more than it has delivered. Be that as it may, Jameson's critique of the text remains convincing. In what conceivable way does it invite the reading which opposes it?

Let us begin with what may strike some as the unlikely matter of disciplinarity. Jameson's analysis very much depends upon a bracketing of textuality *within* the discipline of literary study, and this despite the fact that his initial sketch of the semantic range of textuality includes disciplines as disparate as genetics and telecommunications. If indeed the textual model is "most problematic" within the literary field, then perhaps it is important not to begin by sacrificing one's critical evaluation of textuality to an implicit accommodation of its appropriation by the discipline of literary study.

In the preceding characterization of the ambivalence structuring the concept of the text, it became evident that at the very core of the concept was a conflict driven by, among other things, a discipline (linguistics) at odds both with itself and another discipline, namely, literary studies. As we shall later see, Barthes (who is, after all, Jameson's chief target) explicitly regards the disciplinary dimension of this conflict as cortical to the textual model. What is fundamental here is that the concept of the text did not simply develop in relation to the sort of disciplinary transformations that can be gauged by comparing levels of metaphoricity present in the concept, but that the text's distinctively semiological character was defined by the inscription of a complex disciplinary disruption at its core. Jameson authorizes his critical reading by simultaneously evoking the interdisciplinary richness of the model, while rewriting it in terms of a literary problematic (i.e., modernism). Seen from a theoretical perspective, this gesture comes very close to a recovery of the referent (in this case, the historical "reality" of the disciplinary appropriation of the textual model) which prematurely surrenders everything to it in the name of political pragmatism. Would it not make more sense to acknowledge both that the textual model is internally fissured by a conflicted relation to disciplinarity and that the literary appropriation of this model which has indeed taken place in history has obscured, or at least contained, this conflictual relation? By beginning here it is possible to reinterpret those characteristics of textuality that make it legible as a theoretical articulation of modernism (notably, its refusal of referentiality), as an inscription of the referent, but now understood as mediated by a history of disciplinary crisis—a crisis of which the text's theorists were certainly conscious. The text thus appears as irreducibly entangled in disciplinary politics and not merely as the articulation of an effort to reorganize disciplinary boundaries such as those between linguistics and literature, but as a critical practice seeking to problematize the cultural work effected by the disciplines. If, in fact, it is possible to rearticulate the text and history, it will depend both on securing theoretically the text's link to disciplinarity and on drawing the practical consequences of this linkage as they manifest themselves within the institutional domain of disciplinary power. As I argue in chapter 1, addressing these analytical demands requires that we displace the now familiar emphasis on the text's interdisciplinary character with a perspective that underscores the text's *antidisciplinary* profile. In other words, finishing the text's theorization means radicalizing the significance of the disciplinary disruption animating its core. Or, put another way, the text must be made to oppose the discipline(s) that made it.

On the other hand, there is the question of agency, that is, do the theorists of textuality actually produce something like an ideology for those in a position to exploit the transformation of the social base that conditioned the emergence of monopoly capitalism? Unless the critique of disciplinarity can be summarily reduced to such an ideology, one would be hard-pressed to make a claim like this stick. If, moreover, postmodernity involves (among other things) a fundamental transformation of the base/superstructure relation, then it becomes more difficult than ever to decide whether theory as such is destined to affirm this change or whether the theory of the text in particular expresses the new "ruling" material interests. One need not *affirm* such a change simply by insisting that the historical novelty of the text might well serve as a context for reevaluating, as opposed to reasserting, the categories of historical analysis—particularly when they have arguably been outdistanced by the social process itself. In fact, the labor of reevaluation is precisely what has motivated the development of "post-Marxism," and Jameson himself is often tempted to endorse this project as he struggles to engage the utopian moment of postmodernity.[10]

To conclude I must confront a rather fundamental difficulty raised by my evocation here of "post-Marxism," namely the centrality within it—at least as it has been formulated by Ernesto Laclau and Chantal Mouffe—of the category "discourse." This is important not because it is a particularly controversial category within post-Marxism, but because the task of finishing the text is pointedly *not* the task of finishing discourse. There is, in other words, a question here of giving priority to the notion of textuality instead of discourse. Why? Two issues must be emphasized in response. First, it is important to stress that we are dealing with two distinct phenomena or, at the very least, two different levels of analysis. And second, it is equally important to realize that the historical institutionalization of textuality conditioned the emergence of discourse. As a consequence of this history, the concepts of "the text" and "discourse" pressure each other in ways that require careful delineation. To that end, consider the following formulation from Laclau's "Populist Rupture and Discourse," which invites us to ponder this distinction directly.

> By "discursive" I do not mean that which refers to "text" narrowly defined, but to the ensemble of the phenomena in and through which the social production of meaning takes place, an ensemble which constitutes society as such. The discursive is not, therefore, being conceived as a level nor even as a dimension of the social, but rather as being co-extensive with the social as such. This means that the discursive does not constitute a superstructure (since it is the very condition of all social practice) or, more precisely, that all social practice constitutes itself as such insofar as it produces meaning. Because there is nothing specifically social which is constituted outside the discursive, it is clear that the non-discursive is not opposed to the discursive as if it were a matter of two separate levels. History and society are an *infinite text*.[11]

Here we see the reappearance of the "two texts," one narrow (the linguistic or philological), the other infinite (the semiological). In addition, Laclau explicitly moves to criticize the superstructural designation of discourse in a manner that compels him to draw on textuality as a figure for the interweaving of history (base) and society (superstructure). This enabling gesture of post-Marxism appears nevertheless to subordinate the textual to the discursive, and if such an approach is to serve as an alternative framework for delineating the cultural politics of textuality, this subordination obviously must be engaged.

Laclau's observations bear testimony to a development within cultural criticism, whose roots are often traced to the work of Michel Foucault, in which discourse is made consubstantial with sociality as such. From such a perspective social relations are conceived as *relations* insofar as they are mediated by and through discourse. What is gained here is more than the simple triumph of a hermeneutic (as opposed to a positivistic) approach to society; instead, this perspective envisions the discursive reduction of the traditional bearer of hermeneutic meaning, namely, the subject. In other words, from the vantage point of post-Marxism people no longer simply communicate, they arise as "the people" within the practice of communication. When Laclau moves to dissociate this conception of discourse from the "narrow" sense of the text, he is explicitly attempting to evoke this constitutive aspect of the concept since the linguistic text is, after all, something produced by a subject who precedes its production.

There is, however, the second text, the one that Laclau draws upon to *clarify* what he means by discourse. Though this gesture at one level testifies to the prior institutionalization of textuality (why would one invoke a concept that was even more obscure than the one s/he is attempting to clarify?), it obscures an important tension between the discursive and the textual. Since Laclau makes no effort to specify the context or the structure of this institutionalization, one is left to ponder the necessity of the very allusion to textuality.

To specify what is at stake in this tension, it helps to begin by underscoring the fact that discourse is typically used, as is the case with Laclau, to characterize both the medium and the nature of sociality. Insofar as society is interpretable, it presents itself as an ensemble of discourses. In addition, all that is analytically relevant about society is that which can be interpreted. From this perspective discourse serves as a general name for the class of practices (what, in an older vocabulary, might have been called behaviors and institutions) that define the perceptible surface of society. Cultural analyses conducted from this angle tend to locate particular embodiments of discourse, that is, discourses whose properties and functions are then detailed. For example, all the various "moves" defining a particular style of dress characteristic of a youth subculture might be read as an expression of resistance to the sartorial norms of the dominant class. However, what is clearly not emphasized here is the status of discourse as a disciplinary object, a paradigm that organizes the *way* cultural research is designed, legitimated, and conducted. Instead, discourse designates how a particular type of phenomena presents *itself* such ,that it can become the focus of cultural studies. What remains obscured in the concept of discourse is its relation to an enabling paradigm—a paradigm which, I would argue, derives from the institutionalization of textuality as an interdisciplinary object. Laclau acknowledges this, but shifts the accent in his discussion onto the sociohistorical dimension which, implicitly, rests undeveloped within the concept of the text—whether infinite or narrow. This is a maneuver that harbors a problem whose proportions need to be detailed in order that the priority given here to textuality be fully justified.

Let us come at the issues at stake here from a different direction. Another way to gloss the concept of ambivalence that is cortical to textuality is in terms of the interplay between what takes place within a cultural production, say a particular film, and what, as yet, has no place within the social. In short, textuality seeks to articulate in theoretical terms the construction of what Ernst Bloch might call the "utopic," the nonplace, at the level of a *particular* production.[12] This is not a matter of the "visionary" or "prophetic" dimension of culture which is an interesting problem in its own right. Rather, it is a matter of designating how the specific labor of producing what a society constructs as "culture" touches on processes (psychic and material) which have not been integrated within the prevailing social framework. The concept of discourse, which is, as we have seen, essentially isotopic with the social, not only embodies the phenomenality of the social, but also tends to homogenize society as a discursive field—populated, to be sure, with dominant, marginalized, and oppositional discourses, but devoid of any structural alterity that might give different discourses their specific forcefulness. Without this, political opposition must be derived entirely from the aims and interests of participants—a position which obviates, at a theoretical level at least, the recourse to discourse in the first place. After all, why should we reconceive the social as discourse if, in the final analysis, we are only really interested in the consciousness motivating agents? The immediate political consequences of this will be addressed in my concluding chapter.

The analytical limits of such a perspective are perhaps most apparent in the "reading formation" approach to texts developed by Tony Bennett and others.[13] This theoretical standpoint argues, in effect, that texts are pure context, that is, they are the constructions of the formations that organize their reading. Though argued much more persuasively than many reception-oriented approaches to literary analysis, this perspective has difficulty articulating how readers come to recognize that they are, in fact, engaging some *particular* text over which they may quarrel. If the text is the history of their engagement of it, either there can be no serious quarreling (over what?), or there can be no text, no scriptural embodiment of a linguistic system with its attendant institutional inflections. Implicit here is a certain phobic structure wherein the particular differences that might actually divide and/or galvanize reading constituencies are translated into pretexts for conducting literary interpretation at the level of social analysis alone—*Moby Dick* is in fact little more than the articulation of the contradictions of entrepreneurial adventurism. Again, discourse serves here as the medium of exchange through which specific cultural productions are read as social communications. In the very worst of cases, this type of analysis sacrifices the texture of any particular production for a preemptory political evaluation of the cultural work performed by the discourse in which the production was realized. Obviously, I am not opposed to the labor of political evaluation, which strikes me as unavoidable in any case. Rather, I am concerned that discourse often obscures issues that ought to be part of any thorough political evaluation.

This criticism was anticipated by Julia Kristeva when, in her contribution to *Théorie d'ensemble* entitled "Problèmes de la Structuration du Texte," she contrasted the text and discourse by stressing the latter's rootedness in a communication paradigm modeled on speech wherein a properly capitalist obsession with exchange stripped discourse of its critical power.[14] Though it is true that since this time (1968) discourse has been expanded to include many practices other than speech, it has—through, I would argue, its avoidance of the paradigm problem—continued to undergird the notion of society as a homogeneous, communicative system where all differences are differences of degree, not of kind. Textuality opposes this from two related directions: one, by insisting upon the "utopic" or even "asocial" location that arises in a group's engagement with a particular cultural production and, two, by situating this engagement in the context of a disciplinary struggle where the text is ambivalently split between its particular embodiment and the research paradigm(s) through which this particularity is stabilized. What is advantageous about the textual model, however "unfinished" it may be, is that through it politicized cultural interpretation can engage the texture of a particular production while making the task of doing so assume responsibility for the utopic impulses that emerge within it.

To be sure, the emergence of the concept of discourse has made it possible to see precisely what we risk losing in the text. In fact, as we in the academic cultures of the West have drifted from text to discourse the ontological and ultimately essentialist pretensions of textual alterity have been reigned in and given new value. This more than anything constitutes the vital pressure that discourse as a concept has exerted upon the disciplinary context in which it appeared. But the problem of alterity, which discourse seeks to capture in the notion of resistance, continues to assert itself. Once we abandon the master narratives of enlightenment and liberation, then it becomes both more urgent and more difficult to distinguish resistance from accommodation. Textuality, precisely insofar as it seeks to ground the production of disciplinary knowledge in processes which outdistance the existing framework of disciplinarity, still registers an alterity that enables academics to participate in the political struggle over the present. On these grounds, which are no doubt controversial, I believe we ought to cast our lot with the text and proceed to finish its theorization.

# PART I

# 1

## ✳ Textuality and the Critique of Disciplinary Reason

If the text's relation to history can indeed be rearticulated, it will require that we establish its relation with what I propose to call disciplinary reason. Such a project is, in fact, called for by Roland Barthes in his much discussed programmatic essay, "From Work to Text," [1] though this is now often overlooked by those concerned to determine where textuality stands in the debate over postmodernism. [2] What I find particularly suggestive about Barthes's formulations is that he not only situates the emergence of the text within a specifically disciplinary context, but he links the "nature" of textuality to an important historical moment within this context—a moment divided between its status as a mere development and as an occasion for a decisive critical intervention. Perhaps by detailing the movement of Barthes's argument, we can clarify how the text's constitutive relation to this division invites one to distinguish it from the formalistic reduction of textuality that obstructs the rearticulation called for above.

Two moments in Barthes's exposition seem particularly worthy of our attention. In the first paragraph a shift is announced. It is the shift signaled in the essay's title, from work to text. Most readings of the essay have concentrated on elaborating the difference signaled by this change and as a consequence have tended to marginalize the fact that the shift transpires at the level of what Barthes calls, following strands of contemporaneous discussions within the history of science and political philosophy, [3] the literary object. It is clear from the enumerated distinctions drawn later concerning works and texts, that Barthes believes a deep change has taken place in the way literary scholars conceive of the properties and limits of the phenomena that comprise the domain of literature. Though Barthes does not argue for it explicitly, his entire perspective actually assumes that this change, or shift, is indissociable from an institutional acknowledgment of the existence and function of disciplinary objects as such. In other words, part of what constitutes this change is not merely the displacement of the work by the text, but the recognition that this displacement reaches into the organizing structure of disciplinarity as such. This is why, I would argue, Barthes's effort to theorize the text immediately has recourse to a discussion of disciplinarity as a structural feature of the institutional organization of knowledge. However, to grasp what is necessary and therefore significant about this ambivalent characterization of the text (i.e., as object and as an effect of the recognition of such objects) will require that we consider what I take to be the other significant moment in Barthes's exposition.

In accounting for the emergence of the text, Barthes argues that it resulted from a specific confluence of disciplines (in a later chapter I will have occasion to explore the etiology of this confluence). Rather than specifying the disciplines involved though, he focuses on the confluence as such. Thus, despite the fact that textuality is immediately associated with the literary domain, the shift emphasized in the essay is located within what might more accurately be called an interdisciplinary context. In other words, the notion of a literary object comes to consciousness at precisely that moment when, paradoxically, the domain of the literary discloses the fundamentally interdisciplinary character of its central activities. Given that, as I have suggested, the "discovery" of disciplinary objects occurs simultaneously, it would appear that such objects derive in part from the conflicts that enable disciples to recognize how their membership in a particular discipline actually separates them. In any case, it is this line of reflection that prompts Barthes to set up a distinction between two modalities of *inter*-disciplinarity: one that subsists as a latent feature of the solidarity of disciplines qua disciplines (presumably a reflection of the historical dynamic wherein disciplines develop out of initially undifferentiated if not collaborative intellectual projects), and another which begins "effectively," that is, through a double displacement operating not merely within and among disciplines but upon the institutional grounding of disciplinarity as such. The text thus appears within a confluence of disciplines that enables one to question both their synchronic relations and their sociohistorical supports. Even those inclined to acknowledge the plausibility of the text as a figure of interdisciplinary convergence (an intellectual position previously articulated in terms of the irreducibly hermeneutic character of the social sciences)[4] often fail to recognize the structural moment of the text's sociogenesis that commits it to a critique of the enabling conditions of disciplines as such. Barthes then is not merely describing a shift that has consequences for the way we think about what makes great books great, he is explaining this development in a manner that compels us to rethink what the text must be if it cannot be dissociated from what enables such a shift to occur. What is implicit in this explanation is a theoretical and practical challenge, namely, how should the irreducibly interdisciplinary character of the text be rewritten so as to situate the latter as a critical term within what I have earlier called an *anti*-disciplinary project?

This, of course, reiterates the call issued above for a rearticulation of the text and history, but in a manner that no doubt remains unclear. As we have seen, the formalist reduction of textuality obstructing this rearticulation proceeds either by deliberately exaggerating the domain of the text—as the world—or by confusing it with the term it is meant to oppose—the work. Contrary to those who relentlessly contrast the text and its context (be it psychological, sociological, historical, or cultural), Barthes's essay insists that the text, *even* at the moment where it avoids strict contextual determination, is immanently marked by a crisis within the disciplinary configuration in which it arose. Put differently, the text emerges to name the alterity that simultaneously constitutes and subverts the context of disciplinary reason. Though it would be foolish not to acknowledge that "From Work to Text" was written in the wake of what Henri Lefebvre called "the explosion" that rocked the French state and its educational policies,[5] as well as a major European conference on interdisciplinarity convened by CERI (the Center for Educational Research and Innovation)[6] in 1970 at the University of Nice, it would be equally irresponsible to read the text (either at the level of its intellectual content, i.e., in terms of its properties, or at the level of its disciplinary function) as an immediate reflection of these developments. The text is not merely situated as an intellectual reflex, it comes into existence as an effect of the conflicted and unsettled moment in which it appeared. If its emergence is precipitated by a crisis to which it responds and thus partially constitutes through engagement, then precisely in order to preserve its relation to the context of its sociogenesis it must be understood to refuse the task of directly reflecting this context. Disciplinary crisis does not present itself as a unified phenomenon of reflection, and interpreting such a refusal as a sign of the willful abdication of historical, and ultimately political, responsibility can be shown to embody a tactical maneuver designed, in effect, to rescue disciplinarity in the name of a "radical" historical intervention that spares the conflictual character of the present as a matter of principle. Be that as it may, declaring the necessity of reading the text's emergence otherwise does not, of itself, establish how the text might be mobilized to further an antidisciplinary project. At most, the reading of Barthes's essay that authorizes such a declaration parries the facile denunciation of the text as "ahistorical." But what then can be said of the text's more positive role in the critique of disciplinary reason? The terms of analysis will have to be broadened.

Since the pivotal moment of the critique effected through the notion of the text rests on its status as a disciplinary object, the value of this critique can be better gauged once this latter notion is clarified. Much current research on disciplinarity[7] has recourse to Thomas Kuhn's notion of the "paradigm" introduced in his justly celebrated *Structure of Scientific Revolutions* and modified as the result of critical scrutiny in his "Second Thoughts on Paradigms."[8] This is due to the fact that Kuhn's term permits one to designate that characteristically elusive level of "scientific" experience embodied in the symbolic inscription of community. Without such a phenomenon the banal but inevitable task of drawing up a departmental "mission statement" would be impossible—disciples, that is, the members of a discipline, must have a framework within which even their intellectual differences take on significance, and this is what a paradigm puts in place. Though Kuhn does not in *Structure* explicitly link paradigms and disciplines (he emphasizes the relation between the former and "sciences," even and especially interdisciplinary ones like astrophysics), in his later elaboration of the term he does. In fact, in "Second Thoughts" Kuhn rewrites the notion of paradigm as "disciplinary matrix" and splits it into three components: symbolic generalizations, models, and exemplars. What is to be understood by each of these terms is not, for my purposes, as important as the insight motivating the revision, namely, that what a discipline claims to know arises within a communal framework designed to encounter what lies outside it ("reality") by uncoercively managing the internal dissension about it. In an elaborate explication of the notion of an exemplar, Kuhn makes it clear that even though rules organize what can be claimed about certain phenomena designated as worthy of disciplinary attention, these rules cannot dictate the development of knowledge. If this were the case, science, as a history of the "truthful" construction of reality, would be impossible.

Certain statements produced by discourses interested in being deemed "scientific" need to be held accountable, as it were, to something the producers of these discourses understand to be beyond their influence. Of course, the production of these statements needs to be handled in conformity with certain protocols. All statements are not created equal, and what prevents just *any* claim from being taken seriously is a feeling of appropriateness deriving from the matrix that bonds the disciples who see themselves as committed to the scientific project that depends upon their cooperation. There is, in effect, an abridged "social contract" figured into the functioning of the matrix. It is in this sense that the matrix (which is not, as we shall see, an innocent term) fastens the production of scientific knowledge to the reproduction and contestation of society despite the matrix's apparent abstractness. If disciplinary strictures absolutely constrained research, disciplinary formation would be tantamount to static self-confirmation. At least since the eighteenth century this has constituted an unacceptable view of "true" knowledge, even in the Enlightenment's own terms. However, there are problems with Kuhn's analysis. Before specifying precisely what limits his formulations as a way of furthering the project of antidisciplinarity, it is necessary to spell out how Barthes's notion of the literary object is significantly illuminated by Kuhn's contributions.

In "From Work to Text" Barthes tells us very little about the literary object *qua* object. We learn much about what distinguishes the work from the text, and even though the advent of the text is tied to that of the disciplinary object, we are left in the dark as to the status of the latter within Barthes's analysis. Kuhn provides us with a useful way to conceive of what Barthes might mean by the literary object. He does so by illustrating how something like an object (or a domain of objects) forms as the referent for statements acknowledged as axiomatic, models deemed particularly lucid as doctrinal demonstators, and exemplars thought to be pedagogically effective. Put in this way one can see that the object of a discipline is not necessarily real, it is a regulative fiction that nonetheless *really* works to orient research within a particular field—research which may actually lead to interventions in the real that constitute reality as such.

If one were to extrapolate these ideas in terms of Barthes's notion of the work, it would, for example, be important to identify as an axiomatic statement the claim that "literature" is inscribed within a national or regional language understood as an expressive instrument. Those who study it do not treat literature as a purely private code. On the basis of such a general claim one might further argue that a genre like "the epic" be read as an expression of national striving (however thwarted) that could, once properly understood, model properly "literary" acts of interpretation. Those who study literature do not typically interpret examples without reference (however oblique) to the general type they exemplify. The point is that even for disagreements at the hermeneutic level to arise there must be an enabling framework that permits the disputing factions to quarrel over the same thing. In my example, the "thing" is literature conceived of in a worklike fashion, and it serves as the disciplinary object. What Barthes is claiming in his essay is that there has been a shift at this level of institutional existence and, further, that this shift has taken the form of a crisis in the system or network of disciplines. Thus, what is at stake in, for example, the discipline of literary studies are not just different or even incompatible readings of a Poe short story, but different readings of the framework delimiting the field of the discipline's interpretive practice. Hence one of the reasons that the disciplinary reception of textual theory has been so volatile is because it has problematized the conditions under which intradisciplinary disputes had previously been ajudicated. But rather than respond to this difficulty either by truculently, and therefore vainly, reasserting disciplinary coherence or by finding a way to shore up one's discipline by discovering within it a benign interdisciplinary linkage with jurisprudence, it is more in keeping with the polemical aims of the appeal to interdisciplinarity to underscore the text's relation to the crisis of discipline and refuse to disconnect the local struggle over readings from the broader struggle over their institutional preconditions. However, insofar as this latter point bears fundamentally on the "nature" of the text, it marks the limits of the analogy between textuality and disciplinary matrices. After all, what is required to foster these various struggles is a notion of discipline that designates the general social context wherein such struggles might be waged once they have begun to break down the protective insularity of the academic disciplines.

However useful Kuhn's observations on "disciplinary matrices" are in clarifying at what level of institutional existence the shift analyzed by Barthes takes place, one cannot overlook the fact that the latter's notion of the text exemplifies a decidedly peculiar disciplinary object. So much so, in fact, that precisely in order to register this peculiarity within the terms of his analysis Barthes drops the notion of "object" altogether, replacing it with the claim that the text is to be conceived of as a "methodological field." On the one hand, this tactical maneuver simply anticipates the essay's more familiar typological discussion by presenting the text as an effect of the collective exertions of researchers. As is well known, it was in the name of such a state of affairs that Barthes felt compelled to liquidate "the author."[9] On the other hand, substituting "field" for "object" reflects Barthes's desire to break with the kind of evolutionary assumptions embedded within Kuhn's historicism. Though reluctant to avail himself of the then fashionable trope "break" (*la coupure*), it is clear that the "slide" affirmed by Barthes's essay is designed to underscore the text's relation to a profound rejection of discipline as a horizon for the institutional organization of knowledge. Let me try to clarify this by turning again briefly to Kuhn's discussion of the non-rule-governed development of the disciplinary matrix.

Toward the end of "Second Thoughts," Kuhn repeats a demonstration that appeared in significantly different forms both within the body and the appendix (written eleven years later) of *Structure*. It shows how the member of a discipline (or what I have been calling a disciple) learns to associate his or her membership with a recognition of what is pertinent to that discipline's concerns. Central to Kuhn's demonstration is an example wherein a little boy, under his father's tutelage, learns to group water fowl into classes of appropriate consistency and scope. Kuhn's point is that the boy learns to do this not by following rules whose utility would presuppose the allegiance being explained, but by toying with examples of possible solutions. The right one is the solution that makes the boy feel that he "belongs" where he is trying to achieve recognition. Understood as a plea for humane frivolity within the sciences, I have no particular problem with Kuhn's conclusions, but the analogy he draws touches down in many places, some of which are compromising indeed.

Kuhn introduces the notion of a "disciplinary matrix" in his "Postscript" to *Structure*. Much of what is argued for here is later resurrected in "Second Thoughts," including the example of exemplars. However, what differs in the earlier text is the content of the example. When it is first introduced, Kuhn asks us to consider a situation in which a young boy is confronted with the task of deciding whether or not a woman he has just seen duck into a department store is his mother. Believing that she was at home and thus being somewhat surprised, the young boy pursues the woman only to discover that she is clearly not his mother. He then occupies himself with the epistemic possibility of his confusion, which is precisely the experience of disciplinary training Kuhn values so highly. Kuhn quickly moves on to the now familiar example of the water fowl, making the point that in both cases the boy (read "disciple") has discovered his membership in a disciplinary matrix by playfully testing whether he knows how to situate certain phenomena effectively or not. Since his activities were not guided by a rule that required a prior allegiance to the discipline, the boy's experience seems to pass for a demonstration of the coherence of the noncoercive exemplar.

But what happens if we translate all of Kuhn's analogy into English? Then we recognize the mother, or womb, in the disciplinary *matrix*, and besides understanding that this example operates as a transcendental analysis of disciplinarity as such (that is, the ability to solve this kind of problem is tantamount to understanding the dynamics of discipline in general), we see here the norms of oedipal differentiation infusing what was supposed to be an experience unmarked by the constraints of disciplinary rules. Psychoanalysis is, after all, a form of institutionally reproduced knowledge, and this is true despite the enduring tension between it and the discipline of psychology. Though Kuhn seems prepared to acknowledge the way matrices are distributed across disciplines, in his most general account of their evolution (which, for a historian, forms part of their essence) he argues as if the absence of a *local* disciplinary injunction testifies to a general absence, thus obscuring a decisive aspect of disciplinary reason, namely the point at which rules shade into norms and the entire institutional structure of knowledge connects with other social forms of disciplinary power.

It is this intrinsic commitment to an evolutionary model of history that limits the pertinence of Kuhn's discussion of the disciplinary object, because such a commitment tends to homogenize and segment the disciplinary field and relieve even "revolutionary" historians of the task of formulating their criticisms in relation to the considerably less rational domain of social reproduction and contestation that surrounds and informs the sciences. However if the text, insofar as it resists its status as an object, demands that we formulate its critique of disciplinarity in these terms, then it will be necessary to extend Kuhn's notion of discipline precisely at the point where it turns away from the domain of power. Such a perspective is latent within the work that Michel Foucault produced during the seventies.

What complicates the introduction of Foucault's work in this context is the fact that no less a writer than Edward Said has labored to separate Foucault's interests from those we have come to associate with textuality.[10] My aim here is not to contest this reading directly (though I believe Said decidedly mischaracterizes the text), but to open up another approach to the very texts of Foucault's that Said mobilizes in order to perform his act of critical judgment. To be sure, Foucault cannot be read as a straightforward partisan of the text (though he was an early "friend" of *Tel Quel*), but this does not prevent his work from being read so as to provide a notion of discipline that illuminates what is at stake in the text's antidisciplinary status.

In Foucault's inaugural lecture, "The Order of Discourse," which is the text in which Said locates the seeds of Foucault's most fruitful analyses of cultural politics, there is an important discussion of the notion of discipline utilized by Kuhn. What distinguishes this discussion is the way Foucault situates discipline in relation to two other procedures of what he calls "internal mastery": commentary and, most importantly, the author, since it brings his project in closest proximity to that of Barthes.[11] Specifically, Foucault associates discipline with the two other notions by stressing its productive capacity. If commentary functions to designate a canon through principled exclusion, and if the author is used to tether interpretation to the levels of intelligibility supported by literary commentary, then what is distinctive about discipline is the way it solicits and encourages the proliferation of statements about the domain of objects evoked through the notions of authorship and commentary. Lest one assume from this characterization that Foucault is inclined merely to reiterate Kuhn's rather affirmative, evolutionary assessment, recall that Foucault understands this productive dynamic as an instance of internal mastery, that is, a way of organizing the volatility of the historical process in a manner that preserves the existing balance of political forces.

But aside from the fundamentally different ways Foucault and Kuhn locate the political aspects of their analyses, there is little in what has been said so far that qualitatively differentiates their perception of the disciplinary field. If, however, one reads on in the inaugural lecture to the point where Foucault identifies some of the areas likely to define his future research, and particularly if one then turns to the published results of this prospective activity, then it becomes easier to separate the two projects in a manner decisive to an understanding of textuality. Foucault stresses, both in the discussion already summarized and again later in the lecture, that discipline must be grasped as a productive, rather than a prohibitive, force. Said, who emphasizes that one can detect in the inaugural lecture Foucault's adoption of the theme of power, is too concerned to decry the consequent enervation of historical agency to underscore the fact that in "The Order of Discourse," particularly in relation to the set—commentary, author, discipline—one can see Foucault toying with the rejection of the "repressive hypothesis" that was to ground his later analyses of the prison and the history of sexuality. Only by recognizing how disciplinary formation participates in the social circuits of disciplinary power, can we appreciate what modes of "contextual" engagement are inscribed in the very conception of textuality. This cannot be accomplished if we fail to see that the "productive hypothesis" is what fastens Foucault's early discussion of discipline to the analysis of *Discipline and Punish*.

To understand the so-called productivity of power and its implications for the notion of discipline, it is first necessary to realize that Foucault uses the term "discipline" in this context in order to designate the modernity of power. On a trajectory that has been familiar to Western cultural historians since Weber, Foucault plots the points of power: an early moment where it was articulated as corporeal violence and a later, quintessentially modern moment when power courses through the social body informing it at every level. Though Weberian in its outline, Foucault's analysis shows that the distinctions showcased in the former's history of social rationalization have collapsed with the advent of modernity. This complicates the discussion of discipline because the clarity one anticipates entering a debate with the mention of the word "power" is lost as soon as we realize that historicizing the term has transformed its present meaning. Foucault is not primarily interested in demonstrating that those who belong to disciplines collude with the repressive state apparatuses by virtue of their status as disciples. Rather, and this is what is important for our purposes, Foucault is arguing that the emergence of discipline has been fundamental to a massive historical transformation of the "nature" of power. Though some of his critics have concluded that such a move has made recourse to the very concept of power pointless, I would prefer to argue that Foucault's gesture invites us to reexamine deeply our assumptions about discipline if indeed the latter can be shown to bear the historical relation to power traced out in *Discipline and Punish*.

How then are we to understand the notion of disciplinary power? If what is fundamental to the development of modern power is a displacement wherein, as Foucault says, "the soul becomes the prison of the body" (p. 30), then the multifarious practices that converge to instrumentalize the soul move toward the core of any discussion of disciplinarity. Despite what one might think, models of subjectivity are indeed crucial to the internal coherence of disciplines. Once viewed as an effect of what Foucault likes to call a "political technology," the soul is stripped of its transcendental pretensions and stands forth as an instrument of self-knowledge, if not self-control. As such, the entire analysis of discipline, to the extent that it makes necessary reference to this general historical development, must give priority to those social practices devoted to the production and circulation of knowledge—particularly knowledge about human agency. Central among these are the "human sciences,"[12] disciplines which Foucault roots firmly in the soil of modern power. But before we return to detail the implications of this view for the academic disciplines, let us linger a bit longer on the notion of disciplinary power itself.

I have said that power acquires its status as "modern" when its productive or positive side emerges to reconfigure its other structural and historical aspects. If this process is inseparable from the advent of disciplinarity, then one of the ways to conceive of the "positivity" of power is in terms of the way experiences of human agency are given epistemic shape, are "posited" as socially intelligible phenomena. Foucault prefers not to see this as immediately "repressive" for two reasons: first, because having one's experience recognized as constitutive of society can be an instance of empowerment, for example, seeing oneself as a repository of labor power might well lead one to enter into the wage labor contract and thus acquire a certain level of economic self-determination; and secondly, because if one comes to be what s/he is through this experience, then in a strict sense the point of reference for repression— the to-be-downtrodden self—is not yet constituted and thus incapable of grounding the repressive charge. This does not mean that power lacks a "negative" articulation, of course it does, but disciplinary power in particular remains unanalyzable if it is consistently reduced merely to that which permits it to serve repressive aims. In short then, what distinguishes disciplinary power is the way it participates in what I will call the subjection of human agency, that is, the production and circulation of knowledge that segments, correlates, and thus orders social collectivity around the experiential, but ultimately institutional category of the subject.

Not surprisingly, the very procedural dynamics of segmentation, correlation, and spatiotemporal ordering are what surface in Foucault's description of the sociogenesis of discipline. Affirming Marx's insistence upon the revolutionary character of early capitalism, Foucault links disciplinary power to the sociopolitical task of producing what he calls "docile bodies," that is, agents who see in their submission to the minute and fully reticulated ordering of the field of action (be it labor or desire) the consummation of their productive powers. The point is not that these agents are mystified; on the contrary they are in fact empowered within a particular yet restricted mode of production. The knowledge they have of themselves as subjects of disciplinary power is not false in some absolute sense, it is false (or for that matter true) only in relation to the regime of truth stabilized through the institutionalization of this power.[13] Even so, what are the practices distinctive to disciplinary power that determine the inescapably political character of academic disciplines such as literary study?

Foucault traces two lines, one historical and the other typological. Concerning the historical, he attempts to outdistance Marxism by locating discursive practices formed outside the economic domain that nevertheless subject human agency to compatible codes of self-understanding and control. Specifically, at least as regards the academic disciplines that concern us, he is interested in the relation between monastic and pedagogic discourses as these converge ever more thoroughly in a social context rapidly being redefined by the reproductive needs of a militaristically inflected industrialism. From the typological standpoint what is crucial here is the emergence of the practice of "examination" which is distinguished, as Foucault persuasively shows, by its preoccupation with the establishment of a rule-governed space that enables individuals to gauge their proximity to a standard of performance which, even when met, continues to serve as a convenient, because constantly accessible, target of a certain existential orthopedics.

Lest we forget that this analysis is meant to contribute to an understanding of the birth of the prison, let us recall that examination figures prominently in several practices indispensable to its genesis. It is inseparable from, just to cite some examples, forensic procedure in general, the juridic-legal proceedings of the bourgeois state, the structures and activities of carceral surveillance, and above all, it is crucial to the soul's imprisonment of the body, that is, to the reformation of character thought to comprise the advance constituted by the "modern" penitentiary system. While such claims might not strike one as particularly controversial, what is extremely suggestive about Foucault's analysis is that he locates the birth of the human sciences in the institutional grounding of the disciplinary practice of examination. What is at stake here is not difficult to summarize.

Fundamental to the development of disciplines like sociology or psychology is the reduction of human agency to a repository of potentially objective knowledge. Once this is accomplished the circuit of exchange enabling information to be extracted, rationally ordered, applied to individuals, and then, if necessary, adjusted becomes possible. The presupposition that one can generalize from such conspicuously select cases is authorized less by some flattering conviction about the universal human spirit, than by a recognition that such knowledge production presupposes a certain saturation of society by disciplinary power. In other words, the conditions necessary for the production of objective knowledge about agents require a level of social stability that derives from institutions capable of providing the requisite controls. There is, then, a certain continuity between the internal organization of knowledge production at the level of academic disciplines and the institutional structure of society. *That* we know has a great deal to do with *what* we know, and this has everything to do with the general social function of power.

Contrary to those who have long bemoaned the dehumanization of society, Foucault sees the disciplinary saturation of society as responsible for the state of affairs lamented, but misunderstood by them. In reading the subject as an effect of the cross-referencing that binds together the objects grounding the various human sciences, Foucault regards those who cry out for a reaffirmation of subjectivity—a cry most often uttered by those on the other side of the great disciplinary divide, that is, within the "humanities"—as obeying, perhaps unwittingly, a dictum of disciplinary power, namely divide and occupy. In other words, if the subject is threatened *everywhere,* then the disciplinary forces converging to produce it (even in its absence) are implicitly being invited to occupy those institutional spaces where the prospect of the subject's "preservation" might otherwise have seemed brightest. Once the subject is understood to be a social product of the pursuit of objective knowledge (i.e., knowledge about objects), that is, as an alibi for the unchecked proliferation of disciplinary objects, then the efforts to "rehumanize" society can easily be read as exercises in complicity with power rather than resistance to it.

This then represents the grand stakes of the critique of disciplinarity. It is not enough to attack the parochialism of the disciplines, nor is it enough to affirm interdisciplinarity. Indeed, what Foucault's analysis shows is that, particularly with regard to the human sciences and the humanities, the two go hand in hand. That is to say, the very segmentation of experience that facilitates and requires the coordination of knowledge production contributes immediately to the genesis of an object that is stable precisely to the extent that it is incessantly referred to the diverse, reciprocally legitimating authorities that define the disciplinary field. Appeals to interdisciplinary practices that base themselves on the observation that there is a tragic discrepancy between the fragmentation of knowledge and the totality of social reality often fail to address the question of the sociogenesis of the experience of totality.

Totality is, after all, little more than a concept that seeks to designates what threatens the given social arrangement with something signficantly "around" it. Moreover, what is the tactical point of appeals to interdisciplinarity, to subsume ever more social experience under an academically inflected variant of disciplinary power? Or is it to promote the Hegelian fantasy of a reconciliation between the conditions of knowing and being? Neither of these options seem terribly satisfying. The point of such appeals and the criticisms they harbor is to challenge the political function of knowledge, to confront its institutional organization with a history of those possibilities knowledge production has collaborated to block. If this is so, then the principled refusal of interdisciplinary research advocated by Barthes in his characterization of the coming of the text may be a position well worth mobilizing in the present conjuncture. This is because what the ambivalence of the text enables is a critique of disciplinary reason designed to affect all practical interventions within the academic disciplines by obliging them not to sacrifice their critical character to a depoliticized notion of criticism. Rearranging disciplinary boundaries means little if this rearrangement is not understood to have consequences for the structure of disciplinary power within society at large. Obviously, the contributions to cultural criticism made by such interdisciplinary projects as the sociology of literature or women's studies have become and will remain indispensable, but what I am insisting upon is that such projects continue to confront the task of theorizing and practically addressing the profound consequences of a social divestment of disciplinary power. Such a perspective is what is conveyed in the notion of antidisciplinary research which, I have argued, follows as a tactical consequence of the irreducible ambivalence figured in the concept of textuality.

Of course, the force of these critical claims rests upon the strength of the connection established between the dynamics of disciplinary power and the operation of the academic disciplines. Moreover, the pertinence of my appeal to textuality in this context derives from a reading of it that captures what is necessary about textuality's role in the establishment of such a connection. Before we turn in the ensuing chapters to elaborate the terms of this reading in detail, let us be sure we have addressed the various nuances of these preliminary moves.

Is there not a certain tension between Kuhn's almost commonsensical analysis of disciplinary formation and Foucault's genealogical mapping of disciplinary power? Setting aside their political differences and the fact that Kuhn is primarily concerned with the "natural" sciences, isn't there a serious difference between a paradigm and a subject? It would be foolish not to acknowledge that there is a difference, but is it a difference that has debilitating consequences for the argument I am advancing? I think not and let me indicate why. As already suggested, Kuhn's analysis while forceful seems not to appreciate the complex structure of a disciplinary boundary. A further consequence of this is that he fails to see how the object, that is, the domain ostensibly referred to by axioms, models, and exemplars, is historical not just in the evolutionary sense, but in the political sense. In other words, he does not see that the politically ordered relation among subjects necessary to the disciplinary subjection of agency is what constitutes the existence of the object.[14] It seems to me that Kuhn is certainly sensitive to this issue, as is manifest in his examples which coordinate the ordering of phenomena and the establishment of disciplinary membership, but perhaps because of his willingness to take the subject as that which is given prior to the effects of discipline, he resists the impulse to historicize science thoroughly. Foucault, who often risks conflating history and discipline, nevertheless manages to show how disciplinary objects, particularly through the forms of institutional solidarity established through their generation, are instances of the social production of subjectivity. Once we affirm the thesis that the subject, rather than merely becoming an object, arises where disciplinary discourses precipitate into objects, then it becomes difficult to separate academic disciplines from all the other social practices engaged in the subjection of agency. Foucault's contribution has been to detail the historical framework that authorizes one to accept such a thesis, at least theoretically. Perhaps if we spell out the implications of this thesis at the existential level of a discipline, the connection I see as crucial to the critique of disciplinary reason can be secured, and the implications of textuality as an antidisciplinary "object" clarified. In any case, the tensions that would appear to set paradigms and subjects in opposition can be shown to arise from the difference in scope (and not of "substance") of the analyses of Kuhn and Foucault—a difference that has direct consequences for the force of their respective criticisms.

In order to situate these dynamics at a more concrete level, we need to establish a characterization of discipleship that is attentive to the interplay between the formation of objects and the subjection of agency. If we pursue this in a manner that gets at the tension that arises within objects, then we will have a characterization of discipline that illuminates the specific ambivalence figured in the text. In René Girard's essay, "From Mimetic Desire to the Monstrous Double,"[15] one can glean the outline of such a characterization.

Ostensibly a partial theory of the ritual character of religion, Girard's essay lends itself to my purposes only if one is prepared to read it as a misrecognized theory of the interdisciplinary matrix of anthropology, literary criticism, and the history of religion. My sense is that "violence" plays the central role that it does within Girard's account because he wants to obscure the inescapably modern (cf. Foucault) character of his analysis of the ancient world by projecting the signs of disciplinary power that impinge on his account of discipleship from all sides onto a moment whose "objective" description absolves him of all responsibility to the present. Nevertheless, the theoretical framework of his analysis is suggestive indeed, particularly in its focus on the drama of the disciple.

Girard situates discipleship and thus the agential dynamics of discipline on the triadic grid of mimetic desire. Derived obliquely from Lacanian psychoanalysis, the concept of mimetic desire is distinguished by its triangular structure and the fact that it regards all desire as desire for another, or more precisely, for what the other has. Thus Girard emphasizes the split within desire between lack and envy wherein the articulation of desire is inseparable from aggressivity—the other provokes one to recover what is not exactly "missing." In filling in the triadic grid it becomes evident how this bears on the question of discipleship.

At the apex of the triangle of desire rests "the object," that which is not equal to the other but which appears to be in its possession. At the two points defining the base of the triangle are "the model" (the disciplinarian) and "the disciple" at opposing ends. Narrativized as a description of discipleship, the system operates thus: a collectivity (however restricted) forms when two persons or groups realize that they share an interest in something held by one of them; initially, this object serves to distinguish the two groups and facilitate the exchange between them, but soon the object is subordinated to the rivalry that ensues as the two persons or groups subject themselves to the structure of identification that binds them together—we are the ones who know *this;* under these conditions the object is, in effect, displaced by the dynamics of subjection wherein disciples and models alike struggle to free themselves from the doubling that obscures their distinctive relations to the now lost object— training is nearly impossible without distinction, since someone must truly "have" what the other wants; rather than implode on itself, the collective fixes on a "scapegoat" whose violent elimination restores disciplinary order by establishing a sacred or transcendental instance upon which a prohibition against future acts of violence can rest; significantly the scapegoat usually takes the form of a subject who can double for what presents itself as monstrous in the displaced object, and order is restored when both disciples and models can perceive that their commonality derives from a split between the sacred and the profane that they share, however differently. The disciplinary object thus obscures the subjective tension written into the history of its genesis.

Frank Kermode, in his insightful discussion of canon formation within both the Christian church and the discipline of literary criticism, has pursued similar themes in order to explain the controversy surrounding the shift theorized by Barthes.[16] Though Kermode does not insist upon the distinctive status of the text within his analysis, he does clearly indicate how canons, as structural components of disciplines, become contested terrains where different models of literary interpretation vie for control over the sacred. Moreover, he does draw attention to the constitutional instability of canons (given precisely the dynamics delineated by Girard) and the particularly vicious conflicts that have erupted in the wake of the disciplinary reception of *la nouvelle critique*.

There are several aspects of Girard's narrative that deserve comment. First, the experience of a disciple is bounded by a tension between subjects and the objects they designate as meaningful. Implicit here is a confirmation of Foucault's thesis that the socio-discursive constitution of an object is also, if not primarily, a constitution of subjectivity which devotes itself to the object in order to obscure subjectivity's own grounding in the sociogenesis of objects. This is particularly clear when we consider the scapegoat mechanism, where a relation of doubling is established between a member of the rivaling groups and what is monstrous in the displaced object, namely, the fact that it discloses the social limits of the subject as a particular organization of human agency. As an analysis of disciplinarity, this perspective emphasizes that disciplines are dynamic structures regulating the interplay between subjects and their objects, interplay which is effective precisely to the extent that it is deadly serious. It is perhaps not then surprising that even within humanistic disciplines the passage from the academic status of disciple to that of model is a transfer of power fraught with sufficient tensions that the "sacrificial" discourse that often accompanies it is as comprehensible as it is obnoxious. The dissertator is also the deserter from whom one is entitled to demand his/her "pound of flesh."

Secondly, Girard's narrative invites us to recognize the historicity of discipleship even as a synchronic structure. This can be seen by quickly summarizing the "fate" of the object. Initially, it serves to differentiate two persons or groups. Then it is subordinated to their rivalrous identification. Subsequently, it is projected outward as the monstrous double, only to return as the sacred fetish binding the group together through the rule of the norm. The significance of the object as an instance of the social mediation of human agency cannot be dissociated from the "moments" delimiting its structure. Though these moments seem temporally distributed, they are actually spatially contiguous in the "memory" of a discipline. What this implies about disciplinarity is significant. On the one hand, it indicates that disciplines are traversed by both internal and external struggles; in fact, Girard's account shows that these struggles are coordinated. Put in concrete terms, one might say that the struggles that divide any given discipline have to do with the way the members comprising it situate themselves in relation to the necessarily external conflicts that impinge upon them. Of course, what this means is that disciplines are not irreducibly interdisciplinary simply because of the passage of time, but because of the structural dynamics that define them *qua* disciplines. Girard thus lends support to Foucault's contention that disciplinary power necessarily involves the coordination of different objectal domains—an insight I believe obliges us to appeal to the emancipatory potential of interdisciplinarity with tremendous caution.

Lastly, the characterization of discipleship in "From Mimetic Desire to the Monstrous Double" invites us to designate as one of the most problematic aspects of discipline, the fact that disciplines seem paradoxically to be constructed around a defense against their objects—or, as Paul de Man once said," methodologies that call themselves theories of reading . . . nevertheless avoid the function they claim as their object." [17] Girard formulates this indirectly by showing that the stability of a group or discipline rests on a sacralization of the object, a process which is predicated upon its initial displacement and its subsequent misrecognition. I have presented this in terms of the way the subjection of agency is occluded by the formation of objects designated as such. In either case what is crucial here is that we recognize that disciplines cannot know what they claim to know, and what substitutes for this lack of knowledge is a bureaucratically articulated policing of fidelity. In light of this I would argue that the crisis of judgment that Allan Bloom and others insist we are currently plagued by is not new; it is endemic to disciplines because the latter cannot actually accomplish what their members, simply by virtue of their status as disciples, desire. What is recent, if not new, is the fact that this incapacity is becoming increasingly difficult to separate, particularly within informed opinion, from the social process of instituting disciplines as such. Thus, when I speak of the critique of disciplinary reason, it is precisely with this faint evocation of Kant in mind—disciplines cannot know the "object-itself," the condition of their knowing. This state of affairs is inscribed in the ambivalent core of the text as an antidisciplinary object or field.

Having set out moments ago to respond to some of the nuances in the materials assembled here, and now poised to delineate the history of the text's emergence, the time has come to address the text's relation to the modernity of power and the politics of disciplinary criticism. Barthes, however cannily, clearly argues that the "slide" constituting the text situates it in relation to the European reception of the critical work of Saussure, Marx, and Freud. Foucault, in order to avoid recourse to the "break" (allegedly constituted by the same figures), approaches modernity from a standpoint that leads one to see Saussure, Marx, and Freud, in particular, as theorists whose critical contributions were actually latent within the cultural logic of modernity. Is it really possible then to read the text in a manner that reconciles it with the preoccupations of disciplinary power? Furthermore, is it possible to avoid sacrificing textuality as a tactical term to the fate shared by Saussure, Marx, and Freud at the hands of Foucault?

Let us take the less consequential matter first. Foucault's analysis of discipline in *Discipline and Punish* clearly emphasizes the relation between modern power and the object's role in the social constitution of subjectivity. When Barthes aligns textuality with the notion of "field" and then goes on to embed the earlier conjuncture of the reader and the writer within the conjuncture of the methodologist and his/her materials, he is clearly approaching disciplinarity with an eye toward stressing its implications for the social organization of human agency. Far too often the "birth of the reader" called for toward the end of "The Death of the Author" (1968) is read either as a call for wanton interpretive license or as an anticipation of reader response criticism, but in either case with insufficent sensitivity to the blatantly Foucauldian resonances of the phrase. What is important is not that one recognize the intellectual solidarity here, which would be pointless to deny in the wake of Barthes's inaugural lecture at the Collège de France, but rather that one begin to consider that the theory of the text, even in pieces which predate its elaboration, was also a theory of the subjection of human agency. Without such an hypothesis it is very hard to understand why in Barthes's later development of these issues the opposition between pleasure and bliss becomes fundamental. In any case, what emerges from the early essays is an explicit effort to link the crisis of interdisciplinary research registered in the advent of the text with the task of reconceptualizing the agency of literary experience.[18]

This being so, what is it about textuality that distinguishes it from a merely affirmative critique of disciplinary power? Or, put somewhat differently, in what way does the project of antidisciplinary research provoked by the advent of the text break with the institutional legitimations of modernity?

Barthes, without succumbing to the temptation to accelerate some neurotic plunge into institutional chaos, nevertheless insists upon conceiving of the crisis in disciplinarity so as to foster a contestation of the institutional framework itself. This is precisely what spurs his recourse to the two models of interdisciplinary research, because the second, "effective" model seeks to acknowledge that interests which outdistance the network of academic disciplines need to be factored into a contestation of the academic institutions themselves. This is why the text becomes crucial. It serves, in Barthes's account, to designate that aspect of the objects of disciplinary debate binding them to the circuits of power fundamental to the subjection of human agency. If it has any conceptual integrity at all, the text must then remain in touch both with the specificity of the cultural signifier and the sociopolitical dynamics conditioning its analysis. Without this split theater of operation, the text is easily sacrificed to an institutional reaffirmation of modernity. This is because even though academic institutions might always be in a position to sponsor (and thereby avoid) their own conceptual negation, unless one's critical categories register the necessity of concerning oneself with such questions, it is always possible that academics will believe that such a negation has already been effectively carried out. Textuality registers this necessity by situating cultural study on a ground that is either assumed, and thus *openly* surrendered to the forces of social hegemony, or contested, and thus rendered quintessentially postmodern, that is, unsettled. In what follows I will be attempting to amplify and justify these claims, because I believe that it is worth doing so before the critical possibilities harbored within the notion of textuality have succumbed to the affirmative critiques of the humanities that have actually now entered into public debate about education.

To proceed, let us be clear about what an affirmative critique is. In the tradition of critical philosophy inaugurated by Kant, the concept of critique has focused less on the rejection of prior convictions, be they religious, political, or philosophical, and more on the systematic interrogation of foundations. Nevertheless, in Kant's own work the practice of critique remained immanent to the discipline of philosophy within the conflict of the faculties. As is often argued, Kant worried more about defining the proper limits of philosophical knowledge than he did about the problem of what philosophical discourse presupposed without being able to give an account of it on its own terms. This is not to say that Kant failed to engage knowledge produced in other disciplines, but only that insofar as he engaged this knowledge he did so with an eye toward determining how it might be drawn into the task of clarifying the proper limits of philosophy. Paradoxically, Kant occupied other fields in order to learn about his own.

On one level this procedure is entirely proper—one should seek to question what limits one's project from the inside. But if this questioning only operates to protect and further consolidate a disciplinary project by attempting to pass the gesture of self-scrutiny off as an encounter with what outdistances the project as such, then we have an example of an affirmative critique—a critique which interrogates foundations in order to fortify them against critical scrutiny from the outside. When Marx sought to confront the discourses of bourgeois political economy and German idealism with the various discourses of the European proletariat, he was not merely turning Hegel on his head, he was rejecting the tradition of affirmative criticism inaugurated, in large part, by Kant.

Thus, when I speak of an affirmative critique of disciplinary power, I am thinking of the move toward interdisciplinary study as such. It is not that I object to "blurring the genres" (cf. Clifford Geertz) of disciplinarity—a gesture which is as important as it is unavoidable. But since the radicality of a renewed appeal to interdisciplinary research secures its political credentials by obscuring both the structural and the historical character of the disciplines, it can hardly be considered an effective political critique of the very possibility of disciplinary power. Here, however, is where we run into the heart of the matter. If Foucault comprehends the modernity of power in terms of its transcendence of the repressive hypothesis—an hypothesis that apparently denies the possiblity of any heterotopic site of resistance—and if disciplinarity is the modality of power in its modern configuration, then in what sense is it possible to avoid an affirmative critique of disciplinary power? And more specifically of course, how does the text participate in the avoidance of such a critique?

Let us return, in this context, to the issue of the irreducible ambivalence of textuality. I have engaged this quality in two ways: first, by stressing the disciplinary conflict that wrenched textuality out of the encounter between linguistics and literary criticism and, second, by linking the stubborn particularity of the text to the production of utopic space within the framework of cultural interpretation. I would argue that when Barthes, in "From Work to Text," emphasizes the importance of an "effective" mode of interdiciplinary research, he is giving expression to similar concerns. In other words, to claim—as Barthes does—that the text arose at the point where several disciplines sought to reorganize themselves around an object which eluded each of them in different ways (in this respect the text represents a monstrously "squared" double) is to claim that the text is an ambivalent object, or field. The text is simultaneously shared by several disciplines, while also exposing those disciplines not merely to the borders they share, but to their limits as formations of disciplinary power. The text was not produced by any of the disciplines that came to share it as an object; instead it was produced by a confluence that, to use Freud's term, "overdetermined" it. This means that the text is *within* disciplinarity, but in a manner that captures the constitutional instability of disciplinary power—an instability rooted in the alterity that pressures discipline to develop and expand. For this reason textuality must be distinguished from interdisciplinary research without abandoning it, which is why I have argued that it makes more sense to conceive of the text as an antidisciplinary field.

However, can this notion of the text be reconciled with the modernity of power? I believe it can. If we recognize that the spiral of power and resistance that Foucault drew upon to reject the repressive hypothesis was meant to counter the rather naive notion that the struggle for power somehow took place outside it (without thereby concluding that neither resistance nor domination took place), then such a reconciliation can be effected. As we have seen, Foucault treats the academic disciplines as construction sites where statements can be produced. Some of these will be different, and some will be more of the same. What constitutes the differential character of certain statements has to do with the way they rearrange the lines of force within the rivalrous structure of the discipline. It is on such grounds that Foucault distinguishes figures like Marx and Freud from "authors" in "What is an Author?"[19] Rearranging the lines of force and conflict means shifting the balance of power without, however, doing so by affecting this balance from some Archimedean point of disinterested potency.

But let us factor back in the larger field of disciplinary power, that is, the wider social context in which the academic disciplines operate. Obviously, certain disciplinary rearrangements may work to bring a particular discipline into alignment with power struggles that compromise the gains otherwise thought to have been achieved within a particular discipline. For example, the psychologism that I. A. Richards introduced into literary criticism during the twenties could be seen as an accommodation of the positivist behaviorism that was beginning to sweep through Britain and the United States. By the same token, when disciplinary crises can be made to articulate with other struggles, in other sites, over the structure of disciplinary power within society at large, then what might have been limited to mere institutional "innovation" accedes to the status of "non-affirmative critique," without, however, escaping power altogether. When, in another context, Foucault moves to reintegrate Freud and Marx within the history of modernity (thus resisting the "postmodern" option), he does so on the grounds that the statements they produced, however radical they may have been within the emergent disciplines of psychology and political economy, nevertheless failed to articulate with other struggles, at other levels, in a manner that truly rearranged the lines of force within the framework of disciplinary power—Freud remained ensnared within the apparatus of sexuality, and Marx remained enchained to the anthropologically forged link between scarcity and labor. As scandalously overexaggerated as this claim may be (particularly in the case of Marx), it nevertheless clarifies what I take to be at stake in the anti-disciplinary object of the text.

My point is not, of course, that the text succeeds where Freud and Marx fail—this is why its theorization calls out for finishing. Rather, I want to stress the way the text, as a model for thinking about what disciplines study, can be made to respond to the political demands imposed upon us by the framework of disciplinary power. Far too often the insistence that the interpretation of culture be politicized is restricted, at the practical level, to the introduction of political interpretations of various and sundry cultural artifacts conducted within either disciplinary or interdisciplinary settings. While it is true that this practice, if pursued with sufficient rigor and abandon, can provoke what have been called "curriculum wars," it often does little more than degenerate into curricular innovation. Textuality becomes tactically significant in this context.

As we have seen, the text is divided against itself—not only in terms of the way it straddles the domains of examples and models, but also in terms of the way it links the constitution of examples to the utopic, to the not yet integrated. When we approach particular examples of cultural artifacts as texts (that is, as constructs of the interaction between a signifying practice and a methodological field), we are trying to comprehend how what eludes us in our interpretation has to do with the limits imposed upon our construction by the field in which it is executed. This has the effect of juxtaposing the very texture of an artifact and the struggle against disciplinary power as this power manifests itself in the object or model. What this struggle articulates with beyond the academic framework, textuality does not name. But this is not necessarily an obstruction of those struggles, as some have argued. By virtue of its ambivalent structure, the text insists that artifacts mean both what we make them mean and what others *might* make them mean if we stopped trying to represent their interests for them. Of course, we are in no position to know what this might be, and we have to structure what we do so that it might be pirated by those whose struggle against disciplinarity might well be unrecognizable to us. Thus, the "plural" character of the text (cf. Barthes) has less to do with some bland notion of multiple meanings, than with an empowerment that enables our constructions to be ceaselessly challenged—not merely contested at the level of conclusions, but subverted at the level of disciplinary legitimation. By insisting upon this antidisciplinary dimension of textuality, one can, in effect, institutionalize—that is, render accessible—the conditions for a nonaffirmative critique of the institution. The political character of cultural interpretation is not then reduced to a dispute over "readings," nor is it relegated to extracurricular activities like voting, demonstrating, or striking. Through the concept of the text it may become possible to articulate in a fairly direct way the struggle over interpretation with the struggle to change the world of disciplinary power.

Needless to say we are far from such a position today. My persistent use of the conditional bears silent witness to this. One of the chief reasons for this has to do with the history of the disciplinary appropriation of textuality discussed in my earlier engagement with Jameson's "The Ideology of the Text." As was conceded there, textuality, from its very inception, was swept into the orbit of the literary disciplines, and this despite the fact that it emerged from a crisis within them. This fate had much to do with the fact that within the French context shifts in the institutional structure of intellectual power had begun to menace what Richard Rorty calls the "presiding cultural discipline" of literature. Less a matter of the pure and simple decline of Tradition, than a matter of losing the initiative in the struggle over whether hermeneutics or science was to define the domain of cultural politics, this situation nevertheless prompted the theorists of textuality to enter a Faustian pact with the disciplines of literary study.

In order to sustain contact with one of the few surviving secular practices of cultural interpretation (hence, as well, the enormous importance of psychoanalysis within the theorization of the text), Barthes and others moved to shore up the literary enterprise by giving the perennial literary question of "fictionality" an epistemological spin—a move first worked out in Hegel's reflections on the "genre" of philosophy and then restated in Heidegger's meditation on *poiesis*. Through the deployment of the conceptional weaponry of semiotics and the semiological notion of the text, daily life itself soon became a "legible," if not ultimately a "traceable," phenomenon. Needless to say, this development represented an ambiguous triumph, for concommitant with the preservation of the hermeneutic hedge against positivism came the homogenization of textuality—instead of responding to the ambivalence at its core, the theory of the text ossified into an occupational force which tended to translate all questions of interpretation into variants of literary problems. However, it should be quickly added, that each of the major theorists of textuality struggled energetically with this dilemma. And while none of them really maneuvers the textual model beyond the context of its homogenization, the struggle to do so can be read as an effort to respond to something in the text that resists its literary appropriation. The point is not, at this time, to separate the text from literature, but to attenuate the "literarization" of the model by retrieving and developing the antidisciplinary currents within it.

# 2

## * The Text Goes Pop

**I**

Let us now return to the issue broached in the preceding chapter, namely, that of the structural and historical determinants bearing on the crisis of disciplinarity that precipitated the emergence of the text.[1] As we shall see, reopening this line of inquiry will immediately entangle us in serious methodological questions concerning the very status of the rhetoric of historical determination, the complexities of which invite us to reread one of Barthes's essays in order to get our bearings.

In "From Work to Text" one will find the following curious phrase set off by dashes, "—perhaps even violently, via the jolts of fashion—" (peut-être même violemment à travers les secousses de la mode") (p. 155). It breaks up a sentence in which Barthes is contrasting two types of interdisciplinarity in order to establish the peculiar context for the emergence of the text as a literary object. The phrase, though qualified, offers to explain at the highest level of generality what happened to provoke the shift from work to text he is mapping. I say "highest level of generality" because Barthes does evoke other decisive developments—the crisis of the sign within linguistics, the impact of semiotics on the human sciences, and the encounter between Marxism and psychoanalysis—but once we realize that his account is gesturing toward the extra-academic, it becomes clear that the domain of fashion is the only pertinent such referent offered. This is not to say that Barthes's theory of the text has recourse to some ill-defined notion of the determining last instance of fashion. Nevertheless, after we take seriously the task of reading the advent of textuality as a multiply articulated moment of social history, it is worth pondering what might well be at stake in the priority given to fashion in Barthes's account. It is my aim to do just that in this chapter, not because I am concerned to disclose Barthes's true convictions, but because I believe the text has something fundamental to do with the cultural dynamics of fashion, and this deserves elaboration if we want to know what the text is.

Barthes's phrase invites two sorts of glosses. One that seeks to clarify what is to be understood by his evocation of *la mode,* and another that emphasizes the significance of the relation established between violence and "the jolts" administered by fashion. Ultimately, I believe these glosses can only be separated for the sake of expository convenience, though this may not be immediately apparent.

In 1967 Barthes published the results of a project begun in 1957 under the title, *The Fashion System.*[2] An attempt to elaborate the "discipline" (as he called it) of semiology by reading the discourse of fashion magazines as a complex semiotic system, this book contains a discussion of the relation between fashion and history that helps illuminate what is at stake for Barthes in the notion of fashion. This discussion, entitled "History and Diachrony of Fashion," appears as the book's appendix. What is signficant about it, at least for my purposes, are principally two things. On the one hand, Barthes develops there an analysis of fashion that broadens its implications, making it easier to bridge the apparent distance between clothing and disciplinary objects. On the other hand, and this is what makes the bridgework possible, Barthes uses the notion of fashion to problematize the very historical dimension of cultural analysis. Though initially this takes the rather benign form of indicating how the fundamental dependency of fashion on change complicates the effort to draw analogies between hemlines and the stock market, by the end of the appendix, Barthes has implicitly maneuvered to define fashion as an example of what Althusser had called a "relatively autonomous" instance of the social.[3] As such, history is bracketed not as irrelevant, but as indeterminant in its social causality. Or, put another way, if history is the domain of the economic struggle among classes, then those signifying practices whose constituent elements cannot be reduced to this domain take up relations among themselves which are not immediately historical in the strict sense. In effect, this was how Althusser designated the entire domain of ideology. His aim was not to transcendentalize the superstructure as has often been argued, but rather to diversify radically the social domain. Barthes seems plainly committed to such a view when, as the essay continues, he argues that fashion is touched by history only at the level of what he calls fashion's "rhythm," that is, the tempo and pattern of exchanges occurring among the various levels within its system. In other words, only certain aspects of the fashion system are directly controlled by historical developments in the economy. Thus, the real issue involves where what one calls "the historical" is registered, not whether "it" is effective in some absolute sense. Barthes stresses this when in "Literature Today" (from the period during the writing of *The Fashion System*) he equates fashion and literary history by showing how both subsume the domain of objects under a procession of forms—forms which derive from discursive systems that mediate, and therefore distance us from, the economic dimension of the social.[4]

Though one might be tempted to conclude that Barthes is simply reading fashion as an instance of the merely ideological (however radicalized), this strikes me as misleading. For one thing, Barthes is (at least when the project gets underway) still close to his aggressive rethinking of ideology as myth, and there is simply too much passion displayed toward his material for it to stand implicitly condemned as worthy solely of unmasking. Moreover, the analysis of fashion is completed when Barthes is developing the critique of representation that later played such a fundamental role in challenging the Marxian category of "false consciousness" within media studies. This becomes particularly apparent when one compares *Fashion* with the contemporaneous essay titled "Historical Discourse."[5] There, as a way of grounding the claim that at the level of discourse history and fiction cannot be securely distinguished, Barthes introduces the notion of the "reality effect," which short-circuits the logic of reductive ideological analyses by insisting that discourses traverse and thus undermine the division between the base and the superstructure. Significantly, the conditions for this insight (if not the effect) cited in the essay are precisely those used to elaborate what constitutes the full domain of fashion in the earlier work, namely, the forms and technologies of mass culture, most notably photography. Thus it would seem unlikely, given the importance of the critique of representation in Barthes's later work, that fashion—which is here aligned with the enabling conditions of such a critique—would be attacked as mere ideology. Even so the question remains: what are we to make of the notion of fashion, particularly as it operates in "From Work to Text?"

Semantically, fashion is to be understood as a metonym for the logic of mass culture as a whole, implying that the notion of seasonally organized controlled consumption is consummately embodied in the system of fashion. Structurally, and this follows from its relation to the very logic of mass culture, fashion is understood to embody and thus exemplify the historical development wherein society has so fragmented that historical discourse itself can no longer support the efforts to narrativize experience. The notion of fragmentation is not utilized pejoratively here. Instead, as I have already suggested, it registers the multiple articulations of a social field that resists narrative (including theoretical narrative) mastery, thus realizing a state of what I will later characterize as "openness." Thus, Barthes in "From Work to Text" can be understood to be arguing that the text arose when the symbolic practices of mass culture began to saturate and redirect the institutionally channeled production of knowledge. Contrary to certain influential accounts of this development, the process of saturation actually functions, as we shall see, to proliferate contending discourses and "subject positions" thus contributing to rather than stiffling the heterogeneity of the social. Even if one chooses to give Barthes's phrase the most innocuous of readings, namely, that the text is merely a fad, the brashness of offering this as an explanation for a development upon which Barthes will stake his entire career in effect enunciates the same sort of message as would a pair of "baggies" in the fashion system of the Académie Française—it constitutes an intrusion of the vulgar. That being so, I think we are obliged to take the invocation of fashion quite seriously, especially when, as I have indicated, Barthes himself has continual recourse to fashion throughout the early sixties. Nevertheless, taking fashion seriously does not clarify why jolts and violence are harnessed together in the phrase. Let us ponder this for a moment before elaborating the justification for this reading of the essay.

Of course, one way to read the relation between violence and the jolts of fashion is in terms of an oblique evocation of the popular insurrection embodied in May 1968. I do not believe that this is altogether misleading, but the reservations cited in chapter 1 concerning such a deterministic explanation remain strong and thus require clarification at this juncture.

While Barthes acknowledges the significance of the events of May for intellectual life in Paris, if not Western Europe, he typically specifies this significance by illustrating how the very traditions of scholarship organized around such methodological standards as historicism (whether Marxist or Liberal) were profoundly shaken by these events.[6] Thus, given that Barthes is interrogating the status of historical discourse explicitly in the reference to fashion, it seems unlikely that he would turn around and offer a patently historicist account of the disciplinary crisis. Instead,

Barthes is more likely to be underscoring the *peculiarity* of May 1968 as an historical event—a peculiarity that derives, no doubt, from the fact that it was generated by the new social movements organized by the cultural dynamics of late modernity, and as such unforeseen even by Marxian prognosticators. These movements, precisely because of their explicitly cultural determinations, cannot be dissociated from the opening of the social that resulted, in large part, from the impact of mass culture on the institutions of knowledge production and circulation. For this reason then, Barthes may well be trying to gather the explanatory force of his remarks around the notion of "jolt," understood less in terms of surprise (though this is phenomenologically relevant) than as the means by which the social formation articulates its various moments once its organic and therefore homogeneous nature has been lost. As such, the allusion to violent jolts operates to establish a redundancy in the phrase between "jolts" and "fashion." As a consequence, it operates rather like the double negative of Black American English—it does not negate itself, it materially intensifies the semantic content of the phrase in which it appears.

Barthes's significant precursor in such an analysis is Walter Benjamin, whose germinal reading of Paris in the nineteenth century pivots on the notion of "shock" as a means to designate the experiential specificity of modernism.[7] Though the complexities of Benjamin's position on modernism are notorious, it is fair to say that shock serves to characterize the atmosphere in which the modern subject is interpellated by the traffic patterns, advertising discourses, business cycles, production routines, leisure activities, etc. of the metropolitan space first mapped by Georg Simmel. As one would expect from Benjamin, this atmosphere is properly dialectical in that shock both ravages human agency and prepares it to receive the graft of the efficient and resourceful modern subject. Inscribed in this double function of shock is Benjamin's dialectical appraisal of mass culture as both blessing and curse—an appraisal that, I would contend, he shares with Barthes despite the fact that, like many intellectuals of his generation, the latter knew pathetically little about Benjamin. Such theoretical solidarity would thus imply that the jolts summoned up by Barthes are an analytic expression of many of the same preoccupations reflected in Benjamin's critique of modernity, chief among these being the conviction that the technologies of mass culture have reorganized human experience so profoundly that the legitimated institutional accounts of it, including those accounts which stress the essentially historical character of experience, have been, if not destroyed, then certainly reconfigured. If one of the effects of this development has indeed been the opening of the social, then the jolts of fashion are not best understood as kinetic traits of a particular symbolic practice (*haute couture*), but rather as a *general* designation of the interaction or articulation of practices within the reconfigured social order. Jolts thus refer to the points of contact that organize an ensemble of effects such that these can generate the ensemble's own cause. Not surprisingly, this is precisely the sort of formulation Althusser relied upon in his contestation of historical determinism within Marxism.

But let us move to concretize these general observations by returning to the more pressing task of specifying the relation between fashion and the text. By situating the text as a disciplinary object (at least initially) within a general crisis of the disciplinary framework, and then by offering as an explanation of this crisis the jolts of fashion, isn't Barthes suggesting that insofar as the text comes to designate the engagement of this development it is in effect a "pop" or mass cultural phenomenon? Not in the pejorative sense of a slick piece of social reproduction, but in the sense of an institutional articulation of a popular contestation of the academy. In saying this I do not mean to separate the text from slickness entirely since, as we shall see, this is neither possible nor desirable. But because the prevailing wisdom has been that the text is either a purely vanguard notion or nothing but a publicity stunt, it is important to proceed circumspectly here. What strikes me as particularly insightful and therefore impressive about Barthes's analysis is that he approaches the text by affirming that it cannot be understood either by separating it from the institutional dynamics of disciplinary reason or by separating these dynamics not only from disciplinary power but from the latter's specifically mass cultural inflection. Moreover, Barthes clearly sees that a decisive spur to those interdisciplinary developments that found expression in the text came from an erosion of the border between official knowledge and commodity consumption. While such an account squares with those that seek to affirm interdisciplinarity as an institutional response to the "social totality" that always already eludes academia, what sharply distinguishes it from such accounts is its insistence upon both the intra-institutional crisis provoked by the specifically mass cultural character of the incursion and the methodological responsibilities that followed from this.

Though it is often argued that the text embodies a quasi-modernist commitment to elite culture, this may only be true at the level of its methodological application within the discipline of literary study. The scandal is, of course, that the poststructural reading of elite culture en-

abled by the notion of textuality is not simply an expression of clois-
tered (and therefore inconsequential) vanguardism, but is also, if not
primarily, an expression of mass cultural interests articulated in a critical
discourse previously impervious to them. Put another way, the text did
not simply facilitate a broadening of the cultural canon, it undermined
the conceptual ground of canonicity, making the task of protecting "the
great tradition" (cf. Leavis) from the "unwashed" considerably more difficult. Unless we recognize this dimension of the scandal of textuality,
we risk overlooking certain rather conspicuous developments within recent cultural criticism. Just to take a ready example, there must surely
be something more than an accidental reason for the profusion of "textual analyses" (so designated) of Hollywood films. What I am arguing
is that Barthes's account compels us to consider the possibility that in
some unforeseen way sheer fidelity to the rigors of what has been called
the "immanent critique"[8] of mass culture led analysts to approach these
artifacts through the field of the text.

In the interest of spelling out more fully the implications of this nèw
model of "contextuality," let us begin by detailing some of the more
conspicuous signs of the position I am ascribing to Barthes's essay.

In 1968 Editions du Seuil, a major and respected French publishing house, printed a volume of essays and interviews entitled *Théorie
d'ensemble.*[9] Financed as a title within the Tel Quel series, it was not only
"hip" (*tel quel* in the sense of, "telling it like it is"), it was a stunning as-
semblage of position papers written, for the most part, by the aggressive
young intellectuals associated with, or members of the editorial board of
the journal, *Tel Quel.* Not surprisingly, given its importance to the critical
project of the journal, one of the essays in the collection is devoted to the
systematic presentation of the notion of the text. The essay, "Première ap-
proche de la notion de texte," was written by Jean-Louis Houdebine who
is known to English-speaking audiences primarily as one of Jacques Derrida's more tenacious interlocutors in the interviews gathered together
under the general title of *Positions,*[10] but who at the time was a contributor to *La Nouvelle Critique.* Though I will have occasion to discuss this
essay in some detail later, what requires immediate emphasis is the often
overlooked fact that its first venue was this glossy monthly of the French
Communist Party (PCF). Despite the fact that Houdebine was not then
active within *Tel Quel,* his essay was included among the half dozen or
so contributions from the quarterly whose editors were called upon, as
the cover blurb on the issue inaugurating the feature says, to "respond"
to *La Nouvelle Critique.* Setting aside, for a moment, the conceivably

perplexing topography of such a response, what interests me about this is not that it indicates the compromises French intellectuals are either willing or forced to accept, but rather the fact that one of the earliest attempts to formulate the theory of the text occurred in the context of a deliberate reassessment, on the part of the PCF, of the relation between power and the mass media. By looking at this unusual and limited context, I think we can see to what extent Barthes's formulations illuminate the coming of the text in an as yet unappreciated way.[11]

Seven issues prior to the double issue in which the first of *Tel Quel*'s contributions appeared, *La Nouvelle Critique* divided between an old series that extended back to 1948 and a new series begun in February 1967 that continues to this very day. The motivations for this division are no doubt myriad and complex, perhaps even more so than the editors would be prepared to admit, but at least they attempted to assess them.[12] In the first issue of the new series, the first three pages of the magazine are devoted to an editorial statement in which an analysis of the then current conjuncture was offered as an explanation for the urgency of the new series. Though a typical example of what is one of the more self-aggrandizing genres, the "letter from the editor(s)" does single out a number of themes that deserve our attention.

To begin with it acknowledges that current events are confronting people on the Left with what the editors call "new questions." These are not simply questions concerning how a static body of political opinion is to respond to novel developments. As the editors make clear, the questions confronting their readership include issues of interpretive method, that is, problems concerning the adequacy of the categories used to identify or even pose relevant questions. Significantly, the developments cited that demand such self-reflexivity include the reorganization of knowledge precipitated by the evolution of mass cultural technology. Not surprisingly, the editors then go on to express their concern that one of the chief effects of this evolution has been the proliferation of audiences who are not yet being addressed by the Left. In general, however, it does strike me as surprising that a mass circulation (which is not to say, profitable) periodical could have as explicitly lucid an analysis of its own situation and recognize that the price of such an analysis must be exacted through a transformation of its own material and graphic organization. Hence the new series, complete with its flashy fonts, color photographs, and discontinuous formatting. However much one might be disposed to condemn magazines such as *La Nouvelle Critique* for resorting to "slickness," such a disposition should not be exploited to avoid the issue of whether the engagement of new questions requires an engagement of the technologies conditioning their emergence. In fact, in those cases where this attitude does prevail, one often sees to what extent the critique of mass culture as "spectacle" derives from a transparent disavowal of the very envy thought to be promulgated by slickness.

Thus, toward the end of the first year of its newly adopted profile *La Nouvelle Critique* invites the theoreticians of textuality to address its readers on the question of literary production.[13] Given that the magazine was seeking to attract new readers, one might even say "constitute" new readers, it is not difficult to read the solicitation of *Tel Quel* as an effort to identify a site where an old theme of Marxist scholarship (cultural, or in this case literary, production) is being subjected to new questions. While it is clear from the tenor of the questions posed to *Tel Quel* that the editors are concerned to keep the discussion of production within the orbit of the PCF's concerns, it is equally clear that the debate exposes both parties to the social dynamics thematized in the editorial statement of the inaugural issue of the new series. On one level, of course, this indicates simply that the "media cycle," designated by Régis Debray as the most recent period of French intellectual life,[14] has exerted its characteristic pressure on the writers of both the magazine and the journal, essentially obliging the *Tel Quel* intellectuals to seek this form of "popular" venue. While this is certainly one level on which the pop character of textuality is elaborated, it is not the most interesting or compelling one. If, however, upon examining the content of Houdebine's essay for the characteristics ascribed to the notion of the text, we were to discover there signs of the same preoccupations animating the editorial statement, then not only would we have begun to identify what would qualify as an immanent relation between mass culture and textuality, but we would have also opened a suggestively new line of reflection—one that bears on the text's status as an instance of power within the social dynamics of the present conjuncture. Let us then engage Houdebine's essay in this spirit.

Both versions of this essay (*La Nouvelle Critique* 8/9 and *Théorie d'ensemble*) open by pointing out the constraints that define it. In particular, Houdebine emphasizes the spatial limits of a magazine article that will deprive his piece of a certain thoroughness and "force" him to advertise the work of his interlocutors through bibliographical allusions. This is a formulaic announcement of the presence of mass culture that is readable as such when one recognizes the deferential manner in which it protests against the anti-intellectualism of its immediate context. If it were merely an excuse for the writer's own limits, the essay would surely have disappeared from the collectively edited book, where the board would have had an opportunity to exercise its judgment on such matters rather than compromise the integrity of its own positions. Since the piece reappears in *Théorie d'ensemble* with a new title (it originally appeared under the title, "Texte, Structure, Histoire") and significant but modest revisions, one is entitled to assume that the registration of the mass cultural setting belongs to the text on the text. So too, the fact that the rhetorically inscribed acknowledgment of spatial constraints persists even when they no longer apply in the same way indicates that the hostility toward mass culture such an acknowledgment might seem to embody is qualified if not altogether denied. If we reemphasize that Houdebine's essay was incorporated, as it were, in the Editions du Seuil publication, then the "generic" limits whose operation might otherwise block the hypothesis I am advancing here can be shown to be inapplicable. In other words, the book repeated the magazine article's self-referential criticism despite its lack of immediate relevance. But absence of hostility is one thing; affirmation is another. In what other ways does this theory of the text introject and articulate the logic of mass culture?

Taken in its entirety, the piece is a synthesis of current or relevant prior research that, paradoxically, is presented as nonetheless groping toward an initial position on textuality. Tactically, Houdebine proceeds by introducing those enabling propositions that will require that his presentation of the text question the questions formulated by the editorial board of the magazine. To this extent he is doing exactly what was expected of him. As with most effective narratives, his is organized by a repetition. It opens by designating the text as a result of literary production, thus engaging the theme of the debate directly, and it closes by rejecting the notion of production in favor of a view of the text that has nothing to do with the "work," understood as a fixed product. As such, Houdebine anticipates the distinction later mobilized by Barthes, though he subordinates the latter's historical and disciplinary perspective to a polemical drive for efficient contrastive categories. However, rather than redress what might appear to be the contradiction latent in this repetition by defining the text as such, Houdebine prefers to evoke the text by showing how something exhibiting its properties enables one to attack reflectionist aesthetics whose illegitimate conceptual authority is then held accountable for his necessarily oblique presentation of the text. It is not therefore surprising that when the text is characterized directly (that is, as a positively determined element of a binary opposition) it seems synonymous with that which eludes linguistic determination. Of course, what is so suggestive about such a gesture is that it is exactly like the rhetorical strategy of most commodity advertising where the virtues of one's own product are made to depend on its ability to affirm the system that proffers the competitor as a fair target. This otherwise fortuitous coincidence could be overlooked if it were not for the fact that the two theses on textuality actually advanced in the essay seem informed by some of the same concerns voiced in the editorial statement of *La Nouvelle Critique* analyzed above.

In radically distinguishing the text from the work, Houdebine underscores the text's status as a fragment, that is, as a limited field in which the limitless and reversible process of converting reading into writing transpires. Explicitly underlying this move is the idea that authors and readers no longer have linear access to one another through the stability of an act of cultural communication. Given that the literary evidence for this claim almost always involves those figures we call "modernists" (Joyce, Kafka, Artaud), would it not be reasonable to argue that the dissolution of audiences deemed fundamental to this "literary" practice applies to the theoretical evidence as well? In which case, the opening of the social we have connected with the ubiquity of mass cultural practices is addressed in the very theorization of the text—not just at the level of intellectual content, but also, as I have already suggested, at the level of gesture and scriptural practice.

One's doubts about such claims are dispelled, I think, when we turn to Houdebine's second thesis which draws heavily from Julia Kristeva's reading of Mikhail Bakhtin. To avoid collapsing textuality into a misguided quest for the grail of literary specificity, Houdebine supplements its reading as fragment with the notion of the text's "intrinsic" polyvalency. Following Bahktin, he insists upon the multifariously stratified character of any text, implying not only that anything worthy of the name must be read as comprised of heteronomous signifying instances (e.g., art, politics, fantasy), but that a text *qua* text necessarily positions the reading or writing subject in opposition to regimes whose stability derives from an obfuscation of the heterodox character of their symbolic practices. This state of affairs was analyzed under the heading of the "carnivalesque" in Bakhtin who, in so doing, sought to indicate how the dynamics of popular or "folk" culture operated both within and upon language. Houdebine, in openly appropriating the terms of this discussion, thus fuses the characteristic structural volatility of the text (as an analytic category) with the imbrication of official and unofficial discourses analyzed by Bakhtin. Whether one chooses to make a historical issue of the difference between mass and popular culture or not, it seems to me that the theorization of the text cannot be separated from an effort to respond to the remapping of discursive boundaries precipitated by activities outside the centers of knowledge production—activities' which in the late modern period are ineluctably marked by the presence of mass cultural technologies.

Houdebine's divided allegiances notwithstanding, I do not believe that the text is either misrepresented or misunderstood by him. The reader will recall that Barthes himself sought to locate certain of the enabling conditions of textuality in the mass cultural field, but in a manner that required the sort of specification that the analysis of Houdebine's essay has provided. What seems called for at this juncture is an insistence that the allegedly compromising vanguardism of the text be seriously qualified. However, this need not be carried out by surrendering the text's critical status to the ruthless opportunism of commodity discourse. Instead, if we recognize at what level the categories of elite culture (whether traditional or avant-garde) are informed by the social dynamics fostered by commodity discourse, not only will we be able to focus accurately the inquiry into the text's critical character, but we will be forced to recognize that the evaluative distinction between elite and popular culture is likely to be sacrificed to such an inquiry.

In fact, though I have yet to introduce the historical perspective authorizing this claim, part of the text's critical power derives from its ability to frame the phenomena of cultural interpretation so as to disclose the ways this activity is riven by tensions activated through the collapse of the evaluative distinction between elite and popular culture. Thus, the text is not simply to be branded as a pop derivation, but rather, it is to be utilized as a way of delimiting one's methodological field as a contested terrain marked by the presence of specific and massive forces. So far, of course, I have only stressed the congruity between the logic of the commodity and certain properties of textuality. What remains is to sketch the history of the relation between the intellectual discourses of legitimation and the transformations of the so-called public sphere, with a view toward clarifying how the contextuality discovered by Barthes engages this history. Without this, one would be entitled to conclude that those who reduce the text to a mere trend are not only right, but that the evaluative categories such a reduction presupposes remain historically intact. Let us then turn to an elaboration of these issues, and thus pursue the line of inquiry opened by Houdebine's refusal of the question concerning the text's status as a reflection, namely, its status as an instance of power.

## II

Implicit in the reading of Barthes's invocation of fashion as an explanation for the emergence of the text is an analysis of the impact of mass culture on the sites of official cultural production in Europe during the last thirty years. Though much has been written about the pernicious effects of mass culture on "civilization" as a whole, little has been written (until fairly recently) on the impact of mass culture on the structures and practices of intellectual power, particularly as these are inflected by the disciplinary organization of knowledge. What has been written often fails to generate sufficiently rigorous categories to survive the polemical aims of the individual pieces.[15] To advance my account of the emergence of the text, it will be necessary to draw from the works that constitute exceptions to this general tendency and confront them with the demands of the immediate project which include, of course, the methodological concerns introduced at the outset of this chapter.

With an aptness that might be deemed uncanny, this type of exceptional research devoted to mapping the academic impact of mass cultural technologies has been pursued with remarkable intensity in France. Pierre Bourdieu's recent *Homo Academicus* and the book by Régis Debray cited earlier, *Teachers, Writers, Celebrities*, are ample evidence of this.[16] Debray's book in particular deserves attention in this context because of the explicit manner in which it analyzes the "mediacratization" (this inelegant terms follows Debray's usage of the neologism, "mediacracy," to designate the political culture of the society of the spectacle) of intellectual power in France during the period of the text's emergence. Nonetheless, the pertinence of Bourdieu's discussion of the relation between Barthes's work and the restructuring of the Ecole Pratique des Hautes Etudes is sufficiently obvious that it too merits elaboration in this context.

Though at moments he seems uncomfortable with the task, Debray is attempting to write what Foucault once called "a history of the present."[17] Struck by what he likes to refer to as certain facts, such as the creation in 1970 of the position of "press agent" as a regular and necessary office within major publishing firms, or the surprisingly steady rise since the late fifties of the proportion of the total cost of book production devoted to advertising and promotion, Debray embarks on an attempt to reconstitute the historical developments underlying these phenomena. What he assembles is cleverly reflected in the title of the English translation, namely, three eras in the history of intellectual power where a different social group successively defines the core of cultural authority in France. This is not a story of progress, in spite of (or perhaps even because of) Debray's socialist convictions. What animates his reconstruction is a repressive hypothesis that is neither explicitly evoked (Debray tends to evaluate through ironic inflection rather than declarative utterances) nor, for that matter, demonstrated. If one were to paraphrase this hypothesis, it would resemble a hybrid form of technological and economistic determinism wherein intellectuals are reduced to ulcerous posers by the machines and institutions of the mass media. Stated as baldly as that, the thesis appears either trivial or sufficiently self-incriminating that any intellectual would be obliged to dismiss it as a matter of principle. This is why it is worth temporarily suspending our reading of Debray in order to introduce a discussion identifying the categories that, in being presupposed by him, actually support (without thereby justifying) the position he elaborates. As we shall see, the introduction of this discussion also enables one to specify the political terms of the text's engagement of its sociohistorical moment. This is because the key term of this discussion namely, the "public sphere," enables one to clarify the extent to which academic discourse is marked by the political forces that define its purview.

The general category of the public sphere (presupposed by Debray) was introduced into critical debate by Jürgen Habermas in *The Structural Transformation of the Public Sphere* and subsequently elaborated and modified in several of his later works.[18] In Habermas's initial historical sketch the public sphere designates three distinct, though related, domains—domains which are distributed along a temporal axis that extends from the Renaissance to the late modern period. The first, or feudal, public sphere was constituted as the unstable domain created by the appearance of the monarch outside the court. The second, or bourgeois (also referred to as classical), public sphere was created when those individuals whose interests were formed as a result of private economic initiatives gathered either to oppose or to bargin for the social power invested in the state. The third and last public sphere, which at least in Habermas's initial formulation was not a public sphere at all but rather a sphere of "publicity," emerged when the classical public sphere, which had tended to protect public communication from economic imperatives,

was overrun by the technological resources of the mass media thereby reducing the public to a "target audience" rather than a dialogically formed
collectivity.

Beyond its sociological characteristics, the public sphere refers to a
form of political and cultural practice. Specifically, in its "classical" form
it designates a type of "conversation" wherein certain qualitative features
are said to obtain, notably reciprocity, tolerance, and accessibility. Thus,
this conversation not only exhibits what might be called democratic stylistic features, it takes as its explicit political aim (Habermas tends to tie
his definition to certain pragmatic conditions) the formulation of democratic interests against either the absolutist or the liberal state. One of
the bolder aspects of Habermas's analysis is its insistence upon the connection between the style of this conversation and the universality of
its normative claims. In other words, because such notions as "juridical
equality" and "political freedom" were the intellectual results of what
is alleged to have been a noncoercive conversation, the principles they
embody serve as normative standards for all public discussions worthy
of the name.

What radically separates Habermas's discussion of public life from
most of his predecessors, however, is also what most threatens its conceptual and ultimately political integrity, namely, his insistence upon grounding democratic values in a particular structure of social practice. While
this permits him to break definitively with liberal idealism, it obliges
him to proceed as though democracy were in fact embodied in the social
dynamics that spawned the meanings of the terms that have come to designate its cortical values. Though there are many ways to challenge the
coherence of such a view, what stands forth as a particularly pertinent
issue in the present context is the status of the economic domain in the
determination of the public. What gives this angle its pertinence is the
fact that Habermas seems intent, at least in his early work, on invoking
the normative status of the values generated within the bourgeois public
sphere primarily in order to condemn, in rather characteristic Frankfurt School fashion, the degradation of experience perpetrated by the
culture industry and the sphere of publicity it fostered. By proceeding
in this manner, Habermas can remain true to his pragmatic convictions
while preserving his commitment to normativity. Nevertheless, this sort
of interested defense of normativity cannot protect its own methodological categories from the very intellectual degradation they enable one to
diagnose. Habermas necessarily writes the history of enlightenment from

the standpoint of its agony, and one is entitled to expect him to specify the consequences of doing so.

As we have seen, the bourgeois public sphere forms around private individuals who assemble to formulate common interests on their own terms. Habermas dates it from the late seventeenth century in Western Europe. As a complex institutional configuration it spans from the newspapers read in coffee houses to the offices of public administration that comprise the liberal democratic states. Thus, at a certain basic organizational level this sphere engages the entrepreneurial practices of the class whose name it bears. True though this may be, it is not exclusively at this level that Habermas situates the economy's intrusion upon the public sphere. While it is clear that the discussions that constituted the bourgeois public sphere broke, for the most part, with the values and practices of an aristocracy whose institutionalized authority it opposed (to this extent the bourgeoisie drove a wedge of autonomy between its own concerns and those of "tradition"), these discussions assumed an experience of economic self-determination as their condition of possibility. This was true not only at the level of the social division of gender, that is, men gathered to formulate general interests because women generally saw to it that a certain domestic economy enabled them to do so, but also at the level of the social construction of knowledge. In other words, for the private opinions of individuals to acquire social legitimacy, they had to invoke as what recommended their "generalizability" the enabling condition of those opinions, namely, economic self-determination—as though the fact that the market affected everybody (not immediately true, of course) should be taken to imply that all other articulations of general concerns subsequently became obsolete. Bourgeois public opinion, even when it precipitated into notions like that of "universal suffrage," actually reflected the consistency of the particular interests of those able to capitalize on the liberating forces of the market. The fact that history includes a number of important instances where this state of affairs actually permitted the bourgeoisie to act as a representative social class should not discourage us from examining the obscure debt "democratic" values owe to specific exclusionary practices. Be that as it may (Habermas's own later work indicates that he recognizes some of these problems), what Habermas stresses concerning the crisis wrought by the decline of the "classical" public sphere is that even the *compromised* privacy of the bourgeois individual is imperiled when both domestic and public space are thoroughly colonized by media capable of forming opinion by capitalizing upon the public's dependency on the information circulated by the media.

What then characterizes the sphere of publicity, which emerges toward the end of the nineteenth century, is a tendency to reverse the differentiation accomplished with the instituting of the bourgeois public sphere not by negating it, but by proliferating differences whose social significance derives from the way they uniformly disorient the lives of those who value them. What drives this proliferation in Habermas's early account is the rapacity of the market which seeks to mobilize every available means to generate the needs that will both sustain and stimulate it. Behind this analysis, at least at this rudimentary level, is a clever but risky investment in the assumption that, under certain circumstances, differences in degree culminate in differences of kind. Let us briefly spell out some consequences of such an investment.

As I have already suggested, the economy plays an explanatory role in Habermas's discussion of both publicity and the classical public sphere. Beyond the pragmatic, or even tactical, concerns motivating Habermas's position lies a reconstruction of historical materialism that seeks to dislodge economic activity as the determining instance of historical reality, in order to establish interaction (or what Habermas later refers to as "communicative behavior") as an ancillary, though necessary, point of reference for the critical theory of society. What Habermas wants to do is to renovate the analytic categories of Marxism by narrating a history of the emergence of democratic norms that, while treating them as inseparable from the economy, refuses to reduce them to the latter. The warrant for his emphasis on communicative behavior rests precisely upon his ability to avoid a reduction that would taint the interactive categories, from which the appeal to the norms of democratic discourse derives its urgency, with a troubling (because quintessentially capitalistic) political legacy. Thus we have a reading of the historical emergence of the normative character of interactive concerns that downplays the pertinence of the capitalist economy in what then becomes a "lost origin," in order to mobilize opposition to a threat (i.e., the social and methodological predominance of the economy) which the reading is otherwise intent upon neutralizing. In other words, Habermas both affirms and denies the decisiveness of the economy in his analysis of the public sphere. He affirms it, albeit obliquely, through the very urgency of his historical quest for that which might resist the force of the economy as it manifests itself at present. His denial of it appears in the content of his analysis, where the normativity that recommends the public sphere (or interaction, more broadly) as a form of resistance to the economy in effect presupposes such resistance. Though in many respects these complications simply reflect Habermas's complex relation to Western Marxism, they also signal the extent to which Western Marxism itself has often relied on fairly mechanistic accounts of the economic transformations that define the various phases of capitalism. To his credit Habermas has labored to remain in dialogue with this tradition while also remapping many of its fundamental concerns.

These problems take their severest toll when one attempts to conceive the structure of social articulation on the basis of the model of the public sphere. Due precisely to its thorny relation to economism, the public sphere as an analytic category exemplifies the notion of mediation (as opposed to articulation) in that it tends to function to "express" homogeneous economic contradictions at diverse levels of the social domain. Though we will eventually have to take stock of this, it will remain impossible to do so unless we first recognize and take advantage of Habermas's more fruitful preoccupation with the double threat posed by publicity, namely, its ability to standardize the communicative practices of an entire society, and its ability to organize human agency at the level where individuals are relieved of even those desires that form beyond the range of publicity. In place of a public in dialogue with itself, publicity posits the masses assembled through segmentation and discrete consumptive practices. Though in his later analyses of the legitimation crises of the modern state Habermas considerably nuances this account, it is clear that he continues to align himself with those critical of the social impact of the mass media. What motivates this alignment is his sense that the resources of critical consciousness are being depleted by the influence of mass culture.

Included among these depleted resources are, as Habermas makes explicit in his relatively early essay, "The University in a Democracy,"[19] the institutions of "higher learning" where both the values and the cognitive skills necessary for the identification and protection of democracy have long been cultivated. The precise angle of Habermas's critical intervention suggestively illuminates the pertinence his notion of the public sphere has for someone like Debray, despite the problems I have been elaborating concerning the status of the economic within the former's account. For this reason it is worth detailing.

Against those who merely bemoan the intrusion of mass cultural values within the educational domain and the consequent dispersion of tradition, Habermas stresses the distinctively epistemological aspect of the impact of publicity on intellectual life both inside and outside the university. Echoing Horkheimer and Adorno, Habermas shows how positivist science accomplishes an ideological function entirely compatible with the aims of consumerism. Positivism achieves this by raising to the level of an epistemological fetish the instrumental activity of factual verification. This activity permits the scientist to assume the position of the "man who has everything," that is, one committed to a method capable of transmuting the anxiety that attends every encounter with a previously unknown datum into the satisfaction to be derived from the instantaneous verification of one's world outlook that necessarily follows upon the assimilation of the new datum.

What this represents when examined from the standpoint of the university is an hypostatization of one of the three intellectual functions of education identified by Habermas, wherein the communicative interests fundamental to democratic political life are forced either to recast themselves as instrumental or technical preoccupations (thereby sacrificing their speculative and ultimately critical character) or renounce any claim to epistemic legitimacy. Given that Habermas believes that communication is an irreducibly political phenomenon and that politics (in typical Aristotelian fashion) is fundamentally a matter of "partnership," or the ordering of collectivities, what then is at stake in his analysis of the impact of publicity is the social organization of human agency. If the public sphere is not merely a space of congregation, but a context for the production of sociality as an intractable dimension of human existence, then the very advent of publicity—including, of course, its effects on education—threatens to dismantle the formations of agency requisite to the practice of democratic politics in any realm. In short, "depoliticization" as Habermas calls it, reconciles us to the substitution of needs and goals for desires and interests at the level of social reality. Though Habermas abandons the rather reductive, if not nostalgic, account of the public sphere contained in *The Structural Transformation*, what his framework establishes is a mechanism for analyzing how the conditions of intellectual production cannot be separated from historical events affecting the relations among universities, the mass media, and the market. This reaches beyond the sort of unidimensional thesis that animates Debray's analysis by dispensing with the manipulation paradigm and substituting for it a much more subtle account of the social construction of experience. No doubt this is precisely what has motivated Habermas to ever more insistently underscore the dialectical character of communicative behavior—if one stresses construction in place of manipulation, then some account of resistance is necessary if only to understand the possibility of the *critical* character of one's own analysis. Nevertheless, in outdistancing Debray's categorical assumptions Habermas reveals precisely why the history narrated by the former remains indispensable to the project of situating the theoretical emergence of textuality. As I have suggested however, Habermas's own category of the public sphere needs attention if we are to establish its genuine diagnostic power for such an analysis.

Let us begin then to focus this general discussion more tightly on the current situation, or at least the situation current during the emergence of the text. Once we recognize that the public sphere articulates the domains of academic production and informed public opinion—opinion that to a large extent socializes the relations comprising a mode of production— then if we want to situate an instance of academic production (say, a theory like that of the text), we have to construct the history of the domains articulated and examine that instance for signs of its participation in this structural dynamic. By the same token, it is pointless to construct a history that merely envelopes this participation as its temporal context, particularly when this very notion of history is at stake in the theoretical instance I am attempting to situate. What then do we find if we attempt to specify the state of the public sphere in France during the mid-sixties and early seventies? As I have indicated, Habermas has tended to render his concern with the public sphere more abstract, recasting it as a problem of communicative behavior, and as a consequence has left its detailed elaboration to others. Terry Eagleton and Jean-François Lyotard have each distinctively elaborated some of Habermas's concerns in directions that usefully reorient our return to Debray.

Eagleton, in *The Function of Criticism*,[20] argues that during the sixties the classical public sphere condensed and migrated into the university where it proceeded to repeat, within the space of a decade, its earlier social disintegration. Though Eagleton preserves Habermas's elegiac scenario, he attributes the demise of the public sphere to contradictions—in fact some of the very ones I have underscored—latent within that sphere in its classical form. Moreover, he explicitly links the theoretical revolution that spawned the notion of textuality to the historical unfolding of these contradictions. Beneath this suggestive association, however, is an insight assumed by, but left undeveloped within, Eagleton's approach, namely, that this theoretical revolution took place in the enigmatic zone lying between two domains—academia and the public sphere—that had become connected in a way that fundamentally confused their borders.

Lyotard, in *The Postmodern Condition*,[21] argues in a similar vein when, in contesting the Habermasean preoccupation with consensual discourse, he tries to show that science, in its commitment to challenging the rules of proof, in fact discourages consensus but in a manner that actually encourages the realization of one of the normative aspects of the so-called classical public sphere, namely, justice. Here too the public sphere of the mid-sixties and seventies is read as having migrated into another, more narrowly academic, sphere with the consequence that precisely those theories we associate with poststructuralism and textuality began to appear. As in Eagleton's account, the articulation of domains fundamentally confuses their boundaries, but unlike Eagleton, Lyotard downplays the notion of disintegration, and the contempt for mass culture which it harbors, and instead emphasizes the critique of the categories subtending the public sphere made possible by the development of its articulation with academic science.

Both of these more general accounts square in different ways with Debray's analysis of academic power in France. As we have already seen, this account presupposes something like the disintegration of the public sphere detailed by Habermas, and it contributes to such an analysis primarily by examining it from within the specific historical context of academia in France. What is perhaps surprising about Debray's analysis is that it maps the disintegration of the public sphere in relation to a reversal of what he describes as the French university's traditional preeminence within it. This mirrors, in a strict sense, the findings of Eagleton and Lyotard in that it sketches a pattern of articulation that highlights the same structural displacements. Debray's entire presentation is much too cumbersome to paraphrase efficiently, but since he does situate the emergence of *Tel Quel* explicitly, let us focus our attention there. The broad contours of his project should nonetheless remain visible despite this necessary tightening of focus.

The journal *Tel Quel* appears right at the end of what Debray calls the "publishing cycle" which spanned from 1920 to 1960. Though Debray is careful not to insist upon an absolute rupture between it and the preceding "university cycle," he does insist upon the distinctiveness of the publishing cycle in terms of the historical developments that transformed publishers into what he calls "the authors of [their] authors" (p. 68). Crucial among these were: Napoleon's juridical move to require that every publication within the empire have an *éditeur responsable* (someone who could be sued for the circulation of ideas); the split in 1892 between the unions of booksellers and editors that made publishing into an independent and pivotal moment in the process of literary promotion; and the emergence of the *Nouvelle revue française* (NRF) in 1908 signaling both the consolidation of the three instances of production, distribution, and legitimation and the beginning of the displacement of the Sorbonne as the center of intellectual gravity in France by a group of writers supported and bonded together by a publishing venture. What separated this cycle from the one that superceded it is the fact that though the distribution of cultural capital became as crucial as its production, distribution was not yet governed by the law of profitability. Only when this occurs has the threshold of "mediacracy" been irreversibly crossed, at which point the audience, as a body of consumers, becomes the sole arbiter of values and ideas—a humbling account of reader-response criticism if there ever was one.

During the publishing cycle the review (as a publishing organ) emerges as the characteristic medium of intellectual struggle. As we have seen, Debray sees the NRF as prototypical in this regard, with its coterie of writers (perhaps most notably André Gide), its liberal but essentially aristocratic high-mindedness, and its consequent commitment to a movement that sought not so much to address an audience as to constitute a readership. In effect, during this period there was a profound interdependency between the very existence of movements or schools and the publication of reviews. So much so that one might also gauge the shift from the university to the publishing cycle by emphasizing the fact that the emergence of *mentalité* as the disciplinary object of history probably had more to do with the development of *Annales* (begun in 1929 by Lucien Febvre and Marc Bloch) than it did with the courses taught by its contributors at French universities. What the review thus gives expression to is a tactical practice tailored to generate intellectual influence within a public sphere as yet uncolonized by marketing imperatives and populated by agents with attention spans still greater than those of consumers. Debray uses *Tel Quel* to close the historical parenthesis opened by the NRF. As such, the former stands at the threshold (as one might well have expected from Editions du Seuil) of the period wherein the production of intellectual capital comes to be subjected to the requirement of profitability. The change in tactical posture one would expect to follow from such a development is perhaps best reflected in the emergence, during the sixties, of a splinter Editions du Seuil review pointedly titled *Change*.[22]

Two points require immediate elaboration here. Debray punctuates the cycle of publishing in 1960 and begins the cycle of the media in 1968. This creates an interesting ellipse in his chronology, one that has suggestive implications for the task of locating the theoreticians of the text within his framework. Furthermore, the actual theoretical formulations concerning textuality really do not begin to circulate until the mid-sixties, culminating with a number of decisive interventions in 1968. This suggests that the theory of the text needs to be situated upon a double threshold: one that announced what might be called the "latency" of the media cycle and another which occurred with the onset of that cycle in 1968. Even if we affirm, as Debray insists, that these dates are imprecise, such a state of affairs challenges us to approach the text in a subtle and differentiated manner. For one thing, if we are seeking to identify, within the theoretical presentation of the text, signs of its social inscription, then I think we need to be prepared to encounter a complex dialogic field that registers the "voices" that traverse and animate this double threshold.[23] The attempt to situate the text must locate within it both the "millennial" anguish embodied in the decline of publishing and the mix of contempt and excitement that no doubt organized the French intelligentsia's experience of the emergent cultural hegemony of the mass media. But since I have appealed to Debray's work in order to pose the general problem of articulating the academic and public domains, let us fill in his characterization of the media cycle before we turn either to identifying the general propositions concerning social articulation that follow from it or to rifling the theory of the text for its social inscription.

The core of Debray's analysis of the media cycle is defined by his insistence upon the fact that the production and distribution technologies of mass culture (electronic printing, radio, film, and television) not only have sufficient reach to affect the cultural habits of millions, but their maintenance requires capital expenditures on the part of those reached, thus requiring that the information circulated by such media be organized to stimulate and control its audience. Central to this project is, as several members of the Frankfurt School had observed, the standardization and consolidation of cultural information. Faced with this, French intellectuals either have to cede the contest for influence within the public sphere to the media moguls or pursue it on the media's terms, which is to say, to abandon the quest for *intellectual* influence as such and accept the task of stimulating a public comprised essentially of "smart shoppers." The consequences of this are obvious as they are troubling. However, Debray does not mean to suggest that intellectuals as such have disappeared. As an intellectual how could he? On the contrary, intellectuals are on French television nearly every night, but due precisely to this fact, the form and content of intellectual discourse have suffered. As he makes plain in his discussion of the space constraints of a magazine (as opposed to a review) article, the shape and rigor of a thought is marked by its venue, and though he does not tell us what characterizes a mediacratic theory, he alludes to a privately circulated essay of Gilles Deleuze which offers a number of suggestions about what might.

Deleuze, in "A propos des nouvelles philosophes et d'un problème plus général,"[24] characterizes the discourse of the "new philosophers," whose ascendancy in 1976 he links directly to the growing influence of mass culture in France, as obsessed with what he calls "gross concepts" and a scholarly variant of the cult of personality. By the former he means that the theoretical discourse of the new philosophers is laden with evocations of abstract nouns preceded by definite articles, for example, the law, the subject, etc. Instead of exploiting the intellectual resources made available in the years preceding their arrival, the new philosphers, perhaps under the pressure of the French presidential campaign, chose to formulate their analyses in terms that might comprise effective headlines, "socialism with a barbarous face," for example. By contrast, what had characterized much of the theoretical work prior to this period was an ever more adventurous effort to develop terminological nuances that would capture aspects of problems before they receded into the haze of expository conventions. The term "text" is itself an example of this work. What Deleuze sees in the new philosophers is an abandonment of this earlier project and a return to analyses that merely monumentalize that which they should be seeking to interrogate.

Concomitant with this abandonment of what we might call the signifier of analysis, is a return to the authorial, if not magisterial, subject. By this Deleuze means that, faced with the fact that their discourses were indistinguishable from the "journalese" they competed for space with, the new philosophers resorted to the idiosyncratic aspects of their own personalities as a means to separate their discourses from jingles. Again, instead of seeking to refine and extend the interrogation of agency launched by Lacan, Foucault, Deleuze, and others, the new philosophers not only attempted to reinstate the author of a proposition, but they began treating their own signatures as designer labels, that is, valuable covers for, at best, uneven productions. Not only did this introduce a testimonial or "byline" mentality within theoretical discourse, it obliged argumentation to mimic the sort of rudimentary syllogistic reasoning that has become the hallmark of mediocre investigative reporting, where the disclosure of facts takes such precedence over their explanation that "inquiring minds" never notice the absence of the latter and in fact come to regard the rare presence of explanation as an intrusion of "subjective opinion."

Behind these general characteristics of mediacratic theory stands a logic of consumptive displacement. Though Deleuze tends to formulate this issue in terms of an article's ability to so saturate the reception context of a book that reading the book (not to mention writing it) is rendered superfluous, his analysis is not incompatible with the observations made earlier concerning Houdebine's polemical tactics. There, I stressed the way the notion of the text was used to displace competing notions of the literary object, not by confronting the latter with a carefully defended alternative vision, but by subordinating itself to the system of equivalencies that enables the text to be perceived as challenging the integrity of its competition. Within the phantasmagoria of commodities, "brand X" is almost always avoided on the basis of intimidation, not genuine preference. In effect, *the* text (as Deleuze might say) is made to acquire its conceptual instability, which paradoxically (or conveniently) *is* its definition, by merely parading as a gross concept among other such concepts which nevertheless resist being recognized as such. Of course, once the etiology of textuality is formulated in these terms, it becomes difficult to see how any concept can be saved from the spiral of "mediazation." What, according to Deleuze, the new philosophers resort to in this context is the cult of personality, where one's ability to bear witness to the genesis of his or her concepts becomes their seal of approval. Against this, and here Deleuze parts company with Debray, the former insists upon the importance of taking advantage of the new relays among disciplines and cultural practices made possible by the emergent hegemony of mass culture. Significantly, he elaborates this alternative strategy by underscoring Foucault's critique of the "author-function," [25] whose relation to textuality has already been established. Debray, who also has recourse to this Foucauldian category, seems unwilling to ascribe any internal tension to the mediacracy and as a consequence risks either scuttling his entire analysis or coming embarrassingly close to an endorsement of the subjective heroics of the new philosophers. What remains crucial for Deleuze is the possibility of breaking up the intellectual property system that is grounded in the dynamics of discipleship with its fetishization of the authorized signatories legitimated by disciplinary reason. However, between intellectuals and this utopian possibility stands the cultural dynamic of the logic of consumptive displacement which, in effect, both obstructs and facilitates the breakup of the intellectual property system. As a consequence, an analysis is required that enables one to delineate where the obstructive tendencies manifest themselves, be they in institutional practices or in the concepts intellectuals use to criticize such practices.

Since we have touched once again upon the relation between the sociogenesis of the concept of textuality and the dynamics of the mass-mediated public sphere in France, let us bring the discussion of Debray to a close by spelling out the propositions concerning this relation that follow from Deleuze's and Debray's evocation of the author-function. Doing so will enable us to gauge the extent and character of the inscription of mass culture within the concept of the text, while also broaching a reconceptualization of the public sphere in terms of its status as an instance of social articulation.

Though it is never made explicit in Debray's book, his constant recourse to formulations we have come to recognize as poststructuralist clichés, particularly as ways to characterize the experience of intellectuals within the media cycle, suggests that he believes there to be a tight connection between poststructuralist theory and the enabling conditions of the age of celebrities. The question is, how are we to conceive this connection? As anticipated, we have returned to the vexed question of the structural and historical "determinants" of the text. However, at this juncture we are in a better position to respond to the methodological and theoretical demands imposed upon us by the specificity of the text which, as we have seen, engages its historical context by successfully questioning the models for conceiving the very task of contextualization.

Debray's invocation of Foucault's critique of the author is only one of an entire series of like invocations where Debray implies that, say, Barthes's notion of the decline of the work (p. 113) is merely an intellectual reflection of an existing state of affairs, that is, the triumph of the product within publishing. At one level this invites us to assume that the methodological characteristics of the text are best thought of as directly reflecting the moment of its genesis. On the other hand, Debray's project is, after all, openly grounded in its present. Regardless of how his analytic categories pan out politically, Debray's entire reading of intellectual power in France presupposes their efficacy, if not their aptness. This implies that in the unreflective portion of Debray's project, in the very terms bearing his assumptions, lies a commitment to a rather different way of theorizing the relation between the text and the enabling conditions of mediacracy. Specifically, Debray encourages us to view textuality as emerging within the struggle to analyze and thus constitute the hegemony of mass cultural discourse in France. Consequently, the text cannot be treated as simply reflecting a deeper level of experience which it always deficiently echoes. By the same token, neither can the text be used to subsume the conditions its emergence enables one to analyze. Perhaps what is at stake here can be made clearer by briefly turning to Pierre Bourdieu's discussion of similar issues in his *Homo Academicus*.

As a neoMarxist sociologist Bourdieu is concerned to ground cultural, or more specifically intellectual, production within its sociohistorical determinants. Nevertheless, his discussion of the institutional and political context of the Barthes/Picard affair introduces some material that enables one to clarify certain aspects of the emergence of textuality. Specifically, Bourdieu argues that this controversy was due to an institutional struggle between the Sorbonne and the Ecole Pratique des Hautes Etudes, whose notorious sixth section was to house the activities of Barthes and other key players in the dissemination of French "new criticism." In this respect his analysis mirrors that of Debray. What Bourdieu goes on to emphasize, however, is that the inaugural controversy of the new criticism was less a matter of a transition between "cycles" than an effect of a structural logic that subtended both educational institutions. Defining this structural logic was a drive to secure intellectual prestige in the context of a general devaluation of humanistic knowledge. What for Bourdieu animated Barthes's aggressive response to Picard was the fact that the Ecole Pratique, because of its curricular commitment to the reorganization of traditional academic disciplines—a reorganization precipitated by the social devaluation of humanistic knowledge—was poised to contest the cultural authority of those institutions who, due to their own curricular sclerosis, were incapable of capitalizing on the conditions organized by this structural logic. For Bourdieu then, there was a tight relation between the crisis in intellectual prestige that conditioned the decline of Picard (as a representative of "academic criticism") and the institutionally sanctioned proliferation of those interdisciplinary projects that eventually spawned the paradigm of textuality. This implies that textuality assumed its methodological features (e.g., its commitment to the fundamentally intertextual character of the literary work) in response to the tactical initiatives made available to its theorists through the breakup of the disciplinary order of the *grands écoles*. Barthes, moreover, does not deny this when, in response to a question from Raymond Bellour concerning the genesis of *S/Z*, he stresses that the essay grew directly out of the curricular innovations made possible through the formation of the sixth section of the Ecole Pratique.[26] Nevertheless, Bourdieu, due to his insufficiently self-reflective commitment to the discipline and categories of sociology, interprets this situation as a sign of the complicity between "new" and "academic" criticism. While it is important to understand the structural logic his analysis clarifies, it is equally important not to base one's entire analysis on a model of social determination that it otherwise complicates in interesting ways.

What Bourdieu's analysis can be read to show is that the text *engages* its moment. Thus, the text registers the institutional transformations that condition it by articulating them in a methodological discourse that extends and exports them. At the same time, the methodological field thus constituted alters the way subjects are positioned by the institutions whose transformation conditioned the emergence of the text. Obviously, the text is not unique in this respect. But what Bourdieu overlooks is that new criticism made a difference—a difference that has not been simply reproductive nor, for that matter, merely restricted to the sphere of institutional criticism. Whether this difference is ultimately absorbed or not depends entirely on what is done with the possibilities and dangers created in the fields articulated by the text's emergence. Like Debray, whose compulsive recourse to what I have called poststructuralist clichés belies a certain theoretical apprehensiveness, Bourdieu seems more eager to secure the institutional absorption of textuality (it becomes a variety of "infantile," because humanistic, leftism) than to extend the opportunities its appearance made available within and for cultural criticism.

What these general observations imply for the task of situating the text can now, I think, be stated fairly directly. The theories of the text to be detailed in part two were produced by human agents who could no longer comprehend their own experience as intellectuals in terms of the model of subjectivity latent within what Foucault called the author-function. This is not because they were either stubborn or mystified, but because the social conditions that sustained the coherency of the author as an instance of subjectivity had been remapped during the period of the text's sociogenesis. Precipitating this remapping of the social was the deep structural transformation of what Habermas calls the public sphere, where the theaters of subjectivity, the public and private domains, had been realigned thus provoking a crisis in the categories created by intellectuals within the public sphere to comprehend the experiences organized by it. Within the domain of publicity, whose borders now extend into areas previously either untouched by it or indifferent to its presence, new forms and organs of communication proliferated. These forms reconstituted the public and thus participated in its transformation both by increasing the size of the public at a sheer technological level and by subjecting its intellectual life to new material constraints—the space, time, and speed of, say, a magazine article.

These changes and the forms of their embodiment were not immediately available to human consciousness. In fact, the effort to socialize, that is, render them communicable, could not and cannot be separated from the theoretical constructs generated by those concerned to do so any more than the constructs thus generated can be separated (which is not to say that they cannot be distinguished) from the changes they render social. The text, in its triple preoccupation with play, productivity, and pleasure, was such a construct. It came to embody, as Bourdieu's analysis makes plain, the attempt to confront disciplinary inquiry with the task of addressing what is at stake in the cultural subjection of human agency— a task whose urgency derives from the fact that the process of cultural formation has undergone a fundamental change in orientation, undermining the coherence of the subject as a model for cultural experience. As such, the text is a "pop" phenomenon. It cannot be separated from the reorganization of agency that attended the advent of the media cycle, which is not, however, to say that the text is *merely* a publicity stunt. To claim, as is often done, that this is precisely all the text amounts to is to sacrifice an effective engagement of the text for a sorely misguided analysis of publicity. If there is a "pop" text, it is because publicity has indeed spawned that which makes it legible as a text. But if this is true, then the epithet "fad" applies with equal, and therefore disturbing, pertinence to those analytic categories that refuse to acknowledge the pervasiveness of the domain of publicity perhaps solely in order to obscure the extent to which they are marked by it. Textuality avoids such a refusal, not by simply "affirming the change" as Jameson has argued, but by making what might otherwise present itself as a merely "literary" question resonate with considerably broader implications. It can do so not because its theorists are perversely clever, but because the public sphere itself, and intellectual power more generally, have become subject to the logic of articulation that has come to saturate the entire social field. All cultural phenomena are irreducibly marked by the antagonisms that give meaning to the differences setting them off from one another. However, if we accept the terms of such an analysis, a further question arises: how does this delimit the power of the text?

If one conceptualizes the public sphere as fulfilling a mediatory function, that is, as operating to relay with typically homological precision economic contradictions from the domain of the base to the domain of the superstructure, then the relation between textuality and fashion sketched here strips the former of any critical power whatsoever. This is due to the fact that the very notion of mediation harbors a refusal to complicate the domain of the political. It is essentially designed to solve the methodological problem of connecting the base to the superstructure once it is assumed that historical causality resides exclusively in the base. In other words, given that capitalism survives by perpetually extending the domain of the economic, and given that fashion is clearly an instance of an economically organized signifying practice, once the text can be affiliated with fashion, the logic of mediation captures it in a reproductive dynamic where it functions soley to perpetuate capitalist hegemony. Mediation, even when it is used to accommodate the notion of uneven social development, tends to flatten the various instances of the social, bending them toward a determinant contradiction that orients and defines them.

Habermas, as we have seen, is of at least two minds on such matters. He wants the public sphere to stand in opposition to the economy, at the same time that he derives the normativity of the public sphere (as an embodiment of interactive values) from that sphere's role in the mediation of bourgeois economic interests. Though Habermas's later work has clearly abandoned the commitment to the model of mediation that provoked the nostalgia characteristic of his earliest writings on the public sphere, he has not adequately reformulated the methodological parameters of his later research. In fact, doing so would require the sort of Herculean labors I am not prepared to carry out at this moment. Nevertheless, by briefly bringing Habermas's discussion into contact with the problematic elaborated by Laclau and Mouffe in the name of post-Marxism, we can clarify how the critical power of the text might be conceived within the present conjuncture.

Habermas, Laclau, and Mouffe are all interested in locating the inscription of democracy in social practice. As was suggested in the introduction, Laclau and Mouffe have been compelled—in the name of a radicalization of Marxism—to locate impulses toward democratization in the elaboration of the methodological categories of critical theory itself. This is what led them to their central theoretical notions of articulation and hegemony. Articulation supplements the notion of mediation by underscoring the complexity of the social that appears when the determining instance of the economy is bracketed. Instead of a series of homologous expressive instances (a series that bears remarkable and therefore embarrassing resemblance to Taylorized production), articulation coordinates a collection of noncontiguous frontiers, that is, sites where the massive outlines of the social formation are, as it were, under construction and not therefore "given." If one approaches the notion of the public sphere from this perspective, what emerges is precisely that state of affairs noticed (but not developed) by Lyotard and Eagleton, namely its distinctively blurred contours. This blurring is not the result of some analytic myopia. Instead, it registers the fact that the present historical conjuncture is marked by an eruption of conflicts among groups whose social identities are torn by the contradictory interpellation of race, class, sexuality and gender. What characterizes this eruption at the level of the public sphere is not simply a quarrel within it, but a quarrel about its limits—a quarrel that actually functions to constitute the public sphere as indefinitely bounded. So much so that the public sphere and the debates that traverse it now extend into the terminological repositories of those intellectuals committed to engaging it. In other words, the public sphere does not exist independently of the arguments that constitute it, even when those arguments question its existence entirely. At the most general level, this implies that the boundary between the base and superstructure (itself a theoritical "opinion") is impossible to draw and that all of the methodological assumptions that followed from one's ability to draw such a line have been rendered problematical. At a more restricted level, this means that the sociogenesis of the notion of textuality ought to be seen as an effort to negotiate the frontiers of cultural interpretation that open up once the clarity provided by the determinancy of the economic base had been overrun by the forces of social transformation—forces Barthes had the gall to call by their name, fashion.

Once the public sphere is reorganized around the logic of articulation, the text is no longer reducible to an intellectual gimmick swept up in the reproduction of capitalist social relations. By the same token, precisely because the text is not so reducible, its critical power remains subject to the negotiations it is made to enter as we struggle over its significance. This struggle transpires in the domain of publicity, and as I have said, it *is* the domain of publicity. We did not have to await the de Man "scandal" or the quarrel over "political correctness" to recognize this.[27] What recommends the methodological field of the text as a critical category is the fact that its texture registers this state of affairs without succumbing to it. In fact, it may well be that there is no more challenging way to think the disciplinary conditions of one's object while participating in the struggle

over the public sphere than through the model of textuality. If articulation does indeed define the social under the conditions of postmodernity,
then the text is a perfectly useful way to think the social moment of that
which presents itself to us in the texture of a cultural artifact—whether
high or low.

# PART II

# 3

## * The Text *tel quel*: Derrida's Play

**I**

Though I have already had recourse to the formulation, "the theory of
the text," it will become clear from the diversity of figures to be discussed
in the chapters of part two—Jacques Derrida, Julia Kristeva, and Roland
Barthes—that such a formulation is somewhat misleading. There are and
have been several *theories* of the text, or to put this somewhat more provocatively, there are and have been several texts of theory, several ways
of inscribing what we now rather loosely refer to as the discourse of
*theory,* that seek to delimit the domain of textuality. Nevertheless, due to
the institutional configuration of intellectual power delineated in chapter 2, the quarterly *Tel Quel,* under the editorship of Philippe Sollers, was
able to galvanize and focus the multifarious discussions of textuality in
a manner that warrants the formulation employed in my chapter titles.
Of course, what is important here is not that one justify the use of a
certain phrase, but rather that one specify how and in what terms the
works of Derrida, Kristeva, and Barthes engaged the peculiar community that defined and resulted from their writing. Though only Kristeva
actually served as a member of the editorial board of *Tel Quel* (Barthes
and Derrida often figured as "contributors" and supporters, at least up
to the moment of Derrida's "excommunication" in the midseventies, but
nothing more), it was through the pages of the journal that *le texte* received sufficient discursive elaboration to have an impact on paraliterary
questions of critical methodology and social theory.[1] In a strict sense, it

was through or around *Tel Quel* that the interdisciplinary derivation of textuality exhibited itself publicly, crossing a certain threshold of sociality by appearing in the splay of topics comprising the table of contents for particular issues, some of which, by the late seventies, circulated in print runs of 6,000. Thus, since it has been in relation to the institutional question of disciplinary reason that I have sought to rethink the specificity and significance of the text, it would be misleading not to detail the concept's relation to the *Tel Quel* project even though, as will become evident in what follows, the two cannot be reduced to one another.[2]

*Tel Quel* was launched during the waning years of the French occupation of Algeria. Its founding editors named it after the two volumes of topical writings published by Paul Valéry in the early forties—a provenance that, as we shall see, played a significantly formative role in the elaboration of the journal's problematic.[3] In its founding "declaration" *Tel Quel* was presented as a forum open to scholars interested both in separating literature from ideology and in the theoretical specification of literary specificity.[4] Though this declaration was later used by detractors to justify their own political denunciations of the journal, what is nonetheless remarkable about the project it served to launch are the developments that the declaration spawned. For instance, not long after the quest for literary specificity was announced, the journal took to advocating a rejection of "literature" as such, a rejection whose enabling conditions invite us to hesitate before judging the initial appeal to specificity as a reactionary political gesture. In fact, one of the more intriguing things about the project of *Tel Quel* is the way a distinctly antidisciplinary phenomenon like the text emerged out of a rigorous and highly focused interrogation of the "literary." Perhaps by elaborating the logic of this development we can establish an effective framework for addressing the work of the three theorists assembled in part 2.

What is at stake in the separation of literature and ideology called for in the declaration? Obviously a great deal, but at a certain rudimentary level what is implied concerns one's ability to read a literary text without rifling its content for statements illustrating the text's adherence to prevalent ideological positions. Here, of course, the accent falls on the problem of *particular* ideological allegiances. In the declaration (written by Sollers) he is clearly concerned with this aspect of the separation called for within it. He wants to approach "writing" ("*l'écriture*," though in the Valéryean and obviously preDerridean sense of the term) in a way that would break with the traditions of academic criticism, and in particular with the tendency then prevalent within such criticism to situate literary works in relation to the political or cultural "views" of their authors. Obviously, this is a fairly benign and intellectually unsophisticated appeal. The declaration does not, however, stop there. .

Sensitive to the fact that condemning one set of ideological allegiances invites an ideological assessment of one's own position, Sollers shifts the accent of his criticism so that it falls on the theoretical problem of designating a discourse that can specify the specificity of literature while avoiding the reproach of being ideological. Though he does not yet have at his disposal either the concept of "science" (as it was later developed as a critical category, most notably by Althusser) or the discipline of linguistics, Sollers's characterization of writing as an "entry into matter" (p. 4) suggests that he wants to ground literary specificity in a discourse that opposes itself to ideology, not simply by representing an alternative ideological perspective, but by serving as the discourse through which the domain of ideology is theoretically delimited, namely, historical materialism. Though this explicitly Marxian terminology does not inflect Sollers's writing until the mid-sixties, I invoke it here because it is latent in the Valéryean notion of "literary axiomatics" that Sollers obliquely draws upon to flesh out his category of matter. Clearly, this claim is a much more ambitious and consequential aspect of the appeal to "separatism," and it is not therefore surprising that in articulating this position Sollers finds a way to emplace the quarterly's name, "*tel quel,*" amidst the terms of his analysis. He writes, "sans doute rien ne mérite plus d'attention que ce décalage entre l'objet, le spectacle qui se trouve devant nos yeux, l'ideé que nous nous en faisons, la manière dont nous le recevons habituellement, et la découverte . . . brutale ou progressive de cet objet . . . où nous retrouvons, . . . l'intérêt que mérite ce monde, ce monde TEL QUEL" (p. 4). Significantly, this emplacement occurs at a point where, in stressing the need to embrace any writing that arises within the world as *it is* (here the trope of "science" is smuggled in beneath the ontological "is"), Sollers is able to activate a superimposition that permits the phrase "*tel quel*" both to qualify the noun "world" and to displace it. Thus, the declaration that launches the journal presents the latter as that which coincides with the world while simultaneously protecting literature from the all too worldly concerns of ideology.

Clearly this is posturing, and sadly many of textuality's partisans have mistaken it for a position. Yet rather than sort out the various difficulties inherent in such an appeal to science, I want to explore how such an appeal could be said to provoke, if not require, *Tel Quel*'s eventual abandonment of literature. In spring of 1967 the journal began sporting the regular subheading "Science/Literature." This replaced an earlier one (Summer 1966), "Linguistics/Psychoanalysis/Literature," that had appeared solely to designate a special issue. Without becoming entangled in the general problem of reading the semiotics of subheadings, it is possible to recognize in these isomorphically structured samples an implicit semantic contiguity between science and linguistics. In fact, by the time these subheadings appear, the project of securing literary specificity has already been dropped in favor of a "scientific" (and explicitly historical materialist) rejection of the category of literature as a pernicious aspect of bourgeois ideology. Such a coincidence would suggest that literary specificity is necessarily sacrificed to the pairing of literature and the science of linguistics which, at the time, was understood to provide a materialist account of the sign that supplemented Marx's project in a decisive way. Though there is a long-standing tradition of opposing science and "the humanities" that would warrant just such an assumption, it strikes me as misleading in this case. What is interesting about the impact of linguistics (and the rhetoric of "science") in the French context is that it was mobilized to specify, with all the epistemic force that this term might muster, literary specificity, but in a manner that resulted in a rejection of literature. This occurred because in the intellectual context created by structuralism, with its much touted promotion of the linguistic paradigm, it was not possible to conceive the specificity of anything without inquiring into the character of the research paradigm that governed the methodological field within which specificity was to be specified. In the case of literature such an inquiry quickly turned up a tautology that begged for elaboration. As is well known, moving beyond the circuit of literature as a self-legitimating phenomenon led away from both a psychology of the author and a sociology of the period, but toward an analysis of the structure and effects of language. Yet once language was identified as that which supported and defined the specificity of literature, it was difficult to continue attributing to literature the prestige that separated it from other language practices. In fact, in order to preserve such a value one was forced to appeal to aspects of linguistic experience which, in their heteronomy vis-à-vis literature, frustrated the quest for literary specificity.

In effect, the attempt to specify literary specificity linguistically recast the disciplinary object of literary criticism in a manner that plunged literature back into the vastness of language practices. What emerged within literary criticism, and this is apparent in the epochal quarrel between Barthes and Picard, is a commitment to interdisciplinarity.[5] What prompted this commitment, no doubt, was the fact that once literature could no longer be categorically distinguished from those language practices with which it bore a striking family resemblance and which, not surprisingly, traversed the social field, literary criticism was obliged to turn to the other disciplinary projects that addressed themselves to such practices—and this in the name of the preservation of what was specific to literary practice. Granted, this commitment to interdisciplinarity grew slowly. Barthes, for example, who noticed with ironic satisfaction how Racine was being repartitioned by various critical languages in the fifties, nevertheless took some time to leaven his structuralist narratology with insights from psychoanalysis. But it is difficult to deny that the interdisciplinary incursion of linguistics within academic literary criticism triggered an analytical cascade that forced the latent complexity of the literary object to emerge. And despite the fact that Barthes's essay on the text as a literary object appears a full ten years after the advent of *Tel Quel*, one can detect in the formulations of the declaration—precisely at those moments where Sollers appears to coordinate the tasks of specification and critique—the very sort of insight that was to animate Barthes's reflection on textuality and interdisciplinarity. What, of course, distinguishes the two perspectives at the theoretical level is Barthes's recognition that linguistics is indeed a discipline, an institutional and practical construct, not a "science" (as Bruno Latour would say, "the naked truth"). In short, what in hindsight may have startled Sollers nevertheless spurred Barthes on.

What I have sketched here is familiar to anyone who has read a history of the structuralist movement. Though these histories often avoid specific references to disciplinarity or *Tel Quel*, they uniformly insist upon the promise held out by structuralism for something like a "unified field theory" in the humanities and the social sciences—a promise harbored in the fantasy of a semiotic subsumption of human reality. As we now know, this promise has gone and will remain unfulfilled. But if we are to grasp why these aspects of the activities of those associated with *Tel Quel* effect decisively the theorization of textuality, then another dimension of this all too familiar history of structuralism needs to be underscored. Specifically, it is important to stress that behind the emergent complexity of the literary object stood precisely that state of affairs whose absence is bemoaned by Terry Eagleton when he calls for a reassertion of the importance of literary criticism within national debate.[6] Though marked by a certain self-conscious nostalgia (his critique is ironically couched in terms of a return to "tradition"), Eagleton's remarks underscore the social importance of the struggle over hermeneutics as a discourse within which to conduct public policy debate. As we have seen, he is explicitly attempting to theorize the public sphere of intellectuals so as to grasp how discussion about literature at once participates in this sphere and yet can be made to obfuscate such participation. What I am arguing about *Tel Quel* is that the specification of literary specificity that provoked the interdisciplinary disintegration of the category of literature embodied, at least within the troubled French public sphere, precisely the sort of articulation between literary and sociocultural critique called for by Eagleton. This is not to say that those associated with *Tel Quel* were swept into the center of national cultural debate—though several of them were invited to a much criticized dinner at the Elysée Palace in 1974. Not even Eagleton, whose sense of urgency sometimes becomes indistinguishable from desperation, would affirm such a paltry and artificial sublation of the tension between theory and practice. Instead, I would argue that *Tel Quel*, as an "organ" of public opinion, served (though obviously not in an exclusive capacity) to problematize literature in a manner that, perhaps paradoxically, subjected a number of broad social questions to a novel model of hermeneutic reflection. That is, by connecting the interrogation of literary works to processes whose theoretical derivation emphasized their indissociability from massive psychosocial dynamics, *Tel Quel* was able to participate (certainly not without compromise) in a transformation of the rhetoric of public debate—the reason why the intellectuals associated with the journal sought to sustain a dialogue with the French Communist party, as Kristeva remarks in the previously cited "memoire" (p. 271).

This transformation is emblematically captured in the notion of the text, where a term long associated with the literary critical enterprise came to designate, not so much an entity, but a way of practicing the analysis of entities—an approach that explicitly foregrounded the kinds of skills that would be brought to bear on what, as a consequence of the elaboration of this approach, no longer warranted the name "literature." I am not, of course, suggesting that the pages of *Tel Quel* became the site of a literarily inflected national dialogue, but rather that what transpired in its pages had recognized significance for the terms in which such a dialogue was to be conducted. This is surely the sort of influence that Eagleton wants to see reclaimed by the discourses of cultural criticism. Insofar as the problematization of literature had such implications it participated in the sociogenesis of textuality. To the extent that this problematization was indissociable from the public exertions of *Tel*

*Quel* (the point my reading of the declaration and its subsequent elaboration has sought to establish), then textuality, such as it was or remains, is indelibly marked by the quarterly understood both as a theoretical project and as an institution. If this is so, then should we not be able to detect in the various elaborations of the theory of textuality a series of disciplinary confrontations which in some way pivot around a certain problematization of literature? My answer, of course, is yes.

## II

Though the status of Jacques Derrida's own work does not explicitly number among the many topics broached in "The Law of Genre,"[7] this essay does delineate the problematic within which I want to conduct my reading of his early work. Specifically, Derrida's text(s) invite(s) us to explore its/their relation to the graphic (and therefore material) signifier, that is, the practice that joins philosophy and literature as written discourses. This problematic asserts itself with such tenacity in Derrida's work that many have concluded that the only thing separating "deconstruction" from nihilism is Derrida's struggle to determine the proper *vocabulary* of criticism.

I would argue that Derrida's essays remain within the orbit of the literary precisely to the extent that they problematize this category in a manner that remains most legible and pertinent to those whose work draws upon the notion of literature. Moreover, if one situates this issue historically, then it is not hard to recognize that Derrida's corpus is marked by the oddly philosophical problematic delimited by Philippe Lacoue-Labarthe in "Typographie," where it is argued that at the close of the nineteenth century European philosophy openly encounters the problem of its *Darstellung*, that is, the *form* of its presentation.[8] In any case, since I have linked the conflicted specificity of the literary—the very issue that has consistently agitated literary practice with the theorization of textuality, let us move to test this assertion by turning to Derrida's various articulations of "the text."

The concept (which Derrida treats more like a figure) makes its appearance in Derrida's earliest published essays. In his philosophically bounded dialogue with phenomenology (specifically the Husserlian and Heideggerian strains—Sartre and Merleau-Ponty have been conspicuously neglected by Derrida), the text emerges as a way to thematize what a particular angle of reading permits one to conclude about the phenomenological resuscitation of European philosophy. In this respect,

the text arises at the juncture between a particular philosophical proto-
col of critique, what we might call, following Husserl, "explicitation"
(one translation proposed for the technical notion of "*Verdeutlichung*"
and "explication," an interpretive practice intimately connected with the
institutions of literary scholarship in France. As such, the text not only
straddles two semantic paradigms—referring at once to the phenomenal
"thing" wherein philosophical ideas are inscribed and to the object produced in response to the requirements of a certain critical practice—it
assumes the burden of two intellectual projects, one metacritical (vis-à-
vis transcendental phenomenology and fundamental ontology) and the
other methodological (vis-à-vis literary hermeneutics). Consider the following passage from Derrida's introduction to his translation of *The
Origin of Geometry*.

> The originality of the field of writing is its ability to dispense with,
> *due to its sense,* every present reading in general. But if the text
> does not announce its own pure dependence on a writer or a reader
> in general (i.e., if it is not haunted by a virtual intentionality), and
> if there is no purely juridical possibility of it being intelligible for
> a transcendental subject in general, then there is no more in the
> vacuity of its soul than a chaotic literalness or the sensible opacity of
> a defunct designation, a designation deprived of its transcendental
> function.[9]

This casual superimposition of "writing" and "text" occurs within the
context of an argument that will come to organize much of *Speech and
Phenomena*, namely, Derrida's interrogation of Husserl's elaboration of
the phenomenological theory of signification. Though Derrida does not
move here to extrapolate the relation between writing and the text, he
criticizes Husserl's reductive treatment of the former in many of the
same terms that will later appear to provoke such an extrapolation. The
superimposition of terms in this context merely underscores the literary
insight that pieces of prose can be, and are typically, meaningfully read
in their authors' absence—a point Husserl's discussion of intentionality
unintentionally ignores. What raises this point above a mere quibble,
however, is the fact that Derrida is practicing an *explication* of Husserl
that surpasses critical commentary precisely by demonstrating that the
latter's text "says" more than its author (a most intentional of authors
at that) intended. Though, as I have indicated, Derrida does not proceed
to flesh out this "more" in all its grammatological detail, it is plain that
his preoccupation with the textually mediated network of readers and

writers orients his reading of philosophy toward that which in the phenomenological reflection on meaning will come, almost paradoxically, to problematize the literary practice of interpretation. Thus, despite the fact that Derrida refers at one point to "the *real* text of historical experience" (p. 76), in the introduction to *The Origin* the text is understood primarily as the sort of thing dealt with by literary scholars when exploring the impact of production and reception on literary meaning. The perspective on textuality destined to unsettle the category of literature, and latent within the notion of the text of historical experience, really only emerges in the writing that transpires between this book and *Speech and Phenomena*.

Before, however, we continue with the tracing of the text's emergence in Derrida, it is fitting to pause and consider the appropriateness of my characterization of the "literary" aspect of Derrida's early formulations on textuality. After all, Derrida does not explicitly characterize his work in this way. Setting aside Derrida's thesis topic on the ideality of the literary work (apparently conceived but never executed), let us turn to the 1963 essay, "Force and Signification,"[10] in order to test my characterization.

This essay, an early instance of Derrida's critical confrontation with structuralism, not only brings his earlier reading of *The Origin* explicitly to bear on the geometric Platonism of Jean Rousset's notion of "structure," but it does so in the context of a subtle reading of the discipline of literary study. By showing how the promise of literary structuralism is denied by its necessary sacrifice of force to form, Derrida elaborates the problematic that brings phenomenology and literary criticism into dialogue with each other. As one can see, this dialogue involves more than simply shared terms.

> One must be separated from oneself in order to be reunited with the blind origin of the work in its darkness. This experience of conversion, which founds the literary act (writing or reading), is such that the very words "separation" and "exile," which always designate the interiority of a breaking-off with the world and a making of one's way within it, cannot directly manifest the experience; they can only indicate it through a metaphor whose genealogy itself would deserve all our efforts.[11]

Though the text is not mentioned explicitly here, the interior fissure that conditions the literary act is, through recourse to Blanchot's discussion of literary space, immediately linked to writing which, as we have seen, is the text's twin. Moreover, in the citation one finds the "same" association between the literary act and the dispersion of presence that Derrida had invoked in order to problematize Husserl's subordination of writing to speech. Now, even if one were to conclude that in the network created by these two citations Derrida has merely established the parity between literature and philosophy as concerns access to "writing," it is difficult to deny that, given the persistent recourse to relations between readers and writers, his concerns have an irreducibly literary flavor. So much so, in fact, that Derrida is compelled at the beginning of the essay to identify the transformations wrought upon the "literary object" (his phrase) as a privileged site for the evaluation of the truly significant contributions of structuralist methodology—contributions which, in their impact on the theory of language, clearly made Derrida's "reading" of Husserl possible. Thus, what invites one to characterize Derrida's initial approach to the notion of textuality as literary is this specifically disciplinary interrogation that spills over onto the thematics that animate his critique of phenomenology's mode of enunciation, its "discourse." Insofar as the text functions as a name for the object of a "reading," it would appear to deserve this characterization. Of course, this is not to say that the discipline of philosophy exerted no influence on Derrida's project. Rather, I am arguing that the contours of a literary problematic came to define a question that, once posed, threatened to transform a certain philosophical practice. In effect, the structural critique of the literary object that seemed to necessitate recourse to textuality attacked philosophy from the inside of its outer edge, but it did so by reading philosophy as a text, as a literary phenomenon, not as an antidisciplinary object.

However, during the period from 1965 to 1967 the text approaches this status. Crucial to this development was Derrida's dialogue with linguistics and psychoanalysis, a conversation begun earlier by Lacan and Levi-Strauss. For the purposes of convenience this development can be plotted in relation to three essays: the first part of what was to become *Of Grammatology*, "Freud and the Scene of Writing," and "Form and Meaning: A Note on the Phenomenology of Language"—a circuit which, not surprisingly, brings us back to Husserl.

The first part of *Grammatology* appeared in *Critique* in 1965.[12] It laid out Derrida's analysis of the repression of writing by the traditions faithful to the phonocentrism of Western metaphysics. Specifically, and in accord with a logic detailed in my introductory chapter, Derrida broaches a critique of Saussurean linguistics that evokes, "[the] *text*, in a sense . . . that I shall have to establish" (pp. lxxxix–xc). In this essay we find provocative references to such items as "the text in general as fabric of signs" (p. 14) or "the ultra-transcendental text" (p. 61), but little occurs to "establish" the special significance of the text underscored in the prefatory remarks. What does occur, and this is obviously crucial, is that through the figure of "fabric" the text is brought into relation with the structure of the trace—a relation which both consummates the literary reflection on textuality and situates the text within a specifically psychoanalytic discussion on the psychical apparatus, the very discussion that was to transpire within the pages of "Freud and the Scene of Writing."

In referring to a consummation, I have in mind the fact that here Derrida permits himself the following formulation.

> These precautions taken, it should be recognized that it is in the specific zone of the imprint and this trace, in the temporalization of a *lived experience* which is neither *in* the world nor in "another world" which is not more sonorous than luminous, not more *in* time than *in* space, that differences appear among the elements or rather produce them, makes them emerge as such and constitute the *texts,* the chains, and the systems of traces. These chains and systems cannot be outlined except in the fabric of this trace or imprint.[13]

What emerges in the citation, due, no doubt, to its specific echoing of the discussion of Rousset cited above, is a juxtaposition of the conditions of the literary act and the model of textuality (now worthy of italicization) that outdistances this act by aligning the text and the trace. The term "text" here is used as a hinge—it serves to name the proliferation and dispersion of literary works, while also reaching around them to designate a structure their plurality presupposes. This structure is only detailed, as text, in part two of *Grammatology* and in "Freud and the Scene of Writing." In any case, this passage openly gestures toward a relinquishment of the strictly literary reading of textuality.

What one finds in part two of *Grammatology* (published first in 1966) is a delivery on the promise to "establish" the new significance of the notion of the text. It reads: "No model of reading seems to me at the moment ready to measure up to this text [Rousseau's *Essay on the Origin of Languages*]—which I would like to read as a *text* and not as a document. Measure up to it fully and rigorously, that is beyond what already makes the text most legible, and more legible than has so far been thought." And a bit further on.

This question is therefore not only of Rousseau's writing but also of our reading. . . . And the reading must always aim at a certain relationship, unperceived by the writer, between what he [sic] commands and what he [sic] does not command of the patterns of the language that he [sic] uses. This relationship is not a certain quantitative distribution of shadow and light, of weakness or of force, but a signifying structure that critical reading should *produce*. . . . Yet if reading must not be content with doubling the text, it cannot legitimately transgress the text toward something other than it, toward a referent . . . or toward a signified outside the text whose content could take place, could have taken place outside of language, that is to say, in the sense we give here to that word, outside of writing in general. That is why the methodological considerations that we risk applying here to an example are closely dependent on the general propositions that we have elaborated above as regards the absence of the referent or the transcendental signified. *There is nothing outside of the text.*[14]

Text (in what Derrida will later call the "infrastructural sense," p. 164) thus becomes a way of naming what a certain model of reading produces when it approaches texts (in the "precritical" sense, p. 61) as though the discourses which comprise them obstruct as much as facilitate expression, and in so doing exhaust the resources of human experience. Since this characterization of the text seeks to gloss the now notorious claim that there is nothing outside of it, an elaboration of its implications seems called for.

Faithful to a provenance whose importance I have perhaps already belabored, Derrida moves to establish the infrastructural sense of the text by connecting it with the practice of reading. The figures of "light," "shadow," and "force" explicitly recall the discussion of Rousset cited earlier. Reading, however, is presented as at once suspended between the legible and the illegible and deemed productive of the signifying structure that conditions this opposition. To this extent, reading has acquired a metaliterary significance, for Derrida is not facilely sacrificing the intentions of the author to the intentions of the critic; instead, he is foregrounding the task of specifying the conception of the "read object" that organizes one's reading, the conception that, in effect, orders or produces what one will discover in what s/he reads. The notion of the text attempts to embody the fact that both the reading and the read are marked by a set of precise institutional constraints that unsettle the cognitive sovereignty of both the author and the critic. Be that as it may, why would one then conclude that there is nothing outside the text? In some respects this question is premature since it is in the other two essays from this period that the text is presented with sufficient precision to permit a thorough answer. Nevertheless, the citation invites us to make a few observations that are relevant to this crucial issue.

Instead of assuming that Derrida is making an ontological claim (i.e., that the nature of Being is synonymous with that of the text), which in light of his scathing criticisms of ontological discourse (whether Platonic or Heideggerian) would be unlikely, why not begin by taking the *relation* between the text and reading seriously? In other words, nothing is outside the text, because everything about which people might quarrel concerning its "meaning" can be approached from the standpoint of the text, that is, from a standpoint that insists that one's point of departure intervenes within, and thus unsettles, the meaning s/he assumes such a starting point will enable him or her to discover. If Derrida is confident enough to hope that his reading of Rousseau will be able . . . to draw out of it a signification which that presumed future reading will not be able to dispense with," (p. 149) it is not because he believes that the essay harbors a meaning that his method alone can tap. On the contrary, Derrida's confidence stems from the fact that by foregrounding the production of what he calls a "signifying structure" what his reading makes available is a methodological space wherein the process of generating a text's meanings (regardless of their "sense") can be examined—an examination that does not avoid the text, but which treats the text as a construct for which the critic is to some extent responsible. The elaboration of this space marks the texts treated within it, not with their "truth," but with an approach that provides them with a dimension that indispensably widens the field of their meanings. Thus, one important way to think about the lack of "exteriority" to the infrastructural text is in terms of this disciplinary or institutional notion of its paradigmatic (in Kuhn's sense) function. Nobody knows anything without overpowering it with the institutions that condition one's knowing.[15]

Of course, there is more to the story than this. Why, for example, would one assume that to approach everything textually necessarily implied that, at the moment of doing so, there was nothing left outside the paradigm? Obviously, more needs to be said about that moment in the citation where Derrida links a critique of the "transcendental signified" and the "referent" to what he calls "writing in general." To pursue this while keeping our focus on textuality, it will be necessary to introduce the other two essays I have been holding in reserve, "Freud and the Scene of Writing" and "Form and Meaning."

In "Freud and the Scene of Writing" one finds the following remarks about the text.

> What questions will these representations [those that treat the psyche as a writing machine] impose upon us? We shall not have to ask if a writing apparatus—for example, the one described in the "Note on the Mystic Writing Pad"—is a *good* metaphor for representing the working of the psyche, but rather what apparatus we must create in order to represent psychical writing. . . . And not if the psyche is indeed a kind of text, but: what is a text, and what must the psyche be if it can be represented by a text? For if there is neither machine nor text without psychical origin, there is no domain without text.[16]

In the concluding sentence Derrida once again introduces the problem of thinking beyond the text, but what is distinctive about this formulation is his insistence upon the proximity between textuality in general and the enabling conditions of psychic life. The issue here is no longer whether one can approach everything from a textual point of view, but rather (and this is clearly a more provocative thesis) if theorizing the psyche cannot avoid recourse to textual metaphors, then perhaps what we have called the psyche (its structure and its faculties) is a text, but a text that is as different from what we typically mean by that term as the "psychical" had initially been from the "textual."

Despite the fact that a new problem arises here, namely, how *are* we to conceive the text in its "infrastructural" or "general" sense if its "nature" is obscured by the very blindness that led us to oppose the psyche and *ordinary* texts in the first place, it is plain that Derrida's new account of the limitlessness of textuality rests on the assumption that everything that can be thought is marked by the textual character of the psyche which thinks it. In other words, it is not just because anything *could* be read as a text that nothing is outside the text. Rather, it is because reading (as a psychical activity) necessarily textualizes whatever it reads that nothing can present itself within the psyche without doing so on the textual register. Here the foregrounding of one's approach introduces a complication wherein the strategy of reading the psyche as an instance of textuality has exposed both the psyche and its reading to the consequences of such a strategy. Insofar as such consequences are discussed in the essay, they are treated in terms of the complex border that joins and separates a textually embodied discourse on the psyche and the textualization of the psyche. Though this very interweaving will later serve to characterize the irreducible property of the text as such, here one finds that Derrida is content to link the limits of textuality to the institutional and epistemological problem of separating the known from the conditions of knowing. The psyche *is* textual because it, like any other object of inquiry, is marked by the institutional framework within which it is known. The textual reading stresses this in order to foreground the construction work of analysis.

What again comes into focus here is the problem of discipline. By insisting upon the complex institutional structure of knowing, Derrida is attempting to resist the notion that phenomena have knowable properties (including the predicate of existence) independent of the power we have over them. The disciplines that organize knowledge, and especially philosophical knowledge, necessarily intervene within the known and as a consequence are marked by the epistemological instability such intervention must provoke. Though Derrida's critique of the "transcendental signifier" is often spelled out in strictly semiotic terms, I would argue that it is equally important to grasp the disciplinary character of this critique.[17] That is, if the text can be read as a way of modeling one's analytic practices around a putative object, and if what the text is designed to capture is the interweaving or reciprocal destabilization of the known and the conditions of knowing, then could one not say that the reason that there is no "transcendental signifier," and thus nothing outside the text, is because the known cannot entirely elude the disciplinary mechanisms authorized to overpower it? In effect, if one were to restate the matter more concisely, there is no outside to the text because there is no inside, no secure distance separating the disciplinary framework (including its paradigms) from the space it governs. Perhaps this is why Derrida concludes his critique of literary studies in "Freud and the Scene of Writing" by arguing that "[t]he *sociality* of writing as *drama* requires an entirely different discipline" (p. 227), thereby indicating that fundamental to an elaboration of the consequences of a textualization of the psyche is a transformation of the disciplinary framework within which the challenge of the text arose.

But let us say more about the "nature" of textuality as it emerges in these essays from the mid-sixties. This will enable me to come back at the problem of what lies outside the text from another angle. Earlier, I had underscored the importance of the figure of the fabric, and more recently I have been emphasizing the process of "interweaving." How can these figures help us define the "properties" of the text?

In "Form and Meaning: A Note on the Phenomenology of Language," Derrida resumes his reading of Husserl and refines his earlier criticisms which had been couched primarily in terms of the problematic of writing. Specifically, he continues to pressure the Husserlian account of the relation between signs and consciousness and does so by elaborating further his "new" notion of the text.

> The *interweaving* (*Verwebung*) of language, of what is purely linguistic in language with the other threads of experience, constitutes one fabric. The term *Verwebung* refers to this metaphorical zone. The "strata" are "woven"; their intermixing is such that the warp cannot be distinguished from the woof. If the stratum of the logos were simply *founded,* one could set it aside so as to let the underlying substratum of nonexpressive acts and contents appear beneath it. But since this superstructure reacts in an essential and decisive way upon the *Unterschlicht* [substratum], one is obliged, from the very start of the description, to associate the geological metaphor with a properly *textual* metaphor, for *fabric* or *textile* means *text*. *Verweben* here means *texere*. The discursive refers to the nondiscursive, the linguistic "stratum" is intermixed with the prelinguistic "stratum" according to the controlled system of a sort of *text*. . . . If the description does not bring out a ground that would absolutely and plainly found signification in general, if an intuitive and perceptual ground, a base of silence, does not found speech in the primordially given presence of the thing itself, if, in short, the texture of the text is irreducible, then, not only will the phenomenological description failed, but the descriptive "principle" will have to be re-examined.[18]

The characteristics of the text that emerge here are organized around the implications of the figure of interweaving, a term Derrida teases out of Husserl's analysis of signification. When Derrida introduces the phrase, "if the texture of the text is irreducible," he is not only reiterating the point about the "outside" of textuality (i.e., that there isn't one), but he is explicitly linking this problem to the impossibility of separating consciousness and language. If the two are interwoven, that is, not just indistinguishable but reciprocally destablized, then the disjunctive bond between the referent and the signified that protects meaning from the vicissitudes of social history is rendered dysfunctional. Insofar as the text properly names this state of affairs, it embodies a commitment—articulated as a methodological and analytic category—to a critical practice that seeks to reject, specifically at this level, any such denial of historicity.

The text is thus not only characterized by the process of interweaving, it is also an analytic category designed to produce this impossible border as part of the signifying structure of whatever the textual model is used to read. This does not mean, as is often assumed, that meaning is surrendered to nihilism and ultimately fascism,[19] but rather that meaning is entirely subject to the institutional structures that organize the relations between language and human agency. As I argued in chapter 1, the real issue raised by the notion of textuality concerns the project of formulating categories that enable us to register this situation within them so as to apply them effectively against the disciplinary circumstances in which we deploy such categories.

If one introduces at this point Derrida's remarks in "Semiology and Grammatology" (his 1968 interview with Julia Kristeva) where he explicitly links the notion of interweaving with the structure of the trace, then affinities between "Form and Meaning" and "Freud and the Scene of Writing" become apparent. What nevertheless distinguishes the two essays is the latter's focus on the apparatus—a focus which supplements Derrida's examination of the enunciative inscription of philosophy in a manner that raises issues worthy of further consideration.

In the Freud essay, textuality is situated in the structure and functioning of the psyche. More than a theory about the psyche, Derrida's gesture broaches a reflection about the relation between the text and the notion of technology or apparatus. As we have seen, this reflection attempts to specify the interaction between modes of inquiry (whether those of psychoanalysis or philosophy) and the enabling conditions of psychical experience. What prompts Derrida to read this interaction as nonrepresentational (i.e., he does not treat models of the psyche as reflections of either it or the theories about it) is the notion of the apparatus that supports it. Specifically, by refusing the vocabulary of "paralleling" or "mirroring," Derrida argues for an effective structure or "interface" (as we now say) that both assembles and stabilizes the conditions of knowing. More than a machine, the apparatus organizes, both minutely and regionally, the contours of the life world. Conceived textually, this apparatus stands forth at once as fabric and as fabrication—it is the "zone" of the interweaving of the symbolic and the real, and it is itself a construct marked by its constitution within this zone. Once situated in relation to the apparatus, textuality takes on attributes it acquires by virtue of its role in the history of technology. Thus the text both marks a departure in thinking about technology, and it arises as a particularly effective, and therefore attractive, model at a particular moment in the history of technology—a moment Derrida calls in *Of Grammatology*, "the end of the book." Let us elaborate what is at stake here for the Derridean notion of the text.

Early in the first section of *Grammatology* one finds the following formulations.

> The idea of the book, which always refers to a natural totality, is profoundly alien to the sense of writing. It is the encyclopedic protection of theology and of logocentrism against the disruption of writing, against its aphoristic energy, and, as I shall specify later, against difference in general. If I distinguish the text from the book, I shall say that the destruction of the book as it is underway in all domains, denudes the surface of the text. That necessary violence responds to a violence that was no less necessary.[20]

Thus opens a line of reflection that continues in Derrida's writing up to the present. It is the line of reflection which provoked the unease I voiced in announcing that I hoped to write a book about the text. As should now be apparent, what prompted my reaction is the fact that the opposition between text and book implies that writing the latter perpetuates the era of the book and, furthermore, that doing so violates the very topic of the text. But what is at stake in this opposition, especially for the concept of textuality?

As was stated in the introductory chapter, the book is to be understood as a cultural technology. As a cultural technology, the book subjected human agency to a psychosocial regime of communication and thus participated in the broad dynamics of modernization. Crucial to this regime of communication was a standardization of representation that made reproduction at once invisible and harmless. In effect, and Derrida says as much in his later discussion of Walter Benjamin's analysis of the impact of technical reproducibility on cultural experience,[21] the regime of communication exemplified in the book institutionalized a practice of reproduction that complicates Benjamin's diagnosis of the decline of "aura." While it is true that the book does complicate this discussion, it does so in a manner that essentially confirms Benjamin's thesis. What photography and the cinema (the cultural technologies discussed by Benjamin) accomplish is a practical deconstruction of the benign opposition between the original, animating intention and the medium of its reproductive dissemination. That is to say, though reproducibility is obviously fundamental to printing and therefore to the aura of the literary "masterpiece," it functions to protect the distinction between intent and representation by submitting representation to a technical standard of fidelity that renders the copy exact and therefore strictly dependent. The precision of printing appears to mirror precisely what the author meant for the printed book to say. Do we not still look upon typing up a manuscript in these terms?

Consider, for the purpose of clarifying this point, the difference between a copy of a book and a copy of a painting. Once we assure ourselves that the book is complete and unexpurgated (a determination which assumes its basic legibility), little doubt arises about whether we have "all" the information required to evaluate the work at its own level of existence. This is not true about painting, where one is constantly nagged by the suspicion that s/he is working with less than "exact" reproductions. Granted, there is an important difference between the two signifying practices, but it is not a difference that authorizes one to reject Benjamin's claim, namely, that photography participated in the advent of a new era of cultural technology, one characterized by an overturning and disruption of the opposition between animating original and servile copy.

I would argue that when Derrida establishes an opposition between the book and the "surface of the text," he is reading the book in terms of this sort of organizing opposition. This is why he positions writing as that which is entirely alien to the book in the above citation. By opening a space where not only the "totality" can be named and summoned forth, but where this naming takes place within precise and thus secure borders (i.e., the physical dimensions of the printed manuscript), the book necessarily reifies writing, understood by Derrida, as that which marks every border as precarious and ill-defined. In this context the text designates that which, in its denuding, both precipitates the decline of the book and emerges as the monstrous technology that survives it. What is paradoxical about this situation, of course, is that the text embodies a notion of the apparatus that overcomes the category of technology by refusing the distinction between agent and machine. The psychical apparatus is textual precisely to the extent that it makes human experience, and specifically its interpretation, depend on the immanent operation of a mechanism. Thus the text begins to assume its full function as an anti-disciplinary object by linking the elaboration of analytic categories to the task of intervening within the technological preconditions of the cultural institutions of what I have called disciplinary power.

If there has indeed been a shift "from work to text," it has been due in part to the decline of the book. The "work" was, after all, the unrecognized disciplinary object of literary study during the era of the book. Its unrecognizability derived from the hegemony of the opposition that protected the animating intention of a book from its representational embodiment. In other words, just as the copy of the book failed to affect *the* book, so too the work failed to affect literature. Those who appealed to the category of the work felt entitled to protect literature by raising it above the constraints of discipline. The reason that the "sociality of writing," understood as a text, thus requires an "entirely different discipline" is because the decline of the book has taken place within a sociohistorical context where the cultural technologies of mass culture (photography, cinema, radio, and television) have so destabilized the book that the disciplines which cooperated in its maintenance have themselves been unsettled. In fact, when pressured to clarify the disciplinary implications of his positions on textuality, Derrida responds to Jean-Louis Houdebine that the emergence of the "general text" at once presupposes the complicity of disciplines broadly conceived as "ideological," and confronts them with the task of thinking beyond the notion of "regional delimitation" their organization assumes.[22] Thus, Derrida's preoccupations resonate with issues at stake in the preceding discussion of contextuality and the jolts of fashion.

Once the text is aligned by Derrida with the decline of the book, its literary roots are deeply threatened. What began as an insistence upon the enunciative instance of discourse, forked into a psychoanalytically inflected critique of European philosophy—a critique that subsequently exposed literary analysis to a trenchant disciplinary interrogation—and culminated in a notion of textuality that evokes, without successfully engaging, a post-typographic framework of cultural practices. Along this trajectory, "literature" has served as a sort of pivot, coordinating on the one hand, a critique of philosophy's denial of the linguistic signifier and on the other a critique of literature's unrecognized investment in metaphysics. What is distinctive about this pivot is the way it coordinates an asymmetry. In other words, the two disciplines brought into contact by Derrida's elaboration of textuality are made to disclose their hidden solidarity, and by doing so Derrida perturbs the borders that define the specificity of their intellectual agendas. As a consequence, philosophy and literary research at once seem to mirror each other and yet reflect back images that do not match. This is less because of their differences than because of the equivalent ways that both philosophy and literature are unsettled by what Derrida once called "the play" that marks the discourses of the human sciences. Though not entirely separable from the ludic impulse that animates what Bakhtin has called the "carnivalesque,"[23] Derridean play is perhaps more fruitfully thought of as the "give" that enables a mechanism to operate without succumbing to friction. From this perspective then the text, as the (anti)disciplinary pivot between literature and philosophy, registers the asymmetrical relation it coordinates. This is a specifically Derridean way to conceive of the text's ambivalence. Insofar as the text emerges here as an effect of the functioning and problematization of these disciplines, is it not also legible as a tactic for both identifying and proliferating play? From a tactical perspective the text can be seen as at once "unreal" (it is play in the sense of a "play dough") and deliberate (play in the sense of skillful maneuvering). The text seeks to oppose disciplinarity by enabling its partisans to link the play that prevents disciplines from ossifying and caving in upon themselves to the antagonisms that define the field of disciplinary power. However, in spite of such aims, the Derridean text remains neutralized by the very forces it was devised to oppose, and has, as a consequence, drawn the kind of criticisms discussed in the introductory chapter. Unfortunately, many of those who have risen to defend Derrida from such criticism have only made matters worse by writing as though his text speaks for itself.

# 4

## ✳  The Text *tel quel*: Kristeva's Productivity

Kristeva came to Paris from Bulgaria in 1966 and worked, somewhat uneasily, as a research assistant for Lucien Goldmann. She brought with her an interest in the semiotic debates that had long been preoccupying intellectuals in the Eastern bloc—an interest that prompted her to push for a French translation of Bakhtin's book on Dostoevsky long before he became an intellectual celebrity in the West. In fact, though Kristeva has always been a brilliant literary scholar, her notion of the text derives less from the literary disciplines per se, than from her critical examination of the resources of semiotics as it revolutionized the human sciences during the 1960s. Nevertheless, her elaboration of textuality clearly unfolds within the problematic defined by the linguistic interrogation of literary language, and to this extent it remains linked to the problematization of literature I have identified as being fundamental to the emergence of the text. Moreover, Kristeva, more than either Derrida or Barthes, has labored to specify the literary implications of a commitment to the text, while also detailing those analytic properties of textuality that draw literature beyond itself. In many respects, her insights and innovations are what necessitated M. Wahl's entry in the appendix to Todorov's and Ducrot's *Encyclopedic Dictionary of the Sciences of Language*. As a consequence, the task of summarizing her key formulations is considerably more difficult and will require that we arbitrarily designate a "hub" around which they can be organized. I have chosen the notion of "productivity."

In "Semiotics: A Critical Science and/or A Critique of Science," from her first published book, *Seméiotiké: Recherches pour une sémanalyse,*[1] Kristeva developed a critique of what she later called "semiobusiness" that permitted her to link the Marxian notion of the mode of production to the Freudian notion of dream-work. What attracted her to the Marxian analysis of production was its disclosure of the social processes that constituted the phenomenon of value. In essence, Marx's analysis showed that an object of discourse embodied a social, and therefore intersubjective, relation. By the same token, what necessitated for Kristeva the reference to Freud was Marx's inability to theorize the subjective dynamics of production that preconditioned the social investment in value. Though Kristeva was careful to affirm Marx's insight into the productive character of the body's expenditure of energy and the role played by this expenditure in the structure of class domination, she insisted upon the radicality of the Freudian conception of work elaborated in his discussion of the primary processes. There, work was freed from its "productivist" connotations (i.e., its embodiment in a product) through its connection with the operation of the psychical apparatus and the semiotic determination of the subject. What motivated her insistence upon the importance of the Freudian account of work was her interest in securing a notion of production that captured the fundamentally unstable character of the *social* constitution of the subject. Kristeva's thinking about textuality thus evolves in the context of her effort to sublate the Marxian and the Freudian discourses on production, and for this reason it makes sense to frame the elaboration of her work in this manner.

As I indicated earlier, Kristeva's work as a literary scholar has remained central to her intellectual activities. In fact, her earliest formulations on the text appear in her work on the linguistic and semiological analysis of literature. Within this context the notion of production acquires a restricted, though suggestive, meaning. Consider, for example, the following formulation from *Le Texte du roman*, written in the mid-sixties and published in 1970.

> More than a *discourse,* semiology actually takes as its object *several semiotic practices* which it considers as *translinguistic,* that is to say, elaborated across language and thus irreducible to its categories. From this perspective, we define *the text* as a translinguistic apparatus that redistributes the order of language by relating communicative speech, which aims to inform directly, to different types of anterior and synchronic utterances. The text is thus a *productivity,*

which means: (1) its relation to the language in which it is situated is redistributive (destructive-constructive), and hence the text is better approached through logical and mathematical categories rather than purely linguistic ones; (2) it is a permutation of texts, an inter-textuality, which is to say, in the space of a text several utterances, taken from other texts, intersect and neutralize each other.[2]

Taken from a methodological introduction to a resourceful, yet ultimately linguistic (at least in its motivating preoccupations) reading of an early French prose work, Antoine de La Sale's *Histoire et plaisante chronique du petit Jehan de Saintré et de la jeune dame des Belles Cousines*, these remarks of Kristeva's contain many of her fundamental convictions about textuality, including, of course, its relation to productivity. Though its relation to the problematic of Freudo-Marxism is not immediately apparent, patient elaboration of her formulations will enable us to specify this relation.

Crucial to Kristeva's notion of the text is her sense that it fundamentally serves as an "object" of a particular kind of analytic practice.[3] This idea is reiterated a few years later when, in opening the essay "Le texte et sa science" from *Seméiotiké*, she argues, "religion, aesthetics and psychiatry . . . all claim in turn to capture that 'specific object' . . . provisionally designated as *text* (p. 7). In the context of the previous citation, this point is explicitly connected with the critique and extension of semiotics Kristeva later called "semanalysis." By refusing "discourse" as the object of semiology, not only does semiology take on a new object, but, and this is the crucial issue, semiology itself undergoes a transformation that problematizes its own relation to the disciplines (or, as Kristeva prefers, "sciences") as a result. Insofar as the text designates this new object, it registers in its analytical properties this problematization of semiology as a transdisciplinary practice. Moreover, in the essay, "Semiotics: A Critical Science and/or a Critique of Science," Kristeva explicitly argues that the transformation of semiology wrought by the advent of textuality enables the former to engage in a contestation of science that coordinates an interrogation of its rationality with a practical modification of the institutional structure of science. Or, as she says in "Le texte et sa science," "[t]hrough the semiotic intervention, the system of sciences sees itself decentered and obliged to turn towards dialectical materialism, in order to envisage, in turn, the elaboration of signification, that is to say, to produce a gnoseology" (p. 21). The point is, of course, that the text not only unsettles semiology's relation to the disciplines, but its emergence as an object *within* the sciences provokes the later to question their foundations. In this respect, Kristeva's inaugural meditation on the status of the text as an object quickly links it to a latent politics of antidisciplinarity despite the fact that her linguistic convictions continually pressure her to formalize textuality. Since she never fails to react to this pressure, it will have to be examined more carefully later.

Let us come back to the citation from *Le Texte du roman*. As we have seen, her elaboration of the implications of adopting the text as the object of semanalysis leads to an affirmation of the dialectical materialist task of producing an alternative theory of knowledge. How does this bear on the notion of productivity that operates in the text's relation to language? In the citation Kristeva characterizes the text as an "apparatus" that affects the order of language by confronting its normative, communicative utterances with the processes that are at once presupposed by it (e.g., the functioning of the speech centers of the brain and the circulation of discourses organizing the sociality of speech) and excluded from it (e.g., all those verbal and nonverbal gestures that interrupt or complicate the flow of information in speech as well as those "nonstandard" linguistic practices that silhouette the imposition of the normative model). Though she does not spell out the character of the apparatus here (it has rather obvious affinities with Derrida's), it is plain that, by exposing language to its enabling conditions and exclusions, in short, to its own limits, the text engages productivity in two ways: (1) it discloses the mechanisms through which language realizes its effects, and (2) it dislodges speakers from their strictly representational and instrumental relations with language—relations which when unsettled threaten the very identities of the speakers. In this context, productivity refers to the infrastructure of language that ordinary use simultaneously exploits and represses but through whose functioning linguistic meaning takes place.

What channels this discussion of productivity through the problematic with which I began is not primarily the allusion to the category of infrastructure. Rather, by insisting upon a history of utterances, a historicity endemic to the communicating subject, Kristeva crafts the text such that it bears within its analytic properties an irreducible reference to the social. From this perspective, the notion of meaning is treated much the same way Marx treated value—both are effects of social dynamics that are occluded by their products. Or, as she explicitly argues in "La productivité dite texte," "Textual productivity is the measure inherent to literature [seen as the domain of particular texts], but it is not literature [seen from the perspective of textuality], just as each instance of labor is the measure inherent to value without being value itself" (p. 238). It is these dynamics, if you will, that Kristeva is evoking through the notion of productivity. The text is marked by the psychosocial not by reflecting it, but by serving to designate, and thus make available for analysis, that register of language use that discloses the speaker's emergence within the historical field. Though productivity here preserves its relation to literary artifacts, and to this extent retains its linguistic cast, it scores the formal surface of the artifact with processes that ultimately lead beyond this disciplinary framework. Hence, the explicit rejection of the category of literature that appears in the citation from "La productivité dite texte."

By associating productivity and the redistribution of the order of language, Kristeva accomplishes two significant things. On the one hand, she takes seriously Marx's and Engels's comments on the materiality of language in *The German Ideology*, integrating language within the structure of the mode of production.[4] On the other, she treats language as a specific site within the mode of production where the later encounters, through the vehicle of the subject's unstable relation to language, the possibility of its perpetual transformation. What authorizes the latter move in particular, is Kristeva's appeal to the irreducibility of the human agent who, in acceding to the linguistic signifier, not only assumes a position within a particular mode of production, but does so by activating and thereby revealing the instability of the mode of production insofar as its reproduction (i.e., its historical maintenance) necessarily rests upon the filling of those subject positions deemed essential to its mobilization. This double significance of the agent is what is evoked in the parenthetical phrase, "(destructive-constructive)," that Kristeva introduces to gloss the notion of redistribution. In other words, because the text captures the way language both constructs positions for speakers and subverts those speakers by disclosing the "merely" symbolic character of such positions, its formulation necessarily relies upon an agent who uses, and is used by, language. It is, in fact, the irreducibility of this reliance on the agent that leads Kristeva's notion of textuality beyond linguistics into the domain of historical materialism and ultimately beyond it. Significantly, this drift away from linguistics is explicitly enacted when, in the "Prolegomenon" to *Revolution in Poetic Language*, Kristeva rewrites the passage from *Le Texte du roman* and replaces "discourse" with "text" while comparing the latter's effect upon the subject to a revolution's effect upon society.[5]

By the same token, the insistence upon language as the mediating tissue of the mode of production that animates Kristeva's notion of textuality is what necessitates recourse to psychoanalysis and the critique of what Jean

Baudrillard once called "the mirror of production." [6] Kristeva's emphasis on logical as opposed to linguistic categories, besides permitting her
to exploit the estrangement effects that arise when using mathematical
notation to "represent" literary processes, is meant to associate textual
productivity with the so-called "logic of the signifying chain," analyzed
so extensively by Jacques Lacan whose seminars she attended in the mid-
sixties. What is at stake in this association has been the subject of many
excellent commentaries. [7] For my purposes what is crucial here is that the
text, as the object of semanalysis, is meant to capture the process wherein
the production of meaning, and specifically the appearance of the "I" as
a communicable signifier, slips away from, or eludes, both the speaker/
writer or the listener/reader, in short, society insofar as it is defined by the
subjection of agency characteristic of a particular mode of production.
As she says in *Revolution in Poetic Language*,

> We view the subject in language as decentering the transcendental
> ego, cutting through it, and opening it up to a dialectic in which
> its syntactic and categorical understanding is merely the liminary
> moment of the process, which is itself always acted upon by the rela-
> tion to the other dominated by the death drive and its productive
> reiteration of the "signifier." We will be attempting to formulate the
> distinction between *semiotic* and *symbolic* within this perspective,
> which was introduced by Lacanian analysis, but also within the con-
> straints of a practice—the *text*—which is only of secondary interest
> to psychoanalysis. [8]

In this respect, the text has a contradictory function. On the one hand,
it is introduced to designate, with some methodological reliability, an
aspect of language use. On the other hand, insofar as it designates this
aspect accurately, it must be sufficiently pliant to be, in effect, unreliable,
that is, incapable of recuperating what it designates as irrecuperable.
Because the "irrecuperable," as I have called it, refers to the speaking
subject's shifting (cf., Jakobson) in the register of the signifier, it redis-
tributes the order of language by perpetually marking it as unsettled at
the level of enunciation. Productivity, conceived of redistributively, thus
underscores the way production harbors a modality of expenditure, of
loss, that cannot be grasped through the model of a product, but which
nevertheless participates in the mode of production as its limit. Though
textuality and the notion of semiotics that motivates it are often read as
referring to the "extra-social," I think it is more prudent to read them
as attempts to come to terms with the social production of what outdis-

tances and thus negates the social, or what I have earlier referred to as the utopic. After all, Kristeva herself argues for such a view at the end of the section, "Four Signifying Practices," in *Revolution in Poetic Language*.⁹

The second characterization of textual productivity introduced by Kristeva in the citation from *Le Texte du roman*, intertextuality, continues to extend the concerns of the Freudo-Marxian framework, but by beginning to steer us back toward the formalist preoccupations I emphasized at the outset. As we have seen, the text for Kristeva necessarily evokes, even at the categorical level, a surpassing of limits—the limits of the social, of the subject, etc. It is not then surprising that the productivity associated with the text is subsequently connected with the latter's own "internal" heterogeneity. The text registers the presence of many discourses in the space of a particular artifact. Despite the fact that *Le Texte du roman* pursues this insight by tracing the presence within La Sale's novel of carnivalesque, courtly poetic, and scholastic discourses, intertextuality, like Bakhtin's notion of "dialogism" on which it is explicitly modeled, is not primarily a revision of the literary critical categories of sources and influences. What distinguishes it from such notions is Kristeva's insistence upon intertextuality's relation to productivity. Consider, in this light, the following formulation from her *Revolution in Poetic Language*.

> The term *inter-textuality* denotes this transposition of one (or several) sign system(s) into another, but since this term has often been understood in the banal sense of "study of sources," we prefer the term *transposition* because it specifies that the passage from one signifying system to another demands a new articulation of the thetic— of enunciative and denotative positionality. If one grants that every signifying practice is a field of transpositions of various signifying systems (an inter-textuality), one then understands that its "place" of enunciation and its denoted "object" are never single, complete and identical to themselves, but always plural, shattered, capable of being tabulated.¹⁰

Here productivity is conceived through the notion of transposition. This notion (transposition) supplements redistribution by underscoring the effect of a collision among diverse signifying systems—an effect that is proper to every artifact and which, therefore, marks every artifact as a site where the order of language is brought into contact with practices that, even when articulated through language, unfold beside it. What Kristeva is thus seeking to oppose to the familiar notion of sources is a model of intertextuality that insists upon the way literary texts transform and thus remain marked by, not merely other things like them (i.e., other texts), but other inscriptions of meaning that may even take the form of psychic structures like the ego of thetic (i.e., positional or intentional) consciousness. Moreover, by stressing that texts are sites of an ongoing permutation, Kristeva exploits intertextuality to capture the reciprocal action that constitutes the relations among and within texts, as well as between particular texts and the processes that unfold beside them. This breaks decisively with the critical perspective that comprehends the utility of sources in terms of the antinomy between "tradition" and "individual talent," where tradition (whether literary or cultural) serves as a repository of influences activated by an aesthetic consciousness whose inner force transcends them. Intertextuality, on the other hand, obliges one to approach literary discourse as though its production transforms and thus constitutes not only what should no longer be called "tradition," but also what should no longer be called the "individual." In this respect, Kristeva's position has important resonances with Derrida's, which, as we have seen, also insists upon the textual character of the psychical apparatus. However, by associating this aspect of intertextuality with the notion of productivity, Kristeva remains in closer dialogue with the analytic framework of Marx, confronting the latter's emphasis on the social character of the cultural tradition with the task of grasping, and articulating in categorical form, the theoretical implications of this sociality.

In addition to the specific properties of intertextuality, the tactical elaboration of this notion is also significant. If, as I have argued, the linguistic specification of literary specificity provoked a rejection of literature as a fundamentally ideological category, Kristeva's commitment to the elaboration of a literary problematic—a commitment inscribed in the very notion of intertextuality—suggests that she nevertheless wishes to avoid reducing all cultural discourse to ideology. By recasting the social character of the interaction among discourses in textual terms, and by explicitly extending the domain of the textual well beyond the literary field—thus submitting the latter to a fundamental critique—Kristeva both absorbs and rejects the social preoccupations that underlie the reading of literature as "sheer ideology." Essentially, she rewrites the literary as a transdisciplinary or, as I would prefer to say, antidisciplinary practice that resists ideological reduction—which is not to say that textuality becomes nonideological; Kristeva herself has acknowledged that the text may become ". . . the agent of a new religion that is no longer universal but elitist and esoteric." [11] Rather, intertextuality as a condition of textuality, registers the structural play (in Derrida's sense) that keeps ideology unsettled from within its historically shifting borders. Thus, in spite of the fact that textuality presupposes a sociocultural domain organized by a transdisciplinary practice, it nevertheless refuses to abandon the space of literary (cf., Blanchot again), or perhaps more broadly, aesthetic practice. Instead, however, of grasping this space in terms either of a transcendental differentiation as in Kant or of a historical institution as in Hegel (or, for that matter, Adorno), Kristeva approaches it as a utopic site of expenditure that society seeks to master through rejection. In effect, her notion of textuality registers this revision of the space of literature by invoking the notion of the *chora,* which remaps the domain of literary art without renouncing the critical moment Kant and others sought to attach to it by setting it apart from the social. Tactically then, I would argue that Kristeva's notion of the text is explicitly designed to dislodge a disciplinary specification of literary discourse, not by hammering it into an undifferentiated surface of ideology, but by shifting the supports that permitted such a specification to become institutionalized.

Central to such a reading, of course, is the status of the *chora* and its immanent relation to the textual displacement of literature. In order to elaborate the matrix wherein intertextual signifying practices at once engage and outdistance a particular text, say a poem, Kristeva generates a structural opposition that is crucial to her notion of textuality. This opposition, between the "genotext" and the "phenotext," is at best only latent in *Le Texte du roman* and *Seméiotiké,* and it does not really come to the fore until *Revolution in Poetic Language.* There, she introduces these notions in the following terms.

> We shall use the term *phenotext* to denote language that serves to communicate, which linguistics describes in terms of "competence" and "performance." The phenotext is constantly split up and divided, and it is irreducible to the semiotic process that works through the genotext. The phenotext is a structure (which can be generated, in generative grammar's sense); it obeys rules of communication and presupposes a subject of enunciation and an addressee. The genotext, on the other hand, is a process; it moves through zones that have relative and transitory borders and constitutes a *path* that is not restricted to the two poles of univocal information between two full-fledged subjects. [12]

Obviously, this opposition is meant to capture what might be called the vertical axis of intertextuality, that is, the transfer point between the linguistically organized field of artifacts and the semiotically informed fields of biology and society. Insofar as this axis is precisely what separates intertextuality from "source studies," it is perhaps odd that it would become most visible when Kristeva attempts to address the immanent character of the "literary" text. Yet, this is precisely what occurs, and for reasons that I have already outlined. Nevertheless, to understand what is at stake for the notion of the text in the opposition between the phenotext and the genotext, it must be situated in relation to the more general opposition that it presupposes, namely, the one between the semiotic and the symbolic, where, not surprisingly, the issue of the *chora* assumes its full pertinence.

As we have seen, Kristeva has an ambivalent relation to semiotics—a relation that prompted her to develop the notion of semanalysis as a way to redefine the object of semiotics. In *Revolution in Poetic Language* Kristeva separates semiotics explicitly from those linguistic applications that reduce it to a methodological metalanguage by emphasizing its relation to Lacan's reading of Freud. What is rescued here is the connection between signs (understood as systemically inflected markers of difference) and the drives or forces that animate them at the level of the psychosomatic apparatus. The semiotic for Kristeva, in fact, refers exclusively to the protosystemic inscription of the drives (what Freud enigmatically referred to as the effects of primary repression) that establishes a performative (rhythmic and gestural) envelope for what she calls the symbolic register, that is, so-called ordinary language. She takes the notion of the *chora* from Plato's *Timaeus* and uses it to designate this envelope. As she says, "the semiotic *chora* is no more than the place where the subject is both generated and negated, the place where his [sic] unity succumbs before the process of charges and stases that produce him [sic]" (p. 28). Because this place unfolds between, as it were, the drives Freud linked with the subject's struggle to differentiate itself from the maternal body, Kristeva reads the *chora* as a social locus of the feminine. It is not just, therefore, a space that is bordered by subjects constituted as female within the social division of gender, but it is lived by subjects engendered across this division (by men *and* women) as "feminine" if not specifically "maternal." Here obviously, textuality—insofar as it engages what is at stake in the distinction between the semiotic and the symbolic—seeks to register in its analytic contours the moment and process of "engenderment," a crucial and difficult insight whose elaboration I will defer until the concluding section of part 2.

The symbolic, on the other hand, captures that aspect of the subject that can be articulated through the linguistic signifier. Insofar as one can refer to him or herself with the first person pronoun and experience what such a referral "means," s/he has gained access to the symbolic— understood not in the sense of a discourse laden with double meanings, but in the sense of a discourse through which one can signify one's existence to another. Returning then to the opposition between the genotext and the phenotext, essentially what Kristeva does is align the semiotic with the former and the symbolic with the latter. In other words, the genotext embodies that dimension of a literary text that registers the operation of the performative envelope, the flux of rhythm, gesture, and sonority, tying the text to the subject's struggle to come into its own through aesthetic representation. It was with this in mind that, in the Introduction, I proposed treating textual productivity as a reconceptualization of "creativity." Conversely, the phenotext exists as that part of a work that communicates information and thus lends itself to hermeneutic decipherment. Taken together, and Kristeva insists that they can be separated only for the purposes of exposition, the genotext and the phenotext capture the two registers of an artifact read from the theoretical standpoint of textuality. While they function as quintessentially "intrinsic" or "immanent" categories—and thus remain in dialogue with a certain formalism—the genotext in particular clearly opens the work to an outside, an alterity, that nevertheless remains pertinent to cultural criticism by linking the interior of an artifact to precisely what makes it cultural, namely, the instability that simultaneously attracts the forces of social order and fosters the interminable re-readability of literary practice. In this respect, Kristeva's insistence upon the intertextual character of the text—which, after all, is what is reflected in the opposition between the genotext and the phenotext—at once preserves the social space of the utopic impulse embodied in literature while canceling the designation "literature" by disclosing its supports in specifically nonliterary material.

If we connect these observations about the space of textuality with Kristeva's semiotically inflected critique of science, then one can see that textuality explicitly embodies a rejection of the disciplinary-specific way in which literature has been mobilized to embody a form of social critique that has, in fact, been sacrificed to the task of protecting literature from (and thus raising it above) the discipline or science whose modes of inquiry have in fact constituted it. Instead of reading the *chora,* which Kristeva clearly exploits to designate the "no place" a literary work at once taps into and suppresses, as an ontologically secured alterity, why not read it as a moment within an institutional topography. Doing so saves one the embarrassment of having to contradict one's principles in order to formulate them (as Kristeva herself is obliged to do),[13] and it opens up the possibility of directing the practice of close reading through a particular text and out onto the disciplinary framework that conditions and exceeds one's reading. Once discipline is no longer reduced to the academic activities that cluster around showcases of cultural fetishes and is understood as a social relation organized by the production of objects of knowledge, then the concerns one might have about sacrificing the "radicality" of Kristeva's *chora* to the preoccupations of disciplinarity can be set to rest. I would argue, in fact, that Kristeva threatens to compromise the critical efficacy (which, after all, is what is at stake in the notion of radicality) of textuality by *not* recognizing the conditions of its sociogenesis and thus the limits of the alterity that can be thought under such conditions. If textuality seeks to articulate from within the social that which negates it, the text must operate in the space opened for such a negation and facilitate the identification of what, *within* that space, can be turned against it so as to lead beyond it. In short, textuality needs to direct the study of cultural works toward what I am calling antidisciplinarity.

This aim is inhibited in Kristeva's theoretical work by the specific disciplinary pressures that exert themselves upon it. Whereas in Derrida's work the radicalization of literary analysis leads to a critique of philosophy that delegitimizes any appeal to foundationalism (be it ontic or psychic), Kristeva's desire to remain in touch with the specificity of the literary work (however rewritten) provokes her to confront her disciplinary context with the discourses *it* recognizes as transcending that context, namely, philosophy, mathematics, and psychology (at least in its psychoanalytic variant). Derrida, in effect, rebuffs Kristeva for precisely this strategy when, in "Semiology and Grammatology," he reminds her that, "[w]e must also be wary of the 'naive' side of formalism and mathematism, one of whose secondary functions in metaphysics, . . . has been to complete and confirm the logocentric theology which they otherwise could contest" (p. 35). I believe that only if we were to resist the ontological reading of alterity (cf., Levinas) and reject the pseudonegativity of "pure" semiosis—tactics that bear within them the traces of insufficiently problematized disciplinary legacies—could Kristeva's approach to the text be made to realize its critical potential. By the same token, and here I am only repeating myself, if we avoid the question of situating the social inscription of alterity as a matter of principle, as a matter of cleaving to the philosophically principled rejection of principles, then not only do we risk missing the action taking place in aesthetic practice, but we end up prematurely settling for an ineffective critical practice— one that exhausts itself in institutional renovation. The vitality of both Kristeva's and Derrida's formulations suggests that the text need not be surrendered to such a meager destiny. However, in Kristeva's case in particular, given that her approach to textuality has so profoundly transformed the practice of "formalist" criticism, it is tempting to conclude that sociopolitical neutralization has been the institutional price exacted for such a transformation. Tempting yes, but perhaps also premature.

# 5

## ✳ The Text *tel quel*: Barthes's Pleasure

**I**

Though most of Barthes's now "canonical" formulations on textuality occur in the period from 1968 to 1975, the issues that pushed him toward it were organizing his writing much earlier. For example, if one acknowledges that a certain functional reduction of the author enabled Barthes to conceptualize the reading space of a text (as opposed to the book or the work), then the distinction drawn between the author and the writer in "Authors and Writers" from 1960, though certainly less "funereal" than the one later elaborated in "The Death of the Author," is clearly a precursive development. Or, to take a considerably more repercussive example, in "The Structuralist Activity" from 1963 Barthes identified the role of structuralism (even in its literary form) as the attempt to "reconstruct an 'object' in such a way as to manifest thereby the rules of functioning (the 'functions') of this object,"[1] in essence adumbrating the move that directed his attention to the "work's" status as a literary object and his subsequent elaboration of its textual displacement. Moreover, in this essay Barthes elaborates the procedural categories that are shared by structuralist criticism and literary works and thus justify the denial of a technical distinction between them. Significantly, one of these categories, "articulation" (p. 216), reappears eight years later in the Preface to *Sade/Fourier/Loyola* where, from within a remarkably similar expository context, it is used explicitly to characterize the way the languages discovered by the three writers are open to the "semiological definition of Text."[2]

Though I might be accused of stretching the point, it is also worth noting that in order to exemplify the procedural category of "dissection" (articulation's twin) Barthes has recourse in this essay to the sonoric distinction between s and z—precisely the distinction that Barthes later exploited in his most ambitious demonstration of how one might read "textually," namely, *S/Z*. When we realize that the codes or voices identified in *S/Z* as the texture of "Sarrasine" are used to animate the analysis of the "multiple Text" in *Sade/Fourier/Loyola*, it becomes more difficult to dismiss this tangle of associations as merely fortuitous.

Nevertheless, what these precursive formulations authorize one to conclude is limited. Clearly Barthes, like both Kristeva and Derrida, embarks on the drift toward textuality from within a specific meditation on the limits of the disciplines of literary analysis. He embraces the semiological problematization of the literary object, and as a consequence he adopts and develops many of the same categories as Kristeva (specifically, paragrams, intertextuality, the phenotext/genotext opposition) and Derrida (specifically, writing, the trace, and dissemination).[3] The effect of this point of departure is that it orients Barthes's most provocative contribution to the notion of the text, namely the text's relation to pleasure, around a pivot defined on one side by a fascination with the *enjoyment* of reading and writing and on the other by a desire to specify how the text as a methodological field participates in a society's "use of pleasures." At one level, of course, this pivot articulates the denial of the technical distinction between "creative" and critical writing alluded to earlier. But since it also conditions Barthes's distinctive commitment to the notion that "the discourse on the Text should itself be nothing other than text"[4]—a commitment driven by the desire that Barthes reads as indissociable from textual pleasure—this pivot requires careful elaboration. To proceed, let us turn to those formulations that foreground the problem of pleasure.

The period from 1970 to 1973 is the one during which capitalization seizes the text, marking at the explicitly typographical level the text's emergence as a methodological concept. In 1971 Barthes writes about the text, in what passes for him as "theoretical" discourse, twice, and in both cases he exploits the distinction between the Text (capitalized) and texts. For someone "enraptured with binaries,"[5] this situation embodies something like a minimal pair, and as we shall see, this typographic reduction/ erection of difference (from t to T, as it were) plays a symptomatic role in the elaboration of Barthes's perspective on the text. Perhaps this is what organizes, at the specifically textual level, the ultimately homoerotic structure of Barthean bliss. Consider the following argument from "From Work to Text."

> This leads us to pose (to propose) a final approach to the Text, that of pleasure. . . . Certainly there exists a pleasure of the work (of certain works). . . . But this pleasure, no matter how keen and even when free from all prejudice, remains in part (unless by some exceptional critical effort) a pleasure of consumption; for if I can read these authors, I also know that I cannot *re-write* them . . . and this knowledge, depressing enough, suffices to cut me off from the production of these works. . . . As for the Text, it is bound to *jouissance,* that is to pleasure without separation. Order of the signifier, the Text participates in its own way in a social utopia; before History (supposing the latter does not opt for barbarism), the Text achieves, if not the transparence of social relations, than at least of language relations: the Text is that space where no language has a hold over any other, where languages circulate (keeping the circular sense of the term).[6]

Here, amidst a surfeit of typical Barthean themes (many of which we will simply be obliged to ignore) appears the pivot discussed above, though now articulated around the opposition between the work and the text. In the beginning of the passage Barthes addresses the pleasure one would readily (assuming, of course, one's commitment to the classical dictum concerning art's twin obligation to instruct and to delight) associate with the act of reading a literary work. His aim is not to deny this pleasure, but to supplement it, and to this extent he clearly situates the emergence of textuality within the concerns of literary criticism.[7] Nevertheless, the supplementation of this pleasure effects what I have called a pivot wherein the pleasure taken in the reading of a work encounters the pleasure of the text. What executes this pivot is the shift from a consumptive joy to a productive bliss, and motivating this shift is the very evaluative schema that was to animate the distinction in *S/Z* (p. 4) between the writerly and the readerly text. In this context, the text is to be understood as the framework one must adopt in order to break with a consumptive approach to literary language. But in what sense does the framework effect this break?

Though Barthes explicitly refuses to discriminate between mass culture and elite bourgeois art, it is clear that the opposition between consumption and production—aside from reiterating Kristeva's valorization of "productivity"—expresses, however indirectly, Barthes's commitment to the position taken by Theodor Adorno in the Frankfurt School's debate over the significance of mass culture. In his withering response to Benjamin's "The Work of Art in the Age of Mechanical Reproduction," Adorno, in "The Fetish Character of Music and the Regression of Listening," argued that technological standardization had so saturated the mass cultural sphere that audiences were reduced to groups of consumers, subjects who had regressed to the point where they were incapable of producing unsolicited, and therefore unadministered, responses to cultural activity of any kind. Barthes supports the terms of this argument even as he demurs on its conclusions. By associating the work with consumptive joy, and therefore *mere* pleasure, Barthes explicitly factors the body into Adorno's equation and argues that the sort of cultural experience that makes one "feel good about him/herself" or culminates in "enjoyment" presupposes a model of cultural artifacts (the work as opposed to the text) that promotes passivity and acquiescence to the institutions of cultural production. What permits Barthes to resist Adorno's haughty conclusions, and this is argued at some length in "Pax Culturalis" from 1971,[8] is precisely this focus on the *model* of cultural analysis which either reproduces (consumes) or transforms (produces) the cultural given. In any case, by moving beyond the work and its pleasures, Barthes associates the text with a level of cultural existence that conditions the domain of artifacts (i.e., specific books, films, records, etc.) and in doing so makes available an experience beyond pleasure—bliss. Thus, the text, as a methodological concept, could be said to orient cultural analysis so that we pay attention to those aspects of aesthetic practices that frustrate or surpass enjoyment, and do so as a result of the friction that arises between the textually oriented reading and the semiotic laminations of the specific writing practice made available through the reading. In this respect the text continues to focus reading and writing on the approach that enables them to assume certain traits, leading analysis away from the phenomenal surface regulated by the culture industry and toward the conditions of the institutional production of this surface.

When the text is actually introduced in the passage cited, it is immediately bound to a particular modality of pleasure, "pleasure without separation." Since this characterization is meant to clarify what is at stake in the shift from work to text, it is worth pondering at some length. Clearly, the invocation of "separation" operates to shift the context of Barthes's discussion from literary criticism to psychoanalysis, where the concept of separation enjoys a certain technical status. Thus, the text is once again brought into relation with the dynamics of subjectivity.

Within the context of psychoanalytic reflection, "separation," at least for Lacan (whose discussion is the most pertinent for Barthes), refers to the process whereby a human infant comes to recognize its own existential boundaries—a process that effects the transition from the pre-oedipal to the oedipal phase and bestows upon the infant the psychosocial contours of a precarious subjectivity. In Lacan's *The Four Fundamental Concepts of Psychoanalysis*, the very possibility of desire and ultimately sexual bliss rests upon the fact of separation insofar as both desire and bliss structurally presuppose an impossible distance between the desiring subject and the object of its desire. Though sexual bliss, in effect, cancels momentarily the historical achievement of separation (the stable ego), thus realizing the conditions of a pleasure without separation, its force nevertheless derives from the separation it overcomes and which it ceaselessly reinscribes. By associating the text with a pleasure "without separation," Barthes is explicitly evoking these issues and suggesting that the text enables one to pay attention to the moments, say in a poem, where the subject of the enunciation, the "speaker," is disintegrating, losing control of his/her utterance, in a manner that evokes a return to the pre-oedipal phase—the troubled model of blissful relating—while soliciting the reader to engage the poem at such a moment and, as it were, "make the most" of the subject's disintegration. That is, the textual model invites one to exploit this disintegration so as to disclose the socially organized production of the subject sacrificed within it. Those who insist upon "aestheticizing" Barthes's work (e.g., Susan Sontag) typically overlook the unrelenting association he makes between "bourgeois writing" and texts that, within a certain historical epoch, refuse to problematize the given order of subjectivity. If one keeps in mind the methodological character of the text, then it is easier to see that Barthes has designed it around the tactical assumption that one can disclose the center (in this case, bourgeois cultural hegemony), and thus make it available for criticism, by getting at how it manages that which the center construes as a threat.

Ultimately, of course, it is Barthes's appeal to the "order of the signifier" that obliges one to read "without separation" dialectically. Insofar as language is constituted by a multiplicity of split and arbitrarily joined signs, and insofar as thought cannot be utterly distinguished from language, then there cannot be an experience, thinkable as such, without separation. It is not then surprising that when writing an entry on "the text" for the *Encyclopedia Universalis* in 1973, Barthes's only allusion to the notion of pleasure—and this despite the fact that *The Pleasure of the Text* appeared in the same year—occurs in the context of a discussion of

*signifiance,* Kristeva's reconceptualization of the movement of the signifier.[9] Nevertheless, there is more, substantive support for this reading—
support that will help elaborate the text/pleasure matrix—in Barthes's
other major statement on textuality from the period, namely, his preface
to *Sade/Fourier/Loyola.*

Here the problem of separation is elaborated in a manner that helps
us recognize exactly how Barthes fuses psychoanalytic and literary problems. Consider the following.

> The text is an object of pleasure. The bliss of the text is often only
> stylistic: there are expressive felicities, and neither Sade nor Fourier
> lacks them. However, at times the pleasure of the Text is achieved
> more deeply (and then is when we can truly say there is Text):
> whenever the "literary" Text (the Book) transmigrates into our life,
> whenever another writing (the Other's writing) succeeds in writing
> fragments of our own daily lives, in short, whenever a *coexistence*
> occurs. . . . [I]t is not a matter of making operative what has been
> represented, . . . it is a matter of bringing into our daily life the frag-
> ments of the unintelligible ("formulae") that emanate from a text
> we admire, [and] . . . it is a matter of speaking this text, not making
> it act, by allowing it the distance of a citation, . . . [O]nce again, it
> is not a matter of taking into ourselves the contents, convictions, a
> faith, a cause, nor even images; it is a matter of receiving from the
> text a kind of phantasmatic order.[10]

When Barthes cancels a long string of typical instances of readerly booty
(contents, convictions, images, etc.), he is not only giving precision to his
point, he is also explicitly bracketing the traditional preoccupations of the
literary domain. That is, he is moving to disconnect pleasure from "reading enjoyment." By settling for the notion of a "phantasmatic order" as
that which one derives from a text, he reasserts the importance of psychoanalytic categories in the delineation of bliss. However, in spite of his
now familiar recourse to psychoanalysis, "pleasure without separation"
is elaborated rather differently in this context.

What overcomes separation in the passage from *Sade/Fourier/Loyola*
is comprehended through the notion of "coexistence." Instead of sexual
orgasm, where a subject looses him/herself in a shudder of pre-oedipal
nondifferentiation, serving as the model for bliss, here we have a halluci-
natory model where, in a manner rather like the way one is "haunted" by
a popular tune, the subject is lost to the scripts that invade and reorient

his/her life. In effect, textual pleasure or bliss erupts whenever one can no longer separate him/herself from the effects one's analysis has upon the relation between his/her readings and daily life. Again though, the disappearance of separation does not eliminate difference altogether. As Barthes insists, coexistence is recognized when one is addressed from the *distance* of a citation. In other words, bliss arises not when we think we are talking to ourselves (as in the case of Husserlian autoaffective speech), but when something we have detached from a work uncontrollably returns to us and addresses us in a voice we would like to claim (hence the phantasmatic element) as our own. There is "Text" here, as Barthes says, because only by approaching the work from such an angle can we participate in the production of its effects and affirm what transpires as a result.

Perhaps though, I have been too hasty in differentiating this model from the earlier orgasmic one. In preserving the notion of bliss (*jouissance*), Barthes is obviously bringing his two discussions of pleasure into relation with one another. As a result, orgasm itself undergoes revision. No longer defined by its singular resolution of the division that always operates to separate the subject from a position marked "maternal" (whence a certain massive reduction of femininity), orgasm is now defined by a diffusion and proliferation that at once disperses its phallic organization and places the subject opposite a multiplicity of positions which, even if "maternal," are no longer necessarily feminine at all. However, before we conclude that this is an aestheticization, that is, a denial of sexual pleasure, it is worth recalling that Barthes is indeed insisting upon an intensely charged experience of self-overcoming—an experience that has little to do with a notion of "reading pleasure" modeled on safe-sex eroticism. I would argue that this line of reasoning in Barthes is meant, at one level, to underscore the discursive mutability of bio-physiological phenomena by indicating how the elaboration of other conceptual frameworks for evaluating the social production of pleasure can participate in the alteration of the arrangements that support this production. It is this focus on the framework that links the rewriting of orgasm to textuality.

Let us return though to the issue of separation. In the preface to *Sade/Fourier/Loyola*, the "coexistence" which heralds textuality is defined, quite unexpectedly, in relation to the author.

> The pleasure of the Text also includes the amicable return of the author. Of course, the author who returns is not the one identified by our institutions; . . . he [sic] is not even the biographical hero. The

author who leaves his [sic] text and comes into our life has no unity; he [sic] is a mere plural of "charms," the site of a few tenuous details, yet the source of vivid novelistic glimmerings, a discontinuous chant of amiabilities, in which we nevertheless read death more certainly that in the epic of a fate, he [sic] is not a (civil, moral) person, he [sic] is a body. . . . For if, through a twisted dialectic, the Text, destroyer of all subject, contains a subject to love, that subject is dispersed, somewhat like the ashes we strew into the wind after death.[11]

Here the author Barthes had pronounced dead only three years earlier (cf., "The Death of the Author") returns as a body, as a subject to love and not to know. What distinguishes this notion of the author from the earlier one is its dispersion. Instead of a unifying consciousness that might serve to legitimate a Pouletian reading, the author with whom a reader might "coexist" is a collection of "charms." What links this author with death is its ghostly presence, its status as a body which returns to the text to lure the reader into a dispersion of details, each of which invites him/her to founder on the rocks of coexistence where daily life and its textually derived "captions" can no longer be separated. Of course, one of the motivations for this chain of associations is the enduring literary topos of orgasm as "*la petite mort*," but in keeping with his reframing of bio-physiological orgasm, Barthes is giving greater emphasis here to the task of rewriting death as the dispersion of unified consciousness. Thus bliss remains as the crucial referent point for textuality, and it joins *la petite mort* not at the point where brain functions cease, but rather at the moment when the frame of one's analysis opens itself to the dispersion of the consciousness "behind" the text—a dispersion that brings the ghostly body of the author and the body of the reader into contact. Phantoms are not frightening because of who they represent, but because of what their appearance means to a world which otherwise denies their existence. In effect, they destroy this world.

In this context, pleasure without separation takes on the significance of a traffic in, or the circulation of, bodies—the reading and the written bodies. Again though, bliss (and therefore Text) is not conceived in terms of a transcendence of separation. After all, the author's body appears only discontinuously, in fact, precisely at those moments where the recipient of the author's "charms" surrenders his/her mastery of the work and, in effect, "dies." What the text provides as a methodological field is a way of articulating the interpretive procedures that follow from, and embrace, this collaborative and avowedly sensual dispersal of the consumptive subject. Put in practical critical terms, the text allows us to recognize that if we "love Literature," then not only will our readings manipulate works to fit the measure of our desires, but precisely because our readings fasten on those charms which activate (i.e., assume responsibility for) our desire, we will never "master" (i.e., profess adequate knowledge of) the work we might otherwise be thought to construct in the reading process. Though this elaboration of textual pleasure presents separation (or its overcoming) in psychoanalytically charged terms, it should be clear from this discussion of the author that Barthes's position has direct implications for traditional literary scholarship—a clear indication of the disciplinary dynamics inscribed in the emergence of textuality.

If we move on to the year 1973, when again Barthes discusses "the Text" twice (once in the encyclopedia article referred to above and again in *The Pleasure of the Text*), we find other material that illuminates the cortical themes of pleasure and textuality. Toward the end of *The Pleasure of the Text*, Barthes reiterates points made in the preface to *Sade/Fourier/Loyola*, arguing that the pleasure of the text is "a claim lodged against the separation of the text," where, due to the atopia of bliss, "reading and the risks of real life are subject to the same anamnesis." [12] This is certainly not surprising. However, this opening discussion is also supplemented in a decisive way.

> Whenever I attempt to "analyze" a text which has given me pleasure, it is not my "subjectivity" I encounter but my "individuality," the given which makes my body separate from other bodies and appropriates its suffering or its pleasure: it is my body of bliss I encounter. And this body of bliss is also my *historical subject;* for it is at the conclusion of a very complex process . . . that I control the contradictory interplay of (cultural) pleasure and (non-cultural) bliss, that I write myself as a subject at present out of place, arriving too late or too soon (this *too* designating neither regret, fault, nor bad luck, but merely calling for a *non-site*): anachronic subject, adrift. [13]

In the aphorism directly preceding this one, Barthes discusses the "fiction" of the subject's (not the author's) return as a stimulus to reading pleasure. Here, in the context of a return to the site of literary interpretation, Barthes is directly supplementing his discussion of the author by presenting the body of the *reader* as a body of bliss. Predictably, the issue of separation also returns, and Barthes elaborates it by stressing the technical (vis psychoanalysis) sense of the term as it denotes spatial distinctions among embodied subjects. Thus, what one encounters in the pleasure of the text is the separateness that both joins us to other bodies (we *share* this limit with them) and joins us to our own body (we are the locus of *our* pleasures).

What is interesting about the perspective elaborated here is the fact that "pleasure without separation" is realized through the very structure of separation as it organizes the reader's experience of reading. Whereas before Barthes was intent upon showing how the author might return to haunt the reader, in this case Barthes is showing how, in the act of analyzing reading pleasure, one encounters the bliss that overcomes the separation defining our relation to our own body. In other words, as we reflect upon our reading pleasure, we supplement it with what Barthes called in "Leaving the Movie Theater," a second fascination, a fascination that fastens on the "situation" of our pleasure.[14] This has the effect of exposing us to the categorical assumptions shoring up the divisions that inhabit our bodies, divisions which operate to distinguish, at a basic phenomenological level, the desiring body from the laboring body. Textual bliss, or the text as bliss, thus assumes the significance of a production of pleasure that takes place within literary analysis, driven by the analyst's desire to unsettle the conditions of his/her own analysis while still engaging the work under discussion. While at one level this represents a distinctively Barthesean articulation of the critique of the subject, it also brings his analysis of the text into contact with an aspect of what I have been calling antidisciplinary research. More than a stubborn refusal to ascribe "authorial" power to the reader (a reader whose bodily order is in question would hardly satisfy the authorial requirement of a comparatively stable hermeneutic center), this unmooring of the "anachronic" subject highlights the way institutional borders typically operate to separate bliss from the effort to break up or challenge the analytic consolidation of such borders. Not surprisingly, Barthes moves to emphasize precisely this dimension of textuality and the problem of separation as his discussion unfolds.

> What relation can there be between the pleasure of the text and the institutions of the text? Very slight. The theory of the text postulates bliss, but it has little institutional future: what it establishes, its precise accomplishment, its assumption, is a practice (that of the writer), not a science, a method, a research, a pedagogy. . . . It is not only the inevitably metalinguistic nature of all research which hampers the writing of textual pleasure, it is also that we are today incapable of conceiving a true science of becoming.[15]

This explicitly Nietszchean passage from the aphorism entitled "Science" is provocatively foreshadowed by an earlier one: "How can a text, which consists of language, be outside languages? . . . First, the text liquidates all metalanguage, whereby it is text: no voice (Science, Cause, Institution) is *behind* what it is saying. Next, the text destroys utterly, *to the point of contradiction*, its own discursive category, its sociolinguistic reference (its 'genre'). . . . It is a matter of effecting, by transmutation, a new philosophic state of the language-substance."[16] In the context created by these two passages, one can witness a modest but consequential permutation of the problematic of separation. It is, I would argue, a permutation that explicitly connects the bliss of textuality to a certain engagement of the terrain of disciplinarity.

Organizing the first passage is an opposition between the bliss postulated by the theory of textuality and the institutions of the texts that traffic in bliss. Two things seem to motivate this opposition: (1) the segmentation of "becoming" required by the production of scientific knowledge (the French term, "*science*," implies here "official knowledge" rather than science per se) and (2) the hierarchical structure of metalanguage. The reason that there can only be a "very slight" relation between the text and its institutions is because the latter are organized so as to obstruct what the text makes possible, namely, a practice that traverses, or put another way, refuses to acknowledge, the "separations" among the disciplines. Though Barthes does not make it explicit here, it is clear that the practice produced by the theory of the text is blissful insofar as that practice cuts across or through the institutional structures that typically derive legitimacy from containing or channeling such practices. Obviously, a "slight" relation between the institution and bliss remains because textual practice derives its bliss from a traversal of borders that are nevertheless differentiated in ways that give significance to the traversing gesture. Thus, this discussion too not only has recourse to the thematics of separation, but it insists upon separation as a dialectical precondition, however "twisted," for textual bliss.

The problem of metalanguage introduces another pertinent set of issues. Specifically, Barthes's rejection of the hierarchical status of metalanguage functions to link textuality to the critique of interdisciplinary research that would otherwise appear to be affirmed by my reading of the tension between bliss and the institutions of the text. If we turn our attention to the second citation where the text is conceptualized in terms of a denial of the space between it and the "voices" supporting it from behind, then we can see that two aspects of metalanguage stand out as problematic for Barthes. On the one hand, there is the question of distance, of the separation constituted by the prefix "meta," where reflection on language rises "above," or stands "after," ordinary language. What Barthes finds unacceptable here is the protection this distance provides for theoretical discourse as such—protection which takes the form of insulating reflection on language from the shudder of frivolity that signals the advent of textual bliss. Metalanguage cannot operate if it cannot be taken seriously, that is, if it cannot be read as *really* about, in some rigorously verifiable way, ordinary language. Because, for Barthes, theorizing the text means entering its symbolic economy, he refuses either to conceive of the text as a metalanguage or to treat the text as the object of a metalanguage. The point is not to valorize cavalierly the posture of hedonism (though Barthes is attracted to the impishness of such a gesture—see p. 22), but to underscore the way institutional practices participate, however obliquely, in the social organization of pleasure.

On the other hand, Barthes rejects metalanguage because of the way it operates to overcome disciplinary limitations without problematizing disciplinary reason. If one can generate an analytic discourse, like semiology for example, that permits him/her to survey the collapse of disciplinary borders while, in effect, monitoring the crisis from within a newly secured institutional enclave, then metalanguage can be said to oppose textuality, not because metalanguage redisciplines the text, but because it absorbs the textual critique of disciplinarity within a new institutional topography that merely resegments knowledge along a vertical axis—the axis linking metalanguage and the language practices of various institutions and sciences. Significantly, when Barthes moves to articulate this criticism he emphasizes the need to undermine the very category of textuality, thereby reducing it to the practice that transforms the substance of language by overcoming the separation between our speech acts and the institutionally sanctioned discourses that comprehend them as examples of "language." If the text were to assume the properties of a specific logic (if it were to aspire to the Aristotelian conditions of a noncontradictory language), it could serve as exactly the containment of bliss it was designed to oppose. Is this not why *The Pleasure of the Text* is written the way it is? Rather than parade as a theoretical or metalinguistic discussion of textual bliss, this essay refuses to coincide with itself, its propositions fail to add up, and precisely for this reason it joins the bliss it otherwise appears to discuss. To this extent it explicitly echoes the caveat that appears at the end of "From Work to Text," where Barthes says, "[t]hese few propositions, inevitably, do not constitute the articulations of a Theory of the Text" (p. 164).

But what, I think, prevents us from reading such formulations as mere instances of irresponsible coyness is the fact that they register, at a specific methodological level, the tactics Barthes has pursued in the elaboration of his own research agenda—tactics which, however nomadic, nevertheless embody the very sorts of theoretical commitments animating his notion of the text. One could say that Barthes's disciplinary trajectory—from Marxist literary criticism to semiotics, to psychoanalysis and beyond—or, for that matter, his institutional trajectory—from various high schools throughout France, to institutes in Hungary and Egypt, to the Ecole Pratique des Hautes Etudes and the Collège de France—both conform to the "muscal" pattern (I am thinking here of Barthes's allusion to the fly's flight in the aphorism entitled, "Image-Reservoirs," p. 31) he identifies with the reading of bliss. In short, Barthes associates the text, and the bliss it produces, with a traversal of the institutions whose internal separations are designed to control the production of textuality. Here then, we discover the widest sociohistorical scope of "pleasure without separation," that is, the text. My point is not simply that the text of pleasure, or more specifically bliss, has implications for the internal structure of educational institutions, but that the text, as an instance of bliss, is a particular and to some extent necessary way of engaging and resisting such institutions. This is why, I would argue, Barthes is compelled to open "From Work to Text" by immediately posing the problem of disciplinarity.

Having begun this sketch of the text's relation to "pleasure without separation" by remarking upon the distinctively minimal difference separating "the Text" from "the text," let me conclude by returning to this issue and the question of what has been called, "homotextuality." In tracing Barthes's various formulations of the dialectical logic of separation, I have stressed the way they toy with overcoming the difference between "the one" (be it the reader, the author, the text, etc.) and "the other." In every case, Barthes links textual bliss with an overcoming of this difference that supplements its logical significance (i.e., one cannot comprehend pleasure without separation in the utter absence of separation) with a structural significance. The latter is typically elaborated in terms of an experience, that of reading for example, where two bodies become ecstatic through the discovery that they are less restricted by the stases previously thought to define their limits. What makes this discovery blissful or orgasmic is not the nature of the behaviors that brought the bodies into contact, but the psychospatial enigma of the contact itself. It is as though one has come into contact with him/herself through the other who, it turns out, has done the same. Neither the one nor the other is left in place. I would argue that an austere version of this dynamic is figured into the Text/text relation that fuels Barthes's formulations in the early seventies. In other words, by approaching a literary text from the standpoint of the Text, one discovers that contact between the model (T) and the example (t) projects both the text beyond literature and the Text beyond criticism. What, however, strikes me as particularly suggestive about the fetishistic austerity of such an idea is the way it encourages one to decipher one of Barthes's more scandalous assertions on textuality in *The Pleasure of the Text*, namely, "The text is (should be) that uninhibited person who shows his behind to the *Political Father*" (p. 53).

In later commenting on this passage in *Roland Barthes by Roland Barthes*, Barthes contradicts a critic who scolded him for prudishness (for having said "behind" rather than "ass") by defending the deferential connotation of "behind" (in fact, he makes his comments in the context of a discussion of connotation), saying, "[a] good little devil doesn't show his ass to Mme MacMiche, he shows her his behind; the childish word was necessary, since we were concerned with the Father." [17] Obviously, what is connotatively important for Barthes is the power relation that situates a male child (he permits both the "uninhibited person" and the "good little devil" to bear the masculine pronoun "his") opposite the father. What is curious about the second passage, however, is the way it deflates the critical gesture implicit in the first by paralleling the uninhibited person and the good little devil. "Mooning," as the gesture is called in English, is one of a vast repertoire of prankish insults, and while it is perhaps more amusing than aggressive, it is, nevertheless, a critical gesture of some intensity. By aligning the text and the uninhibited person, Barthes plainly aims to extend his presentation of the text as that which contradicts or challenges the political order symbolized in the body of the father. When the text is subsequently paralleled by the good little devil, this already muted critical component would appear to be even further attenuated. Or is it?

The diminutive oxymoron (good little devil) softens the critical gesture to be sure, but in doing so it invites one to respond to some of the other connotative aspects of this asymmetrical encounter. Specifically, what the good little devil adds at this level is a certain impish, and one might even say flirtatious, connotation to the uninhibited person. Thus, instead of simply insulting the father, the text is devilishly teasing the political order by offering it its behind. The asymmetrical power relation between the father and the boy stressed in the childishness of "behind" openly evokes certain pederastic dynamics of male homosexuality, and even without developing fully Guy Hocquenghem's thesis in *Homosexual Desire*, one might conclude that like Hocquenghem, Barthes takes the male anus to be a fundamentally repressed content of phallocentric capitalism.[18] By identifying the text with the mooning gesture, Barthes is thus both reiterating the dialectical logic of pleasure without separation (the boy and the father confront each other in the same space—the space of the ecstatic tease) and modeling textual bliss on homosexuality. This is why I suggested earlier that the typographically minimal differentiation between Text and text, might be understood to carry an homoerotic charge. Instead of organizing bliss around an onanistic sameness, Barthes proceeds by insisting upon the dialectic of separation while nevertheless preserving sameness, though not by retrieving the autoaffective subject of phenomenology, but by recasting sameness as the homosexual. Even if one attempts to halt this reading before the figure of Mme MacMiche (the married woman who substitutes for the political father in Barthes's commentary and would thus heterosexualize the text), s/he will be disappointed to learn that *miche* is a slang term whose connotations permit a semantic identification between "boobs" and "butt"—a relationship which would connotatively enact the homosexual boy's identification with the mother's sexualized relation to the father.

If we accept such a reading of the text's encounter with the father, then it becomes easier to make sense of other equally suggestive, but opaque formulations in *The Pleasure of Text*, such as Barthes's comparison of writing and "cruising" (p. 4) or his insistence upon the reader's desire for the "formidable paternity" exercised over a work by its author (p. 27). In fact, if one turns again to *Roland Barthes by Roland Barthes* s/he can find explicit confirmation of the position I am developing here. "The opposition of the sexes must not be a law of Nature; therefore, the confrontations and paradigms must be dissolved, both the meanings and the sexes must be pluralized: meaning will tend towards its multiplication, its dispersion (in the theory of the Text), and sex will be taken into no typology (there will be, for example, only *homosexualities*, whose plural will baffle any constituted, centered discourse."[19] Presented in the context of a defense of the very plurality of positions I have associated with Barthes's textual engagement of the institution, this frank insistence upon the connection between the dispersion of meaning mapped by the theory of textuality and the homosexualization of sexuality makes it difficult to avoid the conclusion that textual bliss, or the text as bliss, is conceptualized in homoerotic terms. But what significance are we to attach to this?

Though Barthes once fantasized about writing a book on homosexuality (*Roland Barthes by Roland Barthes*, p. 150), he did not. And though many of his readings of literary works (most notably, perhaps, "Sarrasine") teased out homoerotic threads, Barthes did not place his theory of the text explicitly in the service of gay scholarship, and this despite the fact that during the 1970s such scholarship was beginning to flourish within the West. Rather than conclude, however, that this represents some failure of nerve or lack of commitment on his part, I would argue that Barthes's critical practice was, in fact, engaged in such scholarship, but in a way that reflects his characteristic propensity for reconceptualizing issues. Specifically, by modeling the text around an homoerotically inflected notion of bliss, and presenting the text as a potentially antidisciplinary "reading" strategy, Barthes shifts the terrain of male homosexual politics. Instead of locating gay academic interests exclusively in either the task of identifying the gay contents of works or in laboring to secure the canonical acknowledgment of such works, Barthes's notion of textual bliss both registers gay existence and militancy, thus indicating, through the very urgency of the concept, how extradisciplinary discourses come to be inscribed in analytic categories, and it articulates in disciplinary form a critique which might otherwise never take place there. Put concisely, the text enables one to analyze cultural practices homosexually— not necessarily *as* an homosexual, but in a manner that permits one to participate, at the level of an analytic procedure, in the effort to intervene within the social organization of pleasure and proliferate oppositional sexual practices. Obviously, such a strategy has its costs. In fact, one might argue that emphasis on textuality leads to an institutionalization (i.e., depoliticization) of male homosexual struggles which is why it has become necessary to refocus them on questions of biography, canon, and authenticity. Though such criticism risks sacrificing the political gains of opening an experience to those who, in lacking authenticity, are forced either to appropriate (as has been the case in male feminism) or to avoid it, this criticism does raise the issue of textuality's relation to the "new social movements" as they appear in the current critical preoccupations of race, gender, sexuality, and class. Does the text obstruct or enable these preoccupations? And more importantly, how does the literary appropriation of textuality figure within such considerations?

## II

If the text meaningfully embodies what I have called an antidisciplinary object, then I believe it must be shown either to enable the critical preoccupations with race, gender, sexuality, and class or to complicate these preoccupations in an enabling way. This is because these instances of the social designate precisely those movements that have linked, and begun to contest, the intra- and extra-institutional dimensions of disciplinary power. One thinks here of the proliferation of departments of women's studies, class analysis, and Afro-American studies that have transformed the institutional topography of postsecondary education in recent decades. Since Jameson, Rorty, and Said (among others) perceive the text as an explicit obstruction to such critical preoccupations, let us begin by bringing what in the concept of the text would justify such claims into contact with those aspects of textuality that fruitfully complicate the critical elaboration of race, gender, sexuality, and class.

When Derrida, Kristeva, and Barthes argue that essentially nothing absolutely eludes textuality, they appear to be bracketing the sociohistorical altogether. Why? Because the text is typically understood to be a formal system that obeys an entirely immanent logic, and once the social is itself encompassed by such a logic, it too appears as a formal system devoid of all the temporal and practical density we typically ascribe to society. Setting aside for the moment the criticisms I have already offered concerning this reading, let us consider what invites it. I would concede that such a reading is indeed provoked by two interlocking aspects of the theory of the text: (1) the fact that textuality is consistently used to designate that which outdistances the social and (2) the fact that the theory of textuality is presented as a practice of the text. Since it is not immediately apparent how these two factors interlock, let us consider their relationship briefly.

To begin with, what does it mean to say that the "theory of the text presents itself as a practice of the text?" Though it is less true of Kristeva's work than of Derrida's or Barthes's, the theoretical elaboration of textuality has consistently taken the form of a text, that is, as instances of writing that exemplify the sort of traits the methodological field of the text are meant to disclose. Readers, faced with the obtuse brilliance of the prose in these essays, are obliged to work with them as if they were comprised of the "stereographic weave of signifiers," associated by Barthes with the phenomenal surface of textuality. The theorists under discussion here have exploited this state of affairs, not to question facilely the distinction between criticism and creativity, but rather to alter the "subject position" constituted by critical discourse. In other words, when textual effects erupt within a theoretical argument about textuality, the expository conventions of "philosophical argumentation" are supplemented in a manner that displaces the reader of theoretical criticism. Instead of awaiting the effects of a demonstration, the reader of textual theory is exposed to an experience of the very problems (i.e., connotative undecidability, polyreferentiality, intertextuality, etc.) being addressed in the theory. As a consequence, the "charm" of the propositions thus advanced is intensified by the discursive proximity of the very methodological problems to which these propositions respond. What is challenged by this practice is the psychosocial structure of metalanguage which assumes that the analyst is removed from the immediate domain of the theoretical essay thereby guaranteeing a certain objectivity in his/her approach to it. This feigned removal or detachment creates a space from which the "ideal" or "competent" reader proceeds in order to properly engage the work under discussion. As feminist critics have long observed, this arrangement operates to "engender" the transmission of knowledge. While not rejecting the motivation behind such an observation, Barthes nevertheless opposes metalanguage for other reasons. In fact, he criticizes it precisely in order to implicate metalanguage in the problematic meant to be scrutinized through the notion of textuality—not, as is often claimed, to whimsically abandon the rhetoric of theoretical argumentation altogether.

Typically, however, textuality agitates the surface of the theoretical text precisely at those moments where the latter is straining to designate, in a highly codified social discourse, that which exceeds language in general. As a consequence, the critique of metalanguage deemed crucial to the theory of textuality does appear to situate the sociohistorical at the precise point where the theory's own self-absorption reaches the point of saturation. In other words, an equation is established between that which outdistances the social and that which textual theory has to gesture toward self-reflexively, suggesting that there is, in fact, a convergence between *nonreflexive* theoretical discourse and what falls within the purview of the sociohistorical. Despite the fact that Derrida, Kristeva, and Barthes have never explicitly moved to ground such a convergence ontologically, I would argue that the relation they do acknowledge between the rejection of metalanguage and the textual surpassing of the social, invites one to assume that they are *implicitly* bracketing the sociohistorical and surrendering themselves to the "prison house of language." But let us think about this more carefully.

When Kristeva, for example, argues that the genotextual level of a particular text is linked to the *chora,* the utopic (Barthes calls it "atopic") space of the semiotic, she is not, as we have seen, positing the *chora* (even of her text) in an ontologically secured space beyond language. She posits the "chora" and the social alterity it embodies within the social as that structural instability that constitutes the social as historical, that is, as subject to interminable transformational practices. The text for her is a way of conceptualizing and thereby fostering this structural instability as it arises within the analysis of what she calls "poetic language." Those who would read such an analysis as conditioned by a necessary bracketing of the sociohistorical are therefore misunderstanding the significance of the practical critique of metalanguage. In order to conclude that the social can be conflated with what the nonreflexive text *can* articulate in declarative prose, one has to begin by assuming that the text's self-reflexive gesturing is indeed the *real* locus of an ontologically given alterity of the social. What the example from Kristeva suggests, however, is that the text seeks to register, and thus make available for critical elaboration, the instability that historicizes the social by scoring the latter with the traces of the "not yet"—traces which inhere no less within the discourse on the text than they do within any other antagonistic instance of the social. Thus, instead of implicitly conflating the social and the textual, Kristeva's position actually discloses the pressure exerted by the social upon the theoretical efforts to write about and around its limits. If the theory of the text evokes these limits self-reflexively, it is because the moment of social reproduction inscribed in the regulation of theoretical referentiality is worth problematizing at the discursive level where it operates. What makes such a problematization worthwhile is the fact that it short-circuits the dynamics of naturalization that make the social appear as precisely what lies *beyond* a particular text. Those who criticize textuality for cannibalizing the world often unwittingly sacrifice the world to their conception of what takes place where writing ends.

In effect, the aspects of the theory of textuality that invite the critique of a reduction or abandonment of the social, contain elements of a critique of the notion of society at once animating and obstructing the elaboration of the critical categories of race, class, sexuality, and gender. Let me elaborate this by reengaging Kristeva's discussion of the *chora.* As we have seen, this dimension of textuality is explicitly thematized in terms of gender. Kristeva argues that the space of the *chora* opens within the discourses of representation as that which is to be designated "the feminine"—a name for that moment within the social division of gender that works to convert female beings into "women," that is, the "other" of Man (cf., Beauvoir). By situating a portion of this space within textuality, Kristeva not only indicates that "the feminine" constitutes one of the "not yets" of the social, but she includes within the domain of gender politics the problematization of the social that transpires within the relation between critical theory and poetic language.[20] Like Barthes, whose homoerotic model of bliss enabled him to "homosexualize" cultural criticism, Kristeva develops a reading of gender that distinguishes it from the sexed bodies it arises from, while making the antagonisms that arise over the theoretical categories of social analysis crucial for feminism. Significantly, Kristeva does not treat these antagonisms as crucial because they reflect interests that are more *usefully* articulated elsewhere in the social. Instead, her notion of textuality insists that we consider these theoretically marked antagonisms as instances of the social division of gender—instances whose social character remains obscure precisely to the extent that we refuse to extend the social into the symbolic field.

If textuality is persistently utilized to unsettle the ontic solidity of such antagonisms, it is not because gender, or the social more generally, are deemed "bracketable." Instead, the perspective of textuality helps us to recognize that the whole urgent analytic appeal to "society" risks being sacrificed if, in order to be taken seriously, it has to mobilize a compromised, that is, ahistorical, category. What distinguishes an ahistorical category of social analysis is the fact that such a category vainly resists the ontic reification its reliability as a critical concept actually reflects by presupposing a difference between *mere* symbolic practice (theory) and *actual* society. To put it baldly, the text is a way of acknowledging that the openness of the social is produced, among other places, in our theoretical efforts to think the aesthetic articulations of society's limits.[21] In this sense, textuality extends the critical preoccupation with race, class, sexuality, and gender precisely by underscoring the way these defining instances of the social imply that society is neither rational nor organic, but irreducibly antagonistic. And furthermore, that antagonisms reach all the way into the discourses *about* the social, disrupting referential security on all fronts, since referentiality typically rests upon an ontological warrant of some kind. What the textual perspective actually brackets is any effort to reduce symbolic practice to a pretext for the elaboration of a sociohistorical analysis whose own importance lies less in the political advance it accomplishes, than in the trivialization of the signifying practices its alleged "urgency" authorizes. Insofar as the theoretical elaboration of the categories of race, class, sexuality, and gender fails to emphasize the way such instances problematize the very coherence and integrity of society (either as object or category)—and this failure occurs whenever it is argued that a work *really is about,* say, class—this elaboration deserves to be criticized as antitextual and finally essentialist. Thus, textuality operates to encourage the elaboration of the categorical embodiments of the new social movements precisely by resisting the essentialization of society—ironically, the very phenomenon whose alleged bracketing by the theory of textuality motivated the international critical community's orthopedic appeals to race, class, gender, and sexuality. Moreover, and this strikes me as the crucial issue, if it can be shown that the institutional reorganization of intellectual power that expressed itself in the concept of the text developed in response to pressures exerted by the new social movements in the sixties, then it is fair to argue that the text as a latent antidisciplinary field shares a history with and thus can be made to enable that which is often mobilized against it. Chapter 2 sought to construct the historical relation evoked here.

Though the specificity of the text has been linked to homosexual struggles, by Barthes, feminist and antibourgeois struggles by Kristeva, and anticolonial struggles by Derrida, it remains true that the political effects of textual analysis have been restricted to various forms of institutional renovation.[22] If what I have been arguing about the text's antidisciplinary character is accurate, how are we to explain this undeniable fact? Let me return briefly to the aspects of textuality that encouraged its dismissal on the grounds of its reduction of the social, namely, the relation between self-reflexive gesturing and the utopic. From here I can sketch a provisional response to this question.

The virtue of connecting the textuality of textual theory (or what I have called the self-reflexive gesturing of theoretical writing) to the utopic is that doing so enables the theorist to focus sociohistorical criticism on the sites where specifically discursive modalities of social restraint operate. This enables one to avoid sacrificing a particular text to a reading of what in fact is its context in order to grasp the text's relation to society. By the same token, when this strategic connection is articulated in the context of a systematic problematization of literature, as has been the case in the theory of textuality, one has to be particularly vigilant not to transport the problems that become accessible to us within the field of textuality into those other areas of symbolic practice that this very field allows us to witness operating in the literary work. For example, the subversion of the speaking subject in avant-garde poetry cannot be treated as having an equivalent political value within the context of televisual advertising, where fragmentation is a normative textual feature. If the theory of the text is viable, then the general modes of alterity it enables us to address cannot, as a matter of principle, be approached either practically or theoretically in the manner through which they appear at the level of the *literary* work made accessible through the textual paradigm. What has tended to happen in and with the work of the theorists discussed here is that this has been forgotten. The consequences of such forgetfulness are plain in the textual analysis of film where, despite the disciplinary divide that organizes this activity, the textual analysis of film has remained a "literary" project. Moreover, it has not yet found ways to foster what has been called the "openness" of the social beyond the institutions of media criticism, thereby sacrificing decisive arenas of textual productivity. In short, I would argue that the text has not realized its antidisciplinary potential because its theorists have failed to grasp adequately the disciplinary dimension of their critical practices. As I have argued in chapter 1 overcoming this limit will mean more than disseminating the text throughout the disciplines. It will require nothing less than a definitive settling of accounts with the literary legacy of textuality.

# PART III

# 6

## ✳ The Textual Analysis of Film

Nowhere outside of the disciplines of literary study has the textual paradigm found a friendlier reception than in the disciplines of media criticism, and specifically in the discipline of film studies. In attempting to map the genealogy of the text, it is therefore necessary to examine this development and offer some account of the following three issues: (1) what forces converged to encourage this particular form of interdisciplinary exchange? (2) what happened to the notion of textuality as it emerged within film theory debates? and (3) what does the sort of reconsideration of textuality being undertaken here imply for the practical work of film analysis? As in part 2 I will focus this examination around the work of three prominent theorists: Christian Metz (particularly the period marked by the publication of *Language and Cinema* since *The Imaginary Signifier* makes comparatively little use of the notion of the text), Raymond Bellour, and Marie-Claire Ropars-Wuilleumier. Though in this context one might also think of the work of Thierry Kuntzel and Michel Marie or in the Anglo-American context of Stephen Heath and Teresa de Lauretis, I think those familiar with film studies will agree that the foundational work of Metz, Bellour, and Ropars continues to define the theoretical parameters of what has come to be called "the textual analysis of film." Obviously, in those cases where other figures have made decisive contributions to the theoretical elaboration of filmic textuality, I will draw upon their work in a supplemental manner.

As was suggested by a remark made in the final section of chapter five, despite now twenty-five years of semiological refinement of film analysis, the latter remains a peculiarly literary project. On the one hand, this would certainly help account for why the textual paradigm became so influential within the discipline. On the other hand though, precisely because textuality developed out of a linguistically inspired crisis within the disciplines of literary study, it remains curious that film analysis, in absorbing the textual paradigm, would resist the effects of such a crisis. The conflicted articulation of this resistance marks the entirety of Metz's discussion of the film text, and my reading of his work will trace the starts and stops of this articulation. Moreover, I will argue generally that this conflicted articulation is endemic to the contemporary discipline of film studies and as such filmic textuality plays a decisive role in the literary entrapment of the text. To make this case, let us begin by constructing an account of the tensions within film studies in France that framed the emergence of the text.

What is at stake here is the issue raised above concerning the forces that provoked the "dialogue" between film studies and the literary disciplines. At a very general level it seems to me that film analysis underwent the very same jolts of fashion delineated earlier in chapter two. What distinguishes film analysis in this regard, however, is the fact that its object, the cinema, was already an institution of mass culture. Film analysts could not comprehend their situation by appealing to the violation of a traditionally protected border as was, to a significant degree, the case with literary study. Nevertheless, there is an important difference between the way, say, Gilbert Cohen-Séat and Raymond Bellour practice film analysis. This is due, I will argue, to a shift in theoretical paradigms that was precipitated by the jolts administered to institutionalized film analysis by fashion, that is, by the emergent cultural hegemony of the mass media. Since the affinity between the latter and the very object of film analysis complicates such a claim, let us establish what about institutionalized film analysis in France would have nevertheless made it susceptible to the jolts of fashion. In the process, the groundwork can be laid for understanding how the textual analysis of film has remain bound by literary preoccupations—preoccupations which continue to inhibit the elaboration of the text as an antidisciplinary object.

The historian and theorist referred to above, Cohen-Séat, launched what has been called the "filmology" movement in France.[1] What was significant about this movement is that it explicitly sought to make cinema an object of an interdisciplinary science (in the French sense of the term) and in doing so bring institutional legitimacy to its study. Since Cohen-

Séat, Etienne Souriau, and others, including Edgar Morin (a Marxist sociologist responsible for promoting the systematic study of mass culture), succeeded in getting filmology institutionalized at the Sorbonne in 1948, one would have to say that the movement certainly realized its aim of academic legitimation. As Lowry has noted however, the price of this legitimacy was the constitution of film as a scientific, that is, positivistic, object—a development worth detailing briefly.

When Cohen-Séat wrote his influential *Essai sur les principes d'une philosophie du cinéma*, he was concerned to subject the cinema, which he understood as a revolutionary cultural technology (he likens it to the printing press) capable of tapping society's irrational collective consciousness, to scientific reason. This aim was paramount not because the cinema was necessarily regressive, but because it required an intellectual approach that matched the technical knowledge presupposed by its creation in order for cinema to realize its promise as a civilizing force. Cinema was not, therefore, to be treated as mere amusement, but as a specific social institution capable of wielding tremendous cultural power. Of course, one can detect in such formulations the intellectual commonplaces that have long been used to cast aspersions on all forms of popular pleasure. Nevertheless, what is crucial about Cohen-Séat's position is that it establishes a link between the scientific institutionalization of film study and the general project of specifying "filmic" or "cinematic" specificity, as though such specificity hinged upon one's ability to detach the cinema from the affectively charged (and thus irrational) sites of its popular consumption. Moreover, what is important about this notion of specificity, or science, is the attempt to locate it at a precise interdisciplinary conjuncture.

In the history of the filmology movement this conjuncture of disciplines underwent a gradual but unrelenting reconfiguration wherein the disciplines of psychology and sociology (at this time overwhelmingly Durkheimian in cast) acquired such prominence that aesthetic or hermeneutic concerns were virtually eliminated. This, in conjunction with the institutionalization of Cohen-Séat's famous distinction between the filmic (that which transpires on the screen) and the cinematic (those specific institutions and practices which surround and condition our encounter with the filmic), prepared the way for precisely the sort of specification of specificity that prompted the crisis in literary studies discussed in chapter 3. In other words, the more the disciplines of the social sciences were empowered to specify the specificity of the cinematic object, and the more they sought to ground such specificity in the projected product (the measurable fact), the more the cinematic object became a mere reflection of two disciplinary projects. However, as a result of their encounter with film, the disciplines of psychology and sociology could no longer simply recognize themselves as being *about* either society or the individual, since these were the very elements being bracketed in their exclusive attention to the projected product. In effect, the sciences of psychology, sociology, and even to some extent anthropology were, through the study of film, opening themselves up to the critique of science that was latent within the then emergent analysis of signification, or semiology. The latent implications of this gesture toward the critique of science did not become manifest until the period of the advent of textuality, but what is clear about the history of film study in France is that the notion of filmic specificity was first formulated in positivistic terms.

If we situate these developments in relation to the broad changes in French intellectual power sketched in chapter two, then we can see that filmology and its positivistic object arose in the context of the decline of what Debray has called the publishing cycle. It is not then surprising that with the coming of textual analysis and its rejection of positivism, the institutional center of film study shifts from the Sorbonne to what was to become the Ecole des Hautes Etudes en Sciences Sociales. Though one might expect this to imply that film study was becoming ever more "scientific," in fact, this was not the case. As we have seen, the curricular innovations that made such a shift possible registered the fact that the power of mass culture was beginning to precipitate into specific disciplinary objects—objects which frustrated the methodological categories of traditional disciplinary formations or sciences. The Ecole des Hautes Etudes actually fostered such developments, and when it began sponsoring the activities of Barthes, who with Etienne Souriau was an early semiological contributor to the filmology movement, the critique of social scientific paradigms gained irreversible momentum. It is in this sense that the study of mass culture felt the jolts of fashion as they surged through the institutional practices of scientific legitimation.

As such a context might lead one to expect, the process of the "textualization" of film study was also affected by developments within the sphere of publicity. Clearly an important supplement to the shift from the Sorbonne to the Ecole Pratique, and the reaffirmation of the "hermeneutic" dimension of film analysis that it implied, was the appearance in 1951 of the *Cahiers du cinéma* which, under the direction of André Bazin, mounted an influential, "aesthetically" oriented critique of filmology.[2] Significantly, what emerged from this critique and other writings appearing within the monthly that championed the phenomenological aesthetics of Jean Mitry, was an account of film that rested upon a blatantly literary paradigm—that of the author. I am referring here, of course, to "*auteur* theory" which opposed the positivistic categories of filmology with an analysis of filmic meaning that grasped it as an effect of an author's engagement with the systemic constraints of the cinema understood as a massive social institution. While such a perspective necessarily made much of directorial style and the significance of generic deviation, its historical importance has more to do with the way it, in the context of a general reorganization of the institutional constraints on the cultural production of meaning, provided film study with an explicit, alternative point of disciplinary reference, namely, literature. Though it would appear when Truffaut in 1954 denounced the "tradition of quality" for being scenarist's films that he was precisely opposing film's relation to French literature, careful scrutiny of his manifesto reveals that he was, in fact, most repelled by the "hack" nature of the writing that often mediated between an author's work and the finished film. What he and others wanted to do was to reaffirm the authorial vision that might prevail if the scenarist's power was diminished—a vision that was quintessentially aesthetic and certainly literary. More is at stake here than a mere shift in priorities, and despite the fact that the films of the "nouvelle vague" are virtually littered with literary allusions, I would argue that the real motivating issue here had to do with the necessity of grafting film onto a different disciplinary object—one that had little to do with the quantitative exigencies of positivism. Without this shift in orientation no serious criticism of that which threatened the aestheticism *auteur* theory sought to redeem would be possible.

Summarizing these developments, I would argue that the institutionalization of filmology provoked the textualization of film analysis by forging a link between a general crisis in the disciplinary specification of the object of film study and certain curricular and extracurricular (*Cahiers du cinéma* is certainly not the sort of pedagogical material one would have been exposed to at *les grandes écoles* during the fifties and sixties) trends toward the "literarization" of film study. While this helps us to see why the textual analysis of film might have grown out of such developments, it does not yet explain why, despite all that is at stake in the notion of textuality, textual analysis has preserved its strictly literary character. To pursue this it is important to determine how such a preservation articulates itself within the theories of filmic or cinematic textuality. Let us turn then to our three case studies.

## Christian Metz: The Singular Text

In 1971 Metz published *Language and Cinema*, a full-scale attempt to map the shared border between a semiotically inflected linguistics and film analysis. Characteristically, Metz proceeds both to discourage and encourage those seeking to bring the cinema under the aegis of critical semiotics. For my purposes it is significant that Metz chose specifically to encourage the use of the category of "textuality" in his discussion of film, and though he has since distanced himself from this work, his formulations have been sufficiently influential (Bellour, for example, dedicates his *L'Analyse du Film* to Metz and Kuntzel) that they bear elaborating in the present context.

Strictly speaking, the concept of textuality undergoes a certain semantic transformation in the exposition of *Language and Cinema*. This transformation is bounded on one end by a strictly linguistic understanding of the term "text" (Metz follows Louis Hjelmslev's usage in *Prolegomena to a Theory of Language*) and on the other end by a notion of "filmic writing" that bears obvious resemblance to categories developed by Barthes and others. In light of what we have discovered to be characteristic of the sociogenesis of textuality at the theoretical level, the appearance of this particular transformation is not surprising. Nevertheless, it is worth tracing this development of the concept of the text in order to gauge the pressure exerted upon it by its elaboration within the context of film studies.

The notion of textuality is first systematically explored in chapter five of *Language and Cinema*, significantly titled "From Code to System; Message to Text." I say "significantly" because, written in 1971, it resonates strongly with Barthes's contemporaneous essay, "From Work to Text." Though, as I have suggested, Metz keeps his distance from such an explicitly antilinguistic notion of the text, this distance persistently effects his own elaboration of the concept. To demonstrate this let us begin with how the text appears in its initially strictly linguistic guise.

> When one studies a natural language . . . the structure one finds in each utterance is nothing more than one manifestation of the structure of the idiom . . . which is present in that utterance as in any other and which does not account for its uniqueness. But if one takes into consideration other codes (stylistic, intonational, etc.) represented in this utterance, a structure appears which cannot be confused with the structure of any of the codes which are involved in it, since it

consists, by definition in combining them in a certain way. It is this type of structure which we would prefer to call a "singular system." The corollary of this system on the level of manifestation (i.e., the perceivable discourse in which the system is found) is not *the* message, since it contains several messages, but the text: to be exact *the text of that particular system*, of that single and overall system.[3]

A number of important ideas emerge in this citation. Let us first turn to the corollary that Metz establishes to announce the text. The notion of the singular system that defines one edge of the corollary derives from a linguistic problematic, and it is used to name the structured interaction among codes (be they grammatical or performative) that defines the specific richness of any utterance. Insofar as the text correlates with such a notion, it would appear to name—within the context of film analysis— the structured interaction among codes (sonoric, linguistic, cinematographic, narrative, etc.) that define the utterance of a specific film. Though Metz specifically extends the notion of the text to include more than one film or even a part of one film, the emphasis on singularity that occurs here persists. Thus, the text of a film, at least in this intitial formulation, refers to the precise arrangement (in space and time) of the cinematic and noncinematic codes that permit us to say that a given film is *Alexander Nevsky* and not *October*. In this respect the singularity of the text has much in common with the notion of "uniqueness" when the latter is applied to artistic property. But Metz's aim is not to elaborate the categories that would aid and abet the exercise of copyright law. This becomes obvious when we realize that by "code" he means a conventional, and therefore ultimately social, logic that organizes the production of communicative utterances. Though the text may refer to the codal arrangement defining a specific film, it does not permit one to treat that arrangement as an effect of genius. Rather, the text is meant to provide focus for an analysis that would seek to show how specific filmic utterances result from arranged conventions—arrangements which, in many cases, are dictated by the history of prior uses inscribed in the conventions themselves.

The issue of analytic focus can be given greater precision if we return to the citation and detail the text's relation to the "level of manifestation." When glossing the notion of "manifestation," Metz has recourse to the phrase "perceivable discourse." As such, it is clear that, in keeping with an almost compulsive drive to elaborate and preserve distinctions, Metz is reiterating here a point he makes somewhat earlier when discussing the text's relation to the system where he says, "[t]exts and system thus differ from one another as [does] an actual unfolding from an imputed intelligibility" (p. 76). Thus, "perceivable discourse" as a synonym for the text would imply that the text refers to the phenomenal surface that analysis brings a system to bear upon. Motivating this distinction is, on the one hand, a desire to underscore the structuralist insight into the latent or unconscious presence of structure—a situation that requires the mediation of theoretical analysis to bring structural coherence to symbolic practices. On the other hand, this distinction authorizes the deferral of the *Tel Quel*ean model of textuality which Metz understands in terms of its denial of the neat distinction between the writer and the written, that is, the space of the system (writer in the sense of analyst) and the space of the artifact. In fact, one could say that the whole issue of singularity which is at stake in the text/system opposition is pursued by Metz, not as a way to reaffirm artistic creativity, but as a way to isolate that which analysis is supposed to illuminate. While one can only applaud this drive for specificity, it is important to recognize that the notion of the text is being exploited here essentially to protect both analysis and artifacts from their reciprocal contamination. In effect, Metz is reversing the flow of the shift mapped by Barthes (from work to text) by more or less equating the text and the work. Nevertheless, as I indicated at the outset, Metz's concept of the filmic text undergoes a transformation that reflects its relation to Barthes's sense of textuality, and this transformation is already at work here in a manner that deserves some attention before we attempt a delineation of the degree to which Metz's contribution instances what I have called the literary entrapment of textuality.

Let us consider more carefully the wording of Metz's opposition. He contrasts an "actual unfolding" with an "imputed intelligibility," the text being synonymous with the former. In this insistence on the *unfolding* of the film text, Metz undercuts, to some extent, the significance of its actuality. What receives emphasis as a result is the temporality of the text and the dynamic quality of its structure. This is precisely what Metz emphasizes when, not long after he has introduced his linguistic model, he describes the interaction among filmic codes (both cinematic and noncinematic) as a process of "displacement." Though Metz is not at this point in his intellectual trajectory prepared to elaborate this concept in psychoanalytic terms, it is clear that he wants to bring the textual aspect of film into proximity with the experience of what Thierry Kuntzel was to call the "*défilement*"or "unthreading" of the film.[4] Not surprisingly, as Metz transforms the concept of the text to respond to the film's unfolding, it comes closer to the very model of textuality he earlier had been seeking to defer. Consider the following formulation.

> The only thing which can be said to be distinctive of the system of a film is that it integrates several codes, that it cannot be reduced to any one of them (or to the sum of them), and that it too plays them one against the other. The system of the text is the process which *displaces* codes, deforming each of them by the presence of the others, contaminating some by means of others, meanwhile replacing one by another, and finally—as a temporarily "arrested" result of this general displacement—*placing* each code in a particular position in regard to the overall structure, a displacement which thus finishes by a positioning which is itself destined to be displaced by another text.[5]

This discussion of the text takes place in a section devoted to the elaboration of the general category of displacement. On the page opposite the cited passage, Metz refers to Kristeva's analysis of textual productivity and specifically her formulation concerning the dynamic of "destruction-construction" that defines it. Perhaps that is why here the text sounds rather like the intertext conceptualized so energetically by Kristeva. Significantly, Metz not only acknowledges the vertical dimension of intertextuality (the relations within the film among its constitutive codes), but he explicitly connects this dimension of intertextuality with its horizontal axis—the "destined" displacement of a particular film by other films. To this extent Metz's attempt to specify the dynamism proper to the film text qua text, already confronts the linguistic reading of textuality with the very model he has otherwise been keeping at bay. Let us detail this somewhat more carefully and then attempt to assess its consequences.

In coming to terms with Metz's notion of singularity, we saw that he opposed the text to the notion of system. The latter embodied the intelligibility imputed to a film in the act of analysis. In the passage just cited he refers to what, in light of these remarks, would appear somewhat anomalous, namely, the "system of the text." Though Metz's earlier gloss on the phrase invites us to understand it as a reference to the intelligibility imputed to the text's unfolding and thus belonging to the text, the precise formulation he employs suggests something stronger and therefore more damaging to his initial opposition between text and system, and the project it enabled. Metz writes, "[t]he system of the text is the process which *displaces* codes." Since what he goes on to enumerate are the various levels of displacement *within* and around the text, it would seem that instead of opposing system and text, here Metz is acknowledging that analysis is actually part of the process that displaces codes within the film and, further, that the text is the proper designation for this curious zone of conjuncture between the discourse of analysis and the discourse of film. Of course, once he has recourse to textuality in this sense he can no longer protect his Hjelmslevean understanding of the text from the perspective advocated by those he associates with *Tel Quel* (p. 74). Though Metz makes no reference to any of Kristeva's explicit formulations on theoretical discourse and textual productivity, it is clear that his attempt to absorb her notion of intertextuality as a way to account for the dynamism of the film leads him to transform his notion of the text in response to the theoretical implications of intertextuality. These implications, though never detailed by Metz, force him to recognize that his earlier objection to *Tel Quel*'s deconstruction of the distinction between the writer and the written (Metz insists that since the film is inscribed in a radically iconic signifier, it can never be acted upon by writing) is a bluff at best. The issue is not whether an intelligibility imputed to a film in writing can engage that film in its facticity, but rather whether the messages activated by the film can be read outside of an institutionally inscribed framework of interpretation—a framework that is organized around what I have called a disciplinary object. In his zeal to specify the descriptive categories of filmic interpretation, Metz initially sacrifices textuality to the positivism of filmology which refused to acknowledge the notion of disciplinary objects as a matter of interdisciplinary principle. However, under the pressure of elaborating the descriptive range of textuality as a category, he increasingly retreats from this sacrifice and even moves, in his final chapter, to address the notion of filmic "writing" which shares much with the notion of textuality championed by *Tel Quel*. When Metz later returns in *The Imaginary Signifier* to criticize this presentation of the textual system, it is significant that he only repudiates his claim that each film exhibits *a* textual system, leaving intact the problem of the specifically textual relation between the system as analytic framework and the production of filmic meanings.[6]

The allusion to "writing" that motivates Metz's final elaboration of textuality first occurs in the context of his discussion of the notion of displacement. In fact, when Metz introduces the term (p.100), he uses it as what we later realize is a synonym for the "system of the text." Writing refers to the "process" by which the film modifies and combines its constitutive codes, while playing them off one another as well. When, however, in his concluding chapter Metz discusses writing and cinema at length, he seems to forget the history of affiliations his initial formulations activated (Blanchot, Derrida, and, in 1971, Marie-Claire Ropars-Wuilleumier), settling for a tentative and overly restrained acknowledgment of the significance of writing as an analytic metaphor. Behind this forgetfulness is a polemical impulse which literally overruns his discussion.

Essentially, the chapter on cinema and writing is a survey of all the various attempts, beginning with Alexandre Astruc and ending with Barthes, to bring these two practices into alignment with one another. Organizing the survey is Metz's concern to point out all the ways in which such attempts are decisively flawed, something he manages to do almost effortlessly without, however, really coming to terms with what motivated them in the first place. This becomes particularly manifest in his discussion of Barthes. While Metz explicitly notes that one might turn to Barthes's characterization of writing in order to enlarge the methodological resources one might bring to bear on the practice of film analysis, he zeroes in on a then eighteen-year-old essay of Barthes, "Writing Degree Zero" that simply underscores the taxonomic and fundamentally linguistic approach Metz has been elaborating. Specifically, Metz reads Barthes's notion of writing in terms of its confirmation of the opposition between general codes (organizing a language system) and large subcodes (organizing select actualizations of the system), concluding that cinema is not writing because it lacks the equivalent reservoir of speech which provides writing with a stable general code. Since Metz's appeal to Barthes began by underscoring the need to expand our understanding of the notion of writing, it is odd, not only that he would turn to this essay of Barthes's in particular (recall that *S/Z* had appeared in 1970), but that he would discover in it precisely that notion of writing that would add nothing to the methodological dimension of film analysis. The impression of what can only be called a deferral of textuality is accentuated when, in concluding this chapter, Metz explicitly reminds the reader that Kristeva, Derrida, and others have extrapolated the notion of writing in a way that makes it much easier to understand why theorists, including himself, have been tempted to bring it into dialogue with the cinema—a project which his chapter otherwise succeeds in making appear so ill-conceived as to be absurd.

As we have seen, this deferral leaves its mark on the early moments of Metz's analysis, and this is equally true of his concluding discussion of writing. In the final pages of the book, Metz seems to rediscover what he later called the "investigator's imaginary," by acknowledging that there *is* such a thing as filmic writing and that it needs to be studied in relation to the cinematic language system. What this assertion reveals is that Metz has primarily been objecting to the equation cinema/writing and that the notion of writing as a synonym for "textual system," which motivated his methodological foray in the first place, is in fact coherent and worthy of encouraging. Despite the fact that the appeal to writing initially promised to clarify the dynamics of codal displacement, once Metz unveils the connection between writing and "textual activity" (p. 285), he resists elaborating the implications of this connection for the concept of displacement and instead settles for a reiteration of the distinction between text and language system that organizes his entire book. When he later (in *The Imaginary Signifier*) resumes the discussion of writing and the film text, Metz continues to protect the categorical distinctions that diffuse the methodological significance of writing.[7] Thus, once again Metz reveals that his fascination with the notion of the text seldom lives up to, at the methodological level, the energy provoking it. In effect, even the codal productivity of the text, its irreducible intertextuality, is to be understood in terms of the phenomenal facticity of the film. The implications for the institutional borders of cinematic analysis the concept of filmic writing might have Metz leaves unexamined, and this despite the fact that his entire project bears testimony to the significance alterations of these borders might have for what transpires within them.

What then has happened to textuality in Metz's treatment of it? Though the concept undergoes a certain transformation, under Metz's hand the text tends to designate the structure of message formation proper to a single codal ensemble, say, a film. As such, it functions as a way to ground the notion of specificity, both in the sense of identifying processes proper to something and in the sense of locating those processes in a certain something which can be reliably separated from other things. Significantly, Metz draws a term from a linguistically inflected domain of literary research—the text—to designate the specificity of the object of film study. As I suggested in my opening remarks, this approach registers the pressure exerted by filmology within academic film studies, both in terms of how Metz strives to reintroduce a rigorous hermeneutic component within the later and in terms of how he does so by "positivising" the text. Instead of grasping the text as a "methodological field" and recognizing its systemic character (recall that Metz opposes system and text), Metz attempts to free film from filmology by sheltering it behind a form of disciplinary specificity increasingly ignored by filmologists, the literary text. As a consequence, however, he sacrifices the text which, in the context of contemporaneous literary debates, had become a way of designating the methodological problematic that was undermining the disciplinary hegemony of the positivist social sciences. In effect, by shifting from message to text, Metz reverses Barthes's shift, transforming the text back into the work and encysting within film studies a literary model that was no longer in touch with the changes that were gripping the "literary" disciplines. When Metz turns in *The Imaginary Signifier* to speak of the "text of the cure," he is in effect acknowledging the limitations of his previous analysis, but this acknowledgment comes too late, and it comes in a form that fails to break the disciplinary dependency that entraps the discussion of the text.

### Raymond Bellour: The Lost Text

When Bellour interviews Metz just prior to the appearance of *Language and Cinema* (1971), he both invites Metz to spell out his analytical convictions and, at certain strategic moments, he pointedly criticizes them.[8] Significantly, his criticisms focus on the distinction Metz insists upon preserving between his analytical system (in this case the "general syntagmatic code") and the texts upon which it is brought to bear. As Bellour makes explicit in a later conversation with Janet Bergstrom, he was provoked to emphasize this issue in response to his own effort to explore the way certain films encode, at the level of enunciation, the very segmentation that solicits a system like that of Metz's general syntagmatic code.[9] Though Metz acknowledges the pertinence of such criticism, he continues (during the interview) to defend his notion of the textual system from any effort to blur the border that divides its "internal" functioning from the analysis that delimits the rules of this functioning. As we saw above, this tenacity of Metz's derives from his conviction that an absolute gulf separates analytic and filmic discourses—a conviction ultimately driven by an epistemic need to impart objectivity to analytic discourse. Bellour, in pressuring Metz on this issue, is not immediately interested in contesting the "objectivity" of the large syntagmatic code. Instead, and this is made plain in the quasi-autobigraphical chapter that opens *L'Analyse du Film*, Bellour objects to the consequences Metz's perspective has for the very concept of textual analysis. Nevertheless, when Bellour actually details his own understanding of filmic textuality, he accepts as a presupposition of his discussion the very discursive gulf that led Metz to the perspective Bellour opposes. This state of affairs would suggest either that Bellour is confused about where he differs with Metz or that the notion of textuality undergoes a decisive and perhaps misrecognized transformation in his hands. Judging from one of the questions he puts to Metz in their interview, where Bellour explicitly pressures Metz to reconsider what actually is at stake in the system/text distinction (p. 270), it would appear that the latter explanation is more feasible. Let us pursue it.

Bellour's most systematic and extended discussion of textuality occurs in "The Unattainable Text" from 1975. Included in an issue of the French cultural journal *Ça* devoted to the work of Metz, this essay opens with an evocation of Barthes that explicitly contrasts with that of Metz. Bellour refers directly to "From Work to Text," treating its conclusions as obviously applicable to film. He clearly understand what is at stake in the distinction articulated by Barthes, even citing Barthes's characterization of the text as a "methodological field." However, as one might expect from a theorist who impishly titles an analysis of Hawks's *The Big Sleep* (a film founded on duplicity) "The Obvious and the Code," Bellour quickly moves to complicate his invocations of Barthes by insisting that the text of the film is, in fact, unattainable. Since this feature of the text is its defining trait, it is worth specifying Bellour's arguments for such a claim, keeping in mind that the dialogic field of Bellour's essay is immediately defined by the presence of Metz whose work *Ça* is celebrating.

The argument of "The Unattainable Text" opens with a detour and a suggestive play of hands. Bellour writes,

> But without going into the theoretical labyrinth opened by the notion of the text, I shall stress two things. On the one hand the material possession of the work alone permits one full access to the textual fiction, since it alone allows one a full experience of the multiplicity of operations carried out in the work and makes it precisely into a text. On the other, as soon as one studies a work, quotes a fragment of it, one has implicitly taken up the textual perspective. . . . That is why it is possible, in a slide which is both justified and somewhat abusive, . . . to speak of quoting the text when one means work. . . . In connection with these terms, but without evading them, I should like to emphasize an elementary fatality: the text of the film is unattainable because it is an unquotable text.[10]

Bellour's refusal to enter the "theoretical labyrinth" of the text constitutes a detour whose significance we are not yet in a position to gauge, so let us take up the two issues that receive direct attention. By stressing that possession of the work (i.e., a particular film) gives one access to the text, Bellour appears to be confirming Metz's contention that the text is best understood as the "multiplicity of operations" (to use Bellour's terminology) that constitute the film as a particular or singular work. What nevertheless distinguishes Bellour's position from that of Metz, is Bellour's knowing insistence on the difference between the text and the work. Unlike Metz who unsystematically shifts from text as work to text as a site of unbounded displacements, Bellour underscores the productivity of textuality, arguing that one *makes* the work into a text or that one adopts the perspective of textuality when one *does* something to the work. Nevertheless, when Bellour specifies what that "something" is, namely quoting, he maneuvers into a position of solidarity with Metz.

Once one has a film in his/her possession, Bellour contends that it can be turned into a text by quoting it. In fact, it is by working with the work in this way that one announces his/her commitment to the theory of textuality. Unfortunately, it is precisely as this work unfolds that one realizes that the text of the film, or the film as text, is unattainable or lost. Why? The text is lost because when one quotes a film for the purpose of analysis, the film, as "motion picture," is forced to sacrifice its specificity as a signifying practice. Here Bellour reiterates Metz's point about the gulf that separates the discourses of film and theory. In other words, when one quotes a sequence from a film in order patiently to disclose the multiplicity of operations animating it, one strips it of its filmic, that is, projected, quality. The film's articulation of the "unbounded openness," which Bellour identifies with the text (presumably as "labyrinth"), escapes along with that which makes it filmic. Thus, more than simply re-iterating Metz's point, Bellour reveals his willingness to conflate the text with the singularity of the film even though the point of such a conflation is to indicate the unattainability of the text. But let us pause to consider the precarious solidarity between Metz and Bellour more carefully—a solidarity which ultimately commits Bellour to the literary entrapment of the filmic text.

Despite the fact that Bellour goes on to detail how the discovery of textuality presupposed the homogeneity of discourses underlying the practice of literary commentary—something Metz did not really bother to do—what remains intriguing about his formulations is their presentation of textuality as a dialectical category. As a consequence of this presentation, his notion of the text dilates to engulf the gulf between writing and film. What comprises this dialectic is the fact that textuality can arise only when one is in a position to discover its loss. That is, one has to have the work to quote it (which implies textualization), and to quote it is to lose it as text. This does not necessarily imply, however, that the text is incoherently theorized by Bellour. Instead, it suggests that the text *is* this flickering where its loss is produced. If analysis actually produces this loss, then the gulf between analytic discourse and the discourse of the film amounts to very little—certainly nothing that would justify the incredible privileging of the literary model of textuality in Bellour's essay.

Of course, all this undermines the titular assertion in a profound way. In other words, if the film text indeed manifests itself in its peculiar un-attainability, then strictly speaking the *text* is attainable after all. This is particularly true if the dilation of the text is understood to engulf the ana-lytic practice that "loses" it. Bellour's "text" simply becomes the name for what escapes the institutionally bounded encounter between a film and those studying it, and in this respect his concept potentially shares deeply with Barthes's implicitly antidisciplinary approach to textuality. But if this is so, why then does Bellour persist in referring to the text as "unattainable"? Is there something important for the notion of the text in this persistence? We can proceed to respond to these questions by briefly scrutinizing his analytic practice.

One of the first things such scrutiny turns up is the fact that my charac-terization of the text as a dialectical category is amply justified. Bellour is, along with several others, surely among the first to punctuate their essays with extended "citations" from the films under discussion (see the ex-ample in figure 1).[11]

As one can see, these citations consist of reduced, sequentially ordered (in fact, they are often organized to be read left to right and top to bot-tom—as if they were prose written in a Western language) reprints of still photographs taken from frames within the film. Technically speaking, these images are referred to as photograms. If the text is unattainable (i.e., unquotable), why are such citations so prevalent within textual analyses of films? Obviously, these citations function to indicate that the text is to *some* degree quotable. In fact, the preceding citation of a citation, which is taken from "The Obvious and the Code," is made to function within this essay as something like a presentation of evidence. Initially, of course, this presentation focuses on the task of demonstrating that narrative realism, which depends for its effect upon the containment of its filmic enunciation, is a codally regulated construction. In this regard, the stills both present that which appears obvious (*l'évidence* in Bellour's French title) and, by doing so, enable us to recognize how the obvious is

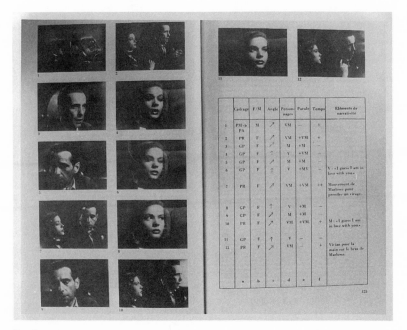

| | Cadrage | F/M | Angle | Person-nages | Parole | Temps | Éléments de narrativité |
|---|---|---|---|---|---|---|---|
| 1 | PM→PA | M | ↗ | VM | – | + | |
| 2 | PR | F | ↗ | VM | +VM | + | |
| 3 | GP | F | ↗ | M | +M | – | |
| 4 | GP | F | ? | V | +VM | – | |
| 5 | GP | F | ↗ | M | +M | – | |
| 6 | GP | F | ? | V | +MV | – | V : « I guess I am in love with you » |
| 7 | PR | F | ↗ | VM | +VM | ++ | Mouvement de Marlowe pour prendre un virage. |
| 8 | GP | F | ↑ | V | +M | – | |
| 9 | GP | F | ↗ | M | +M | – | |
| 10 | PR | F | ↗ | VM | +VM | + | M : « I guess I am in love with you ». |
| 11 | GP | F | ↑ | V | – | – | |
| 12 | PR | F | ↗ | VM | – | + | Vivian pour la main sur le bras de Marlowe. |
| * | b | c | d | e | f | | |

125

**Figure 1**

coded. Since the film text is in large part defined by its *codal* singularity, this presentation would appear to be offering us a glimpse of the "un-attainable" text. Actually, by introducing these stills, Bellour is able to ground and thus justify his reading in much the same way a literary theo-rist would use a citation to do likewise. But this is too obvious, and it is obvious in just the way that "the obvious" is discussed in "The Obvious and the Code." It is not that these observations are misguided, it is that they are simply too tightly focused.

In the essay Bellour wants to teach us that the obvious is not only coded, and coded specifically in a manner that contains or effaces its coding, but that the structure of this coding derives from the scene's (the portion of the diegesis covered by the twelve shots) function in the nar-rative. He also wants to teach us about the utility of textual analysis. To this extent Bellour's essay invites us to read its presentation of evidence, its presentation of what appears obvious, as subject to the implications of the demonstration which this presentation enables him to carry out. However, rather than conclude from this that one should ask, "what then is the code animating Bellour's evidence?" let us consider instead what the evidence he presents might be evidence for. I do not think that it is primarily or even exclusively for Bellour's reading. Instead, I think the evidence contained in the citation is evidence for the textual model as such. Why, and what implications does this have for Bellour's concept of the text?

The stills in the citation are silent and, as their name implies, motionless (except insofar as the "muscal" character of our attention animates them). At the very moment that they present us with what obviously appears in the film, they deprive us of what appears *as* the film. The film text attains its unattainability in the citation, and not surprisingly Bellour makes this observation himself when discussing the use of stills in "The Unattainable Text" (p. 25). At the same time though, the citation occasions a demonstration of textual analysis. Through it, Bellour is able to make the codes organizing the obvious become evident. In fact, in the context of Bellour's essay the stills come to denote the codes his reading constructs beneath them. To this extent that which is specifically textual in film (both in general and in *The Big Sleep* in particular) becomes attainable, not simply through the citation but *in* the citation. In effect, Bellour activates a parallel wherein the deficiencies of the signifier (the absence of sound and motion) are linked to the excesses of analysis, and what is lost as a result is not the specificity of the film text but the "methodological field" that, within a certain institutional context, makes the film mean. From this point of view, what is evidenced in the citation is the flicker between the lost and the found that is the text of textual analysis. What we see in the citation is thus an "analysis-effect" which nevertheless vanishes in the obviousness of the reading, that is, the point at which Bellour's reader goes, "well, but of course." In this respect the citation serves as evidence for the practice of textual analysis, not in the sense of serving to validate its claims, but in the sense of presenting its productivity. What, however, becomes decisive here is the way this approach to textuality invites us to shift our attention away from the filmic staging of what Barthes once called "the obtuse" [12] and toward the disciplinary context that delimits the protocols of evidence.

Though Bellour is careful to connect the unattainability of the film text to the technologies and practices that presently organize its study, it is not until considerably later that he turns the implications of such an insight back onto his concept of the lost text. This is somewhat surprising because, if I am right about what is evidenced in the citation, then one would think that Bellour's sensitivity to the issue of disciplinary constraint would have pushed him to rethink the enabling presuppositions of his theory of the text almost immediately—such may indeed be the pressure exerted by the literary model of the text. What does finally precipitate this turn is the video work of his friend and colleague, Thierry Kuntzel. Bellour's reaction to this material is contained in his piece, "Thierry Kuntzel and the Return of Writing,"[13] where the lost text attains an unanticipated presence.

The essay opens by sounding a familiar theme—the problem of cinematic analysis, and specifically the problem of whether the cinema can analyze itself. Almost immediately Bellour sets up an opposition between two attempts to respond to this problem—filmmakers writing about film and film's which present us with interrogations of their own enunciative mechanisms—an opposition which reminds one of the arguments in "The Unattainable Text." What resonates immediately with this earlier piece is the notion that written analytic discourse (the sort of practice that has something like an "organic" relation to textuality) is manifestly "outside" (p. 31) the film. Nevertheless, what is decisively new about "The Return of Writing" is the way the notion of "writing" is being transfigured in a manner that complicates the earlier argument about the text. As is evident in the title, Bellour wants us to reconsider when and where writing takes place. Not surprisingly, as he pursues his appraisal of Kuntzel's work, he comes back to the work/text relation, but in a way that alters the notion of the text's unattainability.

As we have seen, textuality and quotability are linked by Bellour. What fascinates him about Kuntzel's work is that in the latter's various video pieces a certain form of rigorous film citation is being practiced. Let us trace the exposition of this fascination. After reminding us of the ways Kuntzel's earlier essays on film theory drew our attention to the "other film" that became accessible to us when we recognized the parallel between the cinematic and psychical apparatuses, Bellour argues that the video pieces actually construct visual articulations of this "other film" or, better, of the analysis that permits the relation between the film and the "other film" to appear on screen. Since this relation is a construction of analysis, and to that extent part of the structure of our experience of film, Kuntzel's video pieces can be seen to bridge the gulf that separated the written and the filmed. Moreover, the videos do not misquote. They do not sacrifice the specificity of the filmic medium even as they interrupt it temporally and displace it technologically. By drawing implicitly on the reconceptualization of writing effected by Derrida and Ropars-Wuilleumier, where writing refers to the structure of supplementarity (a structure fundamental to analytic discourse as commentary), Bellour is empowered to argue that Kuntzel is, in effect, recording film analysis *as* video art.

The suggestiveness of this insight can be spelled out in a number of different ways. What I would like to emphasize here is the way this discussion prompts one to rethink the unattainability of the text. Since in many respects Bellour's reading of Kuntzel cancels his prior assumptions about the necessary conditions of textuality, one is entitled to wonder why in this later piece he persists in referring to the notion of the text at all. If, as I have argued, these prior assumptions harbor an unspoken insight about the peculiar attainability of the lost text, then what are the effects of Bellour's reading of Kuntzel on such an insight? What I think emerges in "Thierry Kuntzel and the Return of Writing" is an insight into the disciplinary and ultimately institutional dimension of textual analysis. This is precisely the point Bellour is concerned to elaborate in "D' une histoire" where he draws upon Kuntzel's work on *La jetée* to indicate how the tension between film and analysis explored in "The Unattainable Text" might be resolved.[14] To put it succinctly, the text remains unattainable or, at least, deserves to be regarded as such because the disciplinary organization of film analysis does not recognize the making of videos as "normal" analytic practice. While it may be true that Kuntzel's videos attain textuality, they do so precisely by losing the text to the institutional forces that refuse to recognize these videos as instances of analytic writing—forces which insist upon reading the video pieces as simply "art." Instead of the specificity of the film text eluding citationality, in this case the specificity of the disciplinary contestation of its citational practices is what slips away, or stands silhouetted by the rarity and exhuberance of Kuntzel's example. One cannot see such a contestation if the disciplinary object provoking it is deemed irrelevant to the practice of analysis. What Bellour appears to be toying with in his reading of Kuntzel is his conviction that the text helps us designate what eludes us in the disciplinary framing of film analysis. Thus, the unattainability of the text is rewritten here—hence the "return" of writing—as an institutional effect, not an analytical paradox. What is crucial about video in this context is that it represents the kind of technological development that is obliquely heralded in "The Unattainable Text." More than a mere instance of modernization, video marks a decisive incursion of mass cultural technology within the discipline of film study that solicits that discipline in precisely the way detailed, with regard to a more general level of analysis, in chapter two. In fact, today many scholars engaged in "film analysis" use video technology to do so (though primarily as a convenience), but this is a comparatively recent development. That Bellour, in 1971, was un-prepared to elaborate the implications for his notion of textuality of the technological changes he sensed is not therefore surprising. Nevertheless, I would argue that there is much insight contained in his evocation of the text's relation to the psychoanalytically comprehended object of desire.

In effect, my reading of Bellour presupposes that the unattainability of the text is to be understood through an analogy with the Lacanian object. When, in the essay on Kuntzel, the text is displaced by "writ-ing" and the latter is understood to have "returned," this analogy almost converts into an equation. What seems worth underscoring in this con-nection though is the Barthesean problematic, wherein the text's status as an object is understood, as we have seen, in a specifically paradigmatic sense. Rather than comprehending the object's loss on the model of a trajectory that emanates from and returns to a constitutionally divided subject—in which case the text would function rather like Lacan's notion of the breast[15]—Bellour's discussion invites one to introduce the con-cerns addressed by Girard, where the loss of the object that bonds the disciple and the master is comprehended in terms of the power that orga-nizes the social relations that animate a discipline. As we have seen, this power, or violence as Girard prefers, is lost to those who, in sharing a disciplinary object, remain blind to its constitutive role in the forma-tion of their identities as analysts. When Bellour reads Kuntzel's video work as constituting a return of writing, yet a return that requires the supplement of his own interpretation to acquire its full significance for film analysis, he is comprehending the unattainability of the text in terms of the dynamics of discipleship, that is, in terms of disciplinarity. Yet one wonders whether he was not already doing so when he decided in "The Unattainable Text" to avoid "going into the theoretical labyrinth (dédales théoriques) opened up by the notion of the text" (p. 19)? Let us conclude by returning to the issues raised here.

Now routinely read as a problematic allegory of the containment of heterosexual difference,[16] Ovid's tale of the labyrinth also lends itself to a disciplinary reading. Constructed by one who could set "confusion and conflict in stone," Daedalus' labyrinth was a "prison" built to house the miscegenetic offspring of the queen of Crete. Though certainly not panoptical, the labyrinth nevertheless functioned to sequester an aberra-tion, a mixup. When Bellour chooses to avoid this prison in his discussion of the film text, he is, on one level, simply trying to make his task easier. But at another level he is also implicitly refusing to sacrifice the text, as an analytic figure for plurality, to the labyrinthian order of disciplinarity. Rather than allowing the text to degenerate into a snarled ball of abstract propositions, Bellour refuses to address the theoretical intricacies that his resistant colleagues are waiting to denounce as signs of the text's incomprehensibility. He does not thread the labyrinth of the text, and in doing so he links the unattainability of the text to the institutional, and ultimately disciplinary, conditions of its emergence. In other words the film text is unattainable in part because many of those Bellour, by virtue of his training, knows to be studying film will not fail to misunderstand what the text is, since the latter becomes comprehensible only if one is prepared to suspend the "commonsensical" disciplinary assumptions about the object of film study. If we recall at this point that Jean-Louis Baudry has attempted to read Plato's "allegory of the cave" as a prefiguration of the cinematic apparatus, then we can see how explicitly Bellour's refusal of the labyrinth of the text may bear on his discussion of the text's unattainability.[17] Isn't the labyrinth also readable as a figure for the apparatus, especially in light of Bellour's and Kuntzel's fascination with the *défilement,* the unthreading, of the film that permits it to become a text? Bellour's refusal to enter the labyrinth is also a reiteration of his concern about the technological limits of film study—the unattainability of the celluloid strips that one would thread into a projector or onto an editing table that gives him/her access to the labyrinth opened by the text. Granted, Bellour does not say as much, but I believe this may be due to his reluctance to abandon the Metzian framework (where a film is one thing, and its analysis quite another). When one rereads "The Unattainable Text" in light of "Thierry Kuntzel and the Return of Writing" where this framework is overcome, then it becomes possible to establish the latent connections among Bellour's earlier figures and arguments—connections which invite us to see in the labyrinth a notion of the apparatus that includes the disciplinary issues that Baudry himself left unspecified.

With Bellour's work on textuality then, we see a movement that begins with an affirmation of the gulf that separates the literary text (which knows no difference between itself and the medium of theoretical commentary) and the filmic text. This movement comes to a provisional conclusion with Bellour's rejection of the gulf separating literature and film, but given the attenuation of his disciplinary analysis, one suspects that this rejection, in effect, comes closer to surrendering the film text to literature, than to overturning the paradigm that organized their relation. Textuality thus potentially assumes an identity which ties it to the dynamics of disciplinarity—an identity which ought to permit one to pursue the "close reading" of a film all the way into the enabling institutional conditions of the theorization of film study. Finally though, Bellour hesitates, leaving his notion of textuality to oscillate not merely between attainability and unattainability, but between the literary and the nonliterary. If it is not accidental that Bellour finds it necessary to refer to the "return of writing" in order to think this notion of textuality, then perhaps the relation between textuality and writing needs to be scrutinized further. To do this we must engage the work of Marie-Claire Ropars-Wuilleumier.

## Marie-Claire Ropars-Wuilleumier: The Graphic Text

Of the three theorists considered in this chapter, Marie-Claire Ropars (her name is often abbreviated in this way) is the one whose work on film analysis has most explicitly engaged the Derridian meditation on textuality and writing. While this engagement leads her to theorize the relation between film and writing in ways that go well beyond the limited reflections of Metz, it also firmly binds her to the literary paradigm I have been arguing the textual analysis of film needs to overcome. This is due less to the resourcefulness of her reading of Derrida (among others), than to the point of departure of her analytic project—a point of departure that is defined by many of the concerns I have associated with the disciplinary struggle against filmography. Since Ropars's work represents, in many ways, the most extreme radicalization of filmic textuality, it is worth characterizing this point of departure in order to gauge what forces operating there inhibit this radicalization.

Ropars's earliest film criticism appeared in the Catholic monthly *Esprit* during the late fifties and through the sixties. As Dana Polan has pointed out, this work bore the intellectual stamp of its venue.[18] Though not specifically Catholic, Ropars's essays are clearly engaged in an unabashedly humanistic affirmation of aesthetic expressivity, and Polan rightly argues that her initial interest in the relation between writing and film is founded upon this affirmation. In one of the more "theoretical" pieces from this period, one finds the following discussion of writing.

In effect, in the order of writing the gulf is going to widen between a linguistic system of communication which makes use of language and does not survive the transmission of a thought, and a linguistic system of creation which disengages the word from its concept in order to carry it towards the image, and to struggle with a transitive syntax that gives rise to an intransitive and durable vision:

through the resistance that a style and a structure oppose to the immediate givens of language, the literary work realizes itself in an aesthetic object, where signification can only be perceived through the apprehension of this new form.[19]

What emerges here, despite the absence of an explicit reference to film, is a treatment of writing wherein its distinctive embodiment of a split in the social use of language is used to privilege it as a reference for delimiting what Ropars calls "cinematographic expression." Not only does Ropars reiterate the long-standing equation between formalism and modernist aesthetics, but she later draws upon this equation in order to ground filmic specificity in the expressivity exemplified in that writing which renounces the task of communication: writing which favors the creative use of language, that is, literature. Though this evocation of writing is a far cry from the elaboration of it that characterizes Ropars's later work, it is clear that even here writing has a privileged relation to both the work which is properly filmic and the signifying practices which can no longer be comprehended through the linguistic account of language. When, in the contemporaneous *De la littérature au cinéma*, Ropars discusses the relation between film and writing at length, she consolidates these insights, making writing essentially synonymous with the aestheticization of film once the latter's specific dependency on the practice of montage is affirmed.[20]

In light of the disciplinary context I have sketched for comprehending the emergence of filmic textuality, Ropars's emphatic embrace of "literature" is not surprising. It represents her critical engagement with the tradition of filmology. Significantly, when Ropars discusses work that appears in the *Revue Internationale de Filmologie*, she focuses (albeit briefly) on Amédée Ayfre's essay on neorealism, criticizing it for rejecting montage as a technological compensation for the mimetic limits of the medium. What is interesting about this maneuver is that Ayfre is actually a critical historian, someone who recognizes the importance of preserving filmology's relation to aesthetics.[21] In attacking his work, Ropars places all that more distance between herself and filmology. By establishing montage as the aesthetic practice of film, and by designating Ayfre (and Bazin) as one who is prepared to sacrifice this practice, Ropars challenges the adequacy of filmology's internal reflection on the relation between positivism and art. Thus, what might otherwise strike one as an aside can be read, given the significance of Ayfre's position vis-à-vis filmology, as a forceful rejection of the tradition of film analysis connected with this movement.

Another important aspect of this discussion, of course, is the appearance within it of the name of Bazin. This is because by grouping Ayfre and Bazin as "realists," Ropars implicitly moves to distinguish her notion of the "literary" dimension of film from that of Bazin's, who in his role as editor of *Cahiers du cinéma*, helped to generate the discursive context that supported the "*politique des auteurs.*" Though both Bazin and Ropars make much of the notion of stylistic rigor as a way to conceive the aestheticization of film, Ropars wants to break definitively with the model of the aesthetic subject that implicitly orients Bazin's discussion. Though in certain respects Bazin kept his distance from auteurist criticism, his championing of figures like Flaherty and Renoir differed from such criticism only to a degree. Specifically, Bazin unequivocally affirmed Renoir's ability to submit the technological resources of film to an austere enunciative realism where the spectating subject was "free" to engage the image directly. Not only did Bazin treat Renoir as what Truffaut would have called an *auteur,* but he un-self-consciously presented the spectatorial positions generated by Renoir's films (on his reading of course) as though they were modeled on the controlling consciousness of an author—a perspective that essentially gave the viewer the same direct access to the spatiotemporal order of the image as Renoir. Later remarks of Ropars's make it clear that, at the level of a particular analysis, she is willing to associate nearly everything occurring within the orbit of the *Cahiers de cinéma* with this sort of auteurism.[22]

Thus, even in these early pieces of Ropars's, one can see her gingerly moving the notion of writing away from its disciplinary basis in literature, and this despite the fact that she is drawing upon this very basis in order to save film from the positivistic tendencies of filmology. Clearly what she does not like in Bazin's work is the way his realist response to the question "what is cinema?" imposes a model of cinematic subjectivity that inhibits the elaboration of the concept of filmic writing—a concept she believes better specifies what is specifically filmic in film. It is not, however, until Ropars discovers the grammatological meditation on writing that she is able to take full advantage of the interdisciplinary structure of her reflection on film art. As we will see, the complexity of this structure ultimately impinges upon Ropars's project, and it impedes her ability to elaborate the antidisciplinary potential of textual analysis.

This discovery is steadily elaborated during the midseventies, and it is marked by Ropars's more persistent recourse to the notion of the text. In *Muriel: histoire d'une recherche* from 1974, which Ropars writes with two colleagues, one can witness this process in a fairly direct way, sensing some of the difficulties that she is seeking to overcome through its elaboration. Toward the end of her contribution to the chapter, "Sens et idéologie: le texte de *Muriel*," Ropars brings writing and textuality into alignment in the following way.

> *Muriel* can be considered a text to the extent that the work inscribes within its plot the image of its own working. But this representation which permits us to see the cinema as a mode of referentiality, permits us equally to read the referent itself. The self-representation of the film, which qualifies it as a text, does not, for all that, cut it off from historical reality—it only permits the film to maintain a maximal distance between the representation of reality and reality itself. . . . Hailed by this double working, the viewer thus accedes to a productive activity. The decipherment of a writing which is ceaselessly *different* turns the signified into a question where the solution, at once proposed and exposed, transports the spectacle towards the viewer by leaving open within it a place for the viewer's intervention.[23]

Here, writing no longer refers immediately to the literary domain. Instead it has acquired a technical connotation that is connected to Ropars's theorization of the text. In fact, during this period, writing and the text become nearly synonymous. When presenting this research to a colloquium at Harvard in 1977, Ropars makes this explicit when she says, "[the] text's meaning calls for a global analysis of [the] signifying process, or writing."[24] What separates this from a narrowly literary treatment of writing is Ropars's reliance upon Kristeva's work on textuality and, obviously, the grammatological reconceptualization of writing. When in the preceding citation Ropars appeals to the viewer's accession to "productive activity," she is drawing directly on Kristeva's discussion of the "productivity called text." Despite Ropars's focus on the problem of filmic self-representation, it is clear from the context of the passage cited, that a film is textual insofar as it unsettles, while constituting, the subjectivity of the viewer. Though her appeal to the viewer's intervention reminds one of Bazin's rationale for his preference for sequential editing (as opposed to montage), it is plain she understands the consequences of such intervention very differently. Under the influence of a textual model the intervening viewer discovers his/her placement within the rigors of the film's referential strategies. Even historical realism is disclosed as subject to the ceaseless differing that characterizes the filmic text.

Surprisingly, these then novel reflections on filmic writing are contained in the chapter devoted to the "text" of *Muriel* that is divided into sections named "Text," "Context," and "Pre-text (*Hors-texte*)." Though Ropars only writes the first section of this chapter, her introduction to the book refers to these divisions as if, despite everything the preceding citation problematizes concerning the status of the text's "outside," they still made sense. Consequently, in the work from this period one can see Ropars poised between the text of literature (i.e., the "work" literary scholars would situate in its "context") and the text of writing (i.e., the productivity that theorists of signification would exploit to complicate the very logic of contextualization). What appears to resolve this interdisciplinary tension is Ropars's absorption of the critique of linguistics detailed in an earlier chapter. Again, quoting from her talk at Harvard, Ropars says specifically that "The theoretical field in which I am working concerns the filmic text. What is text? As you know, the term falls into many different oppositions, building various definitions. Here, I will retain the specifically semiotic sense, and limit it little by little: for now, text can be considered as [any] system of signification—pictural, [oneiric], filmic, as well as literary—whose devices of meaning go beyond the linguistics of the sign."[25] Setting aside momentarily the problem of the different ways the listed systems of signification go beyond linguistics, it is worth underscoring that the general condition of textuality is identified here with those semiotic processes that elude the linguistic meditation on the sign. In chapter 3 I argued that the discovery of these processes in the context of a quest for literary specificity precipitated the emergence of textuality by provoking a crisis within the literary disciplines. In order to overcome the aestheticism of her early discussion of filmic writing, Ropars needed to come to terms with this crisis. This is clearly what is evidenced in the preceding citation, and not surprisingly this development took place in the context of a struggle to specify the specificity of a signifying practice that existed in a transdisciplinary field—a struggle which I am arguing remains unresolved.

But let's come back now to the problem set aside above and draw upon its resources to flesh out Ropars's textual model of filmic writing. In the work examined so far, writing (the domain of filmic specificity) is equivalent in many ways to what Eisenstein meant by "montage." Developed in tension with both Meyerhold and Pudovkin, Eisensteinian montage referred primarily to the conflictual articulation of the semiotic properties of each film image within a sequence. In typically phallic rhetoric Eisenstein characterized successful montage as a "series of explosions of an internal combustion engine." Though Eisenstein thought long and hard about what he called "vertical montage" and the "synchronization of the senses," he tended to apply a graphically derived model of montage to voice, music, and noise with surprisingly little sensitivity to the heterogeneity of sonaric signifiers. This is a most instructive oversight, the consequences of which will require a separate chapter to detail.

Ropars, in aligning writing and montage, essentially locates filmic writing in the effects of shot linkage as these are generated in the enunciation of the image. On the one hand, this reflects an important desire to oppose the fetishization of the image in film analysis, both in terms of its function as a reductive privileging of one filmic code and in terms of the image's role in the interpellation of the viewer—a mode of fetishization that leads to a reductive critique of mass cultural technologies as uniformly and efficiently repressive. On the other hand, Ropars's coordination of the critique of the image's iconic integrity (it was undermined by the "shock" of enunciation) with her discovery of writing tended in the early work to orient her analyses around what might be called horizontal relations, that is, linkages established by dissolves, jump cuts, paralleled sequences, etc., which transpired on the same iconic level. This is why throughout *Muriel: histoire d'une recherche* almost compulsive attention is given to the methodological implications of dividing the film into levels. Though this is understood to be required by a reading of the "text" of the film, the case for filmic writing is most urgently argued for as it operates on a specific level, as though the "scriptural" character of the vertical relations *among* levels was either sufficiently obvious to go without saying or nonexistent, and this despite the painstaking delineation of the codal complexity existing at each level. Consider again, for example, the point made in the immediately preceding citation, where the textuality of the film is demonstrated by an appeal to the fact that in the narrativization of the image one *sees* a representation of a film whose incompleteness marks the film *Muriel* with the impossibility of the latter's own narrative closure. This is not a claim about the structural friction among levels; it is a claim about the iconic enunciation of the narrative statement. As such, it tends to present writing or textuality as localized at the level of visual montage, and to this extent the critique of the fetishization of the image is compromised.

Needless to say, however, Ropars's reflection on filmic textuality does not simply remain fixed at this level of elaboration. In fact, her theoretical absorption of the critique of linguistics does ultimately propel Ropars beyond the montage-oriented discussion of writing, and this is evident, to some extent, even in the citation from *Muriel: histoire d'une recherche*. What received emphasis there was what Metz, in a similar theoretical context, called displacement, that is, the dynamic instability of the structural relations among the codes that define the singularity of the film. Ropars links textuality with the fact that Resnais's film is narratively organized in such a way that its relation to history and the viewer constantly operates to inhibit the film's closure—*Muriel* ceaselessly fails to coincide with itself and is *therefore* textual. This treatment of the text invites one to consider the ways this lack of coincidence articulates itself throughout the "open" (cf., Eco) film. It is precisely in response to such an invitation that Ropars's later work responds.

*Le Texte divisée* appeared in 1981. As its title suggests, it is divided into two, predictably unstable, parts. In the first of these Ropars lays out the theoretical terms of her more recent perspective on filmic textuality. Though she has written a great deal since then, this book continues to set the parameters for her analytic practice. In the first chapter we find the following, remarkably synoptic, characterization of the text. "But the side taken—that of the text—appeals by definition to a decentering: the text is, we shall see, a frontier space, that is, a negation of proper spaces, a place of tension and encounter where writing, traditionally confined to the linguistic domain, and cinema, too frequently defined by the image and sound, can exchange, without confusing, their specific demands."[26] This passage abounds with now familiar themes. There is, for example, the reiteration of the concern over specificity which Ropars here ties to the task of taking writing beyond the disciplinary preoccupations of linguistics. Significantly, this follows upon her characterization of the text as a "frontier space" which resonates strongly with Barthes's notion of the "methodological field" (Ropars's explicit discussion of the work/text opposition in *Le Texte divisée* more than invites this comparison). What is immediately interesting about such a formulation is the way it rebounds upon the context of Ropars's own book, rendering the latter a place of tension and encounter between that which negates every *proper* space and the *specific* demands of writing and cinema. On the one hand, this formulation opens a question which, while crucial to Ropars's more recent account of textuality, we will be forced to set aside for now, namely, the interactive economy of filmic analysis and filmic writing. On the other hand, and this is what deserves to be stressed here, Ropars's emphasis on "space" (with all of its Derridean implications) and "exchange" presents textuality as addressing precisely what I have suggested was undeveloped, if not missing, in her earlier analysis—the vertical axis of montage. As we shall see, clarifying what is at stake in the spatial model enables one to evaluate the relation between Ropars's project and the task of what I have been calling antidisciplinary research.

What are we to make of this metaphor of the "frontier space"? In attempting to flesh it out herself, Ropars draws directly on the grammatological analysis of the relation between "spacing" and "writing," making her abandonment of the literary, aesthetic model of writing quite clear. In exploring the grammatological categories in relation to film, Ropars reinforces her earlier critique of the priority of the film image by first showing how its effacement of the spacing (the enunciative ordering) that conditions the image (as a recognizable visual phenomenon) makes film complicit with phonecentrism, that is, the ideological system that, among other things, reduces writing to a seamless representation of speech. Once the complicity between phonecentrism and iconic fetishism is established, Ropars then exploits the play this introduces into the concept of writing in order to bring the latter to bear on that which encompasses the relations among all the montage elements that comprise a film: the image, the voice, the music, the noise, the script. By referring to that which encompasses these relations as a "frontier space," a space which negates the properties of other spaces, Ropars is directly modeling her notion of the film text on Derrida's analysis of the trace. As we have seen, the structure of the trace is such that every element of a system is marked by, that is, defined and thus compromised by, that element's relations with all the other elements that comprise the system of those elements. Ropars is treating both the montage elements of any film and the disciplinary space of film and analysis as though they conform to this model. At the level of a film, this invites her to consider the way an image and a voice, for example, are reciprocally marked by the space that conditions their relation. This is not a space that preexists this relation. It arises through relating, an activity that takes place along the border or frontier between film production and film analysis. This, according to Ropars, is the space of the text.

More than a reiteration of Metz's and Bellour's notion of the text as the precariously singular ensemble of the codes constituting a particular film (or group of films), Ropars's later view of the film text insists upon its *lack* of particularity, its inability to coincide with itself—even at the level of narration. Though it is true that Ropars tends to associate this general model of textuality with certain productions of the Western avant-garde (Eisenstein, Rocha, Duras, Resnais), she does so in the same spirit that Derrida reads a comparatively obscure essay of Rousseau's as symptomatic of the aims of his entire corpus—if avant-garde texts *can* systematically fail to coincide with themselves, this is because such a possibility is *necessarily* endemic to that which we call the cinema. In order to refine and further specify the notion of the filmic text as a frontier space, Ropars connects the film's lack of particularity with the concept of the hieroglyph—a concept she develops out of her reading of Eisenstein and Derrida. In many respects the hieroglyph represents the fullest articulation of Ropars's meditation on writing, and its conspicuously "archaic" quality helps diffuse the vanguardism implicit in her approach.

What had persistently compromised her early discussion of filmic writing was the absence of something like an "organic" relation between the two media. To overcome this Ropars essentially coordinates Eisenstein's discussion of the "coupled hieroglyph," where the emphasis falls on the cinematographic generation of cognitive meaning, with Derrida's insistence upon the hieroglyph's graphic embodiment of a cohabitation of figurative, symbolic, abstract, and phonetic elements. Thus, the very heterogeneity of the hieroglyph as a conceptual model is exploited to get around the problem of the distance between two signifying practices, without thereby simply canceling this distance. From this perspective, filmic writing qualifies as "writing," not because it generates aesthetic effects (like literary writing), but because it is, in many ways, a consummately "modern" articulation of the heterogenous spacing that comprises writing *in general*. If what defines the hieroglyph is its ability to designate the signifying activities that prompt meanings to arise in the experiences of perceivers without, however, evaporating into those meanings, then the hieroglyph is an immediately appropriate model for approaching film. This is what Ropars's argues in her summary of the hieroglyphic proposal.

> A hieroglyphic interpretation of cinema drives this tension [between writing conceived of as representation and as figuration] back into the heart of the scriptural hypothesis: this interpretation is what confronts in the text, regardless of the text's materials, a mimetic current—where figuration would subtend the adequation of sign and

thing—and a process of montage—where the only motivation [in the linguistic sense] that could be constituted would remain internal to the play of signifiers.[27]

Aside from the fact that here we see Ropars sound many of her major themes very quickly, it is important to note that she pairs the hieroglyphic interpretation with the object of the text, wherein she claims one will encounter the diversity and tension that defines the domain of writing. Significantly, the text becomes the space *of* the encounter between montage and mimesis—a development that separates the text from writing (in the earlier sense of montage as such). What then makes the hieroglyph so decisive is that its elaboration finally enables Ropars to thoroughly reconceptualize montage. Beyond simply allowing her to use writing as a means to talk about the relation between montage and mimetic representation, the hieroglyph permits film analysis to connect methodologically the production of this relation to the articulation of all the codal elements that define a film. On a practical level, Ropars exploits this insight to examine, for example, the way proper names or signs which seem mimetically anchored in things are graphically dispersed and narratively recharged within the dynamic unfolding of a film.[28] Thus, under the influence of the hieroglyphic proposal, textuality comes to designate the site, or the space, where the divisions that both constitute and subvert the audiovisual phenomenality of the film take place.

Nevertheless, the pairing identified in the citation between the text and a hieroglyphic interpretation raises an issue that requires further clarification. If this pairing leads to a separation between writing and textuality (as has been suggested), then are we authorized to see the text as a singular empirical phenomenon, much in the same way Metz did? Ropars explicitly refuses such a proposition when she writes, "There is, then, no text in itself. There is only a textual reading where the materiality of the works under consideration will limit its extension without conditioning the orientation of the reading a priori: this follows from a choice which can be defined theoretically, and which can be confronted with other choices."[29] Here, in a manner that echoes all of the theorists discussed in part two, Ropars links textuality to the productivity of a reading practice, thus marking the text as an effect of practice, a construct, not a formal entity. By separating the text from writing, however, Ropars is not interested in establishing an opposition between reading and its other— writing. Her point is rather that a film can be approached in such a way that our attention to filmic writing (both vertical and horizontal montage) will prompt a reading that is productive, that is, a reading capable of disclosing both a film's codally organized production of meaning, and the viewer's constitution and subversion in the generation of filmic meaning. Though not known primarily as a psychoanalytically oriented film theoretician, Ropars's alliance with such a position here becomes visible.

However, what is more important for Ropars is the question of the gulf between a film and its analysis. By insisting upon the grounding of textuality in reading, she counters the positions of both Metz and Bellour on this issue. In fact, Ropars explicitly criticizes Bellour's discussion of the "unattainable text" saying, "couldn't the same be said for any text?" (p. 92). Her point is that the heterogeneity which a reading produces in its engagement with a work arises just as readily in a piece of literature as its does in a film, and the protection of analytic discourse qua discourse that the denial of such an insight has authorized is totally illegitimate. For Ropars, textuality means that, as with the codal relations within a film, the relation between a film and its analysis is radically open and unsettled. This does not, however, imply that film analysis is either inconclusive or aimless. In fact, anyone familiar with any of Ropars's painstakingly detailed readings knows that her work is anything but aimless. Instead, by insisting upon the unsettled character of the space of analysis, Ropars seeks to underscore the fact that analysis is disfigured by the very material it works with and by the institutional context in which that work takes place. It is as though for Ropars textuality means that the relation between analysis and its object, a particular film or group of films, must of necessity be conceived as a montage relation. The space of analysis is thus a frontier space, a site of border conflicts where a film challenges and transforms the very theoretical framework that permits one to isolate the signifying activities that would otherwise go unnoticed in its absence.

In this respect, Ropars openly endorses the linkage that both Metz and Bellour more cautiously explore between filmic discourse and the discourse of analysis. Doing so permits her to extend the textual model in ways that were not envisioned by those who based their allegiance to it upon a strict division between literature (or prose, more generally) and film. This is to some extent surprising in light of the trajectory of Ropars's theoretical development—she, after all, began by insisting upon the quasi-redemptive function of literature in the context of film studies. What is perhaps even more surprising though is the way Ropars's notion of textuality, which in many ways should have led her to an openly antidisciplinary position, has nevertheless tended to stall her within a literary problematic. In, for example, "Film Reader of the Text" from

1983, the issue animating the essay concerns the possibility of "developing the return effects of filmic textuality on literary textuality."[30] Though
Ropars begins by assuming the presence of "genuine" textuality in both
discourses, her aim is to show how the frontier space of the text can be
traversed in a way that primarily illuminates the activity of reading literary writing. This is carried out by constructing a "parallel montage"
(p. 29) between *Hiroshima mon amour* (a film) and *L'arrêt de mort*
(a "novel")—a montage that, among other things, reveals the extent to
which a film's reflexive "reading" (hence, rewriting) of its screenplay can
guide a reader toward the semiotic vortex that simultaneously enables
and erases a literary narrative. In the context generated by this construction, textuality becomes a way of coordinating processes that are taking
place in other signifying practices and facilitating our reading of a literary
thematic that might otherwise remain illegible. Here, it is as if Ropars is
paying off a disciplinary debt; returning to literary analysis something of
what it once donated to film study.

There are two problems with this otherwise provocative and resourceful analysis. On the one hand, there is the implicit reduction of the text's
heterogeneity to the two-way traffic that comprises the border between
film and literature. On the other, there is the pressure this reduction
obliquely exerts on the reading of vertical montage in particular. The
implications of this criticism can be sorted out best if we begin by considering the second issue first.

In the reading of *India Song* that closes *Le texte divisée*, Ropars addresses at some length the vertical relations between the soundtrack and
the image track. In discussing the soundtrack, which Ropars believes
plays a predominant role in the structuring of the film as a whole, she
concentrates on the voices which intertwine in the opening sequence.
Her point, which is amply demonstrated, is that the play of voices and
their "presence" off screen bleeds into the narrative images and prepares
us for the invisible staging of an impossible and ultimately unspeakable
desire. Thus the dialogic code operates vertically to accentuate, within
the image track, a fissure that opens within the code of the gaze that
organizes the specular presence of the characters to one another and to
the viewer. As she proceeds to elaborate this reading, Ropars discusses
the way the voices themselves divide between phonetic sense and noise,
arguing that after a certain point they "lose their meaning value, becoming mere sounds, just like the music."[31] In the context of a general
exploration of the relation between Duras's work and that of Derrida's,
this implicit characterization of music as lacking in meaning value is

to be seen positively—music as a signifying practice collaborates with figural writing to disrupt Western logocentrism. Nevertheless, when one notices the technical care with which Ropars, in her *découpage* of the film's opening, describes Carlos d'Alessio's title song, one wonders why it was so important to strip music of meaning value.

The point here is not that music is valuable—that should go without saying. Rather, the point is to insist that even mere sound is not without meaning value—it is simply organized by different disciplinary and ultimately cultural institutions. D'Alessio's song participates *textually* in the hieroglyph that structures the vertical (and horizontal) montage of the opening, and not merely by acoustically mirroring (a relation Ropars, in this piece in particular, should have been sensitive to) the voices that accompany it on the soundtrack. The issue I what to emphasize is simply this: what would happen to "textual analysis" if one were to acknowledge that a shift comparable to the one from work to text might take place in the discipline of musicology? What would the textuality of music be like? By posing these somewhat rhetorical questions at this juncture, I am suggesting that Ropars's discussion tends to use textuality as a way to locate a confluence of processes whose significance as a disruption and reorientation of various cultural codes is determined in relation to a *particular* set of disciplinary preoccupations. What is missing here is not a recognition of music as an aspect of the film text qua text, but an engagement of the disciplinary heterogeneity that may be inscribed in music if read as a specific embodiment of textuality as the latter might be understood within musicology.

To compensate for this deficiency, I am arguing it is necessary to appeal to the notion of *intratextuality* which supplements intertextuality by underscoring the presence of conflicting disciplinary histories and agendas within the frontier space of any text. In other words, the heterogeneity of texts qua texts is not due exclusively to their semiotic properties. It is due, as well, to the agonistic power plays that are animating the different instances of textuality that comprise them and the social relations of those who study works as texts. Because Ropars seems bent upon keeping her meditation on filmic writing within the orbit of a certain linguistically grounded literary problematic, she tends to subsume all instances of textuality under a hieroglyphic figure that renders the text synonymous with that which, for literary scholars and philosophers, constitutes the crisis of language. This is why, in spite of all her advances, Ropars continues to shuttle back and forth between film and literature, rather than opening an interrogation of the disciplinary conditions of this relation as they become readable in her objects of study. Through a consideration of musical textuality, I will attempt to sketch out what film analysis might be like if one were to pursue such an interrogation.

I do not mean to suggest that Ropars is blind to the disciplinary and institutional dimension of her work. In many ways she is more articulately aware of the way these forces mark the "intrinsic" character of her research than Bellour, whose embrace of Kuntzel's televisual critical apparatus suggests a certain profound, if unconscious, comprehension of such matters. It is nevertheless surprising that someone who so clearly understands the text's relation to the disciplinarily organized practice of reading would fail to extend the text's disruptive lack of closure back onto the disciplinary context itself—not as a contextual gesture, but as a consistent and rigorous articulation of a specifically textual reading.

What I have argued throughout this chapter is that this failure is not due to personal limitations, but rather to the historical unfolding of the discipline of film study in the French context. Because of the precise ways that different disciplines were drawn into the conflict over filmic interpretation, even the surpassing of literary models left their mark within the concept of filmic textuality. Regardless of how important it was to displace the positivist approach to cinematic meaning by appealing to the concept of "reading" a film, it has now become urgent to pressure the very limits of reading themselves. In other words, filmic textuality ought, at long last, to submit to its own "openness" and assume the task of articulating an antidisciplinary project.

# 7

## ✳ Toward the Textual Analysis of Music

**I**

The aims of this chapter are several. First, I will elaborate a reading of the discipline of French musicology that illuminates the institutional impact of the textual paradigm in music analysis. Strictly speaking, this impact remains latent not only in France but here in the United States as well, and part two of this chapter will be devoted to exploring the extent to which this latency is due to the "literarization" of the text we discovered in the practices of film studies. Second, I will develop a "textual analysis" of Sergei Eisenstein's and Sergei Prokofiev's *Alexander Nevsky* that pursues and elaborates the insight concerning *intratextuality* introduced at the close of the preceding chapter. And third, on the basis of this analysis I will set the stage for a concluding discussion of antidisciplinarity and textual politics that stresses what might be gained from a textualization of music.

When the first volume of Claude Lévi-Strauss's *Introduction to the Science of Mythology* (*The Raw and the Cooked*) appeared in 1964, it bore the distinctive epigraph, "To Music," followed by eight bars from the score of a song written by Edmond Rostand and Emmanuel Chabrier.[1] In the pages which follow, an entire series of musical terms appears, suggesting that there was a profound affinity between the structural science of mythology and music. For the most part this affinity is figurative, though it is true that the "Overture," as it is called, does contain and introduce most of the thematic material to be developed in the book, including the self-reflexive theme of musical analysis. To the extent that this discussion goes beyond the "merely" figurative, it does so by suggesting that Lévi-Strauss's approach to myth was to be governed by a syntactic understanding of meaning production. In his lengthy discussion of serial music, Lévi-Strauss attempts to show how mythic meaning can be understood to arise as the result of certain codal permutations within a sign system in much the same way that musical meaning arises in relation to manipulations of tonal and rhythmic codes defined by the system of Western repertory composition. Of course, this argument was thought to contain a triple scandal: Lévi-Strauss was denying hermeneutical agency to the indigenous peoples who "spoke" the myths, while also modeling "the science" of mythology on an "art" (a properly epistemic scandal), but he was also claiming that even serial music was as saturated with meaning as mythic discourse.[2]

As with many specifically French scandals, the ones created by *The Raw and the Cooked* amounted to little—what was indeed noteworthy about this volume was the institutionalization of structuralist anthropology that it initiated, not the fact that its methodology reflected somewhat novel aesthetic concerns. This was no doubt due, in part, to the fact that there was nothing particularly scandalous about basing the science of mythology on the art of music.

In 1965 when *L'Arc* published its special issue on Lévi-Strauss, this was made particularly clear in Célestin Deliège's contribution where he traced the impact of structuralism upon French musicology, only to find, perhaps unintentionally, that the latter had been well on its way toward the very positivism that structuralism was suspected of threatening music with.[3] In other words, Lévi-Strauss's epistemic gambit was immediately compromised by the fact that music, at least from the standpoint of the discipline devoted to its study, was *already* aspiring to be a science. Though we often associate the advent of specifically "structuralist" musicology with the work of Jean-Jacques Nattiez and Nicolas Ruwet,[4] Deliège's article suggests that this work (inspired as it was by Lévi-Strauss) primarily effected a shift away from mathematical models of structure toward linguistic ones—and specifically those informed by the semiological critique of linguistics. It did not by any means introduce the concern for structure as such into musicology. In this respect French musicology during the 1960s would appear to be forced to confront the same sort of disciplinary displacement wrought by the intrusion of linguistics within literary study. Though there was indeed a confrontation, it differed importantly from the one in literary study we have already examined.

In the disciplinary context of literary analysis, linguistics provoked a crisis within the drive to specify literary specificity. At the very moment when it seemed possible to specify the literary object in all its particularity, that object disintegrated into the field of other signifying practices made accessible through structural semiotics. In musicology the linguistic turn began to reconnect the object of musical analysis to the field of meaning production. And while this involved a displacement of what musicologists understood to be specifically musical about music, it functioned to renew confidence in the cultural significance of their object. In fact, I would argue that it is precisely this kind of confidence that moved Lévi-Strauss to regard even serial music as being every bit as saturated with meaning as myth.

Perhaps the most distinctive aspect of the intrusion of semiological linguistic paradigms within musicology is the fact that it brought with it the work of Noam Chomsky along with that of Saussure and Hjelmslev. Specifically, both Ruwet and Nattiez attach great importance to Chomsky's notion of generative grammar because of the way it seeks to link syntax and semantics, while comprehending how language users come to be creative within the medium. This is deemed important not only because of the way it addresses the inventiveness that befits an aesthetic medium like music, but because it permits musicologists to reconnect their analyses of the message/code relation to meaning production at the level of the human subject, the language user. While it is true that neither Nattiez or Ruwet go very far with this line of inquiry (both prefer to describe research, such as that of Barthes,[5] rather than actually elaborate what is at stake within it), their work reveals the extent to which French musicology was already open to the advent of the textual paradigm, where the problem of subjectivity as an aspect of the production of meaning explicitly arises.

The appearance of the textual model within musicology begins in the early 1970s, where it is developed in the work of the writers and intellectuals either on, or affiliated with, the editorial board of Editions de Seuil's music journal, *Musique en jeu* that was founded in November 1970. Perhaps due primarily to the institutional provenance of the journal, the theoretical inspiration motivating its contributors was the work of Barthes, Derrida, and Kristeva among others (notably Adorno and Jean-François Lyotard). With the publication of Jacques Attali's *Noise* in 1977, and perhaps even more so with its translation into English in 1985, this history has been obscured, despite the fact that Attali's central category, "noise," had been explicitly theorized in relation to textuality by Daniel Charles in two early contributions to the journal, "L'écriture et le silence," and "La musique et l'écriture."[6] Surprisingly, this occlusion of history is abetted by Jameson when, in his introduction to the English translation, he argues that Attali's book should be read in the context of a "resurgent" historicism which he otherwise tends to regard as precisely what had been sacrificed by French theorists in the heyday of textuality. Though it was not, in fact, until Ivanka Stoïanova published her *Geste, texte, musique* in 1978 that the textual model was thoroughly fleshed out, there are certain theoretical achievements of Charles's that bear elaboration here, particularly since they in many ways enable the work of Stoïanova.

For English-speaking audiences, Charles is perhaps best known as John Cage's "collaborator/interlocutor" in *For the Birds*. Cage, and the musical avant-garde in general, have long been decisive points of reference for Charles, and it is not therefore unusual that the former figures prominently in Charles's early work on musical textuality. In these essays the work of Cage provokes Charles to examine the institutional economy of musical discourse. But the two insights pursued by Charles that are crucial to the emergence of the musical text are: (1) the semiotic and therefore systematic character of musical discourse—an insight that enables him to discover how the notation/performance polarity arises within a social context where something rather like Derridean "writing" is subordinated to the requirements of musical expression—and (2) the fact that, in relation to such requirements, the mute and therefore "silent" presence of their enabling conditions appear as the "noise" that simultaneously underwrites and undermines the production of musical meaning. As Charles puts it, "[w]e interpret writing as noise tracing itself," presumably on the musicologically generated surface of music.[7] What authorizes this seemingly paradoxical association of noise and silence is the fact that Charles sees musicology as a discipline which protects its object, the musical artifact, by considering anything which historically conditions human access to this object as essentially interference or, in the vocabulary of information theory, noise. In most cases this "noise" is embodied in mute structures, like the enforced normality of the Western European system of tonality, which never become audible in the music as such, hence the notion of a silent inscription of a writing whose repression is musicologically justified in terms of the need to control interference.

By linking musicology's evaluative term of protective self-justification (noise) to our experience of music's phenomenal surface (what is heard, versus what is silent), Charles indicates that the effort to think music's relation to the theoretical category of writing, or as he says, "the semiotic text,"[8] necessarily involves an interrogation of the disciplinary paradigm that founds musicology. Though Charles never goes on to elaborate this disciplinary critique in any detail, his attention to the enabling conditions of music as a semiotic system clears the conceptual space for a fully elaborated textual analysis of music.

As indicated above, this work is systematically carried out by Ivanka Stoïanova, who worked with Charles, Kristeva, and others, joining the *Musique en jeu* editorial group toward the end of the seventies. Not surprisingly, *Geste, Texte, Musique* makes much of another category that also played an important role in Charles's analysis—the category of gesture. In "L'écriture et le silence," gesture is exploited to designate the dimension of musical discourse which registers the inscription of the body—that of the listener (and in some cases, the dancer) as well as that of the composer. As such, it exemplifies an aspect of the mute writing that both constitutes and subverts musical works. That is to say, gesture is thought to constitute the musical work because it belongs to the very phenomenological surface of a performance. By the same token, it subverts musical works because gesture is precisely what musicology excludes from consideration in the elaboration of musical meaning (a minuet is not typically analyzed—if at all—in relation to the dance steps performed along with it, even when they dictate the time signature of the piece or movement).

In Stoïanova's work gesture retains this "dialectical" function, while also designating one of the semiotic strands that traditional musicology overlooks when it refuses to think its object—the musical artifact—in terms of textuality. By pursuing musical analysis using a textual model, what Stoïanova insists draws our attention is precisely the network that brings graphic notation, practical execution, and listening pleasure into relation with one another as gestures. What is important about such a pursuit is not primarily that it is a "fuller" description of music (which it happens to be), but that it connects the analysis of music to a social account of the conditions of music in a manner that transforms such an analysis into a mode of social criticism. In Stoïanova's hands this critique is articulated in conjunction with her elaboration of a theory of the avant-garde, broad enough to include European art music and North American pop minimalists.

In light of her points of theoretical reference, it is not surprising that *Geste, Texte, Musique* opens by refusing the distinction that isolates musicology from literary criticism, namely, their mutual and altogether typical insistence upon the utter incommensurability of music and literature (except, perhaps, at the level of song lyrics or a libretto). Her point is not, however, to deny that there is a difference between the two (Stoïanova takes this to be noncontroversial), but to insist that we understand in what way the differences that separate music and literature belong to a sociocultural framework that affects both practices— a framework that must be considered within the analyses that are conducted by either musicologists or literary scholars upon their respective objects. Though she does not reiterate the now familiar argument about the effect of semiotic linguistics upon literature, the initial moves of her argument nevertheless suggest she realizes that the indefinite expansion of literature's sphere of disciplinary influence has direct implications for the study of all signifying practices. One such implication is that music, like literature, can indeed be conceived textually. Here is one of her initial programmatic characterizations of the text.

> The notion of *the text* designates the functioning of the signifiers/ signifieds recast by one another, that is, the functioning of *signifiance* that traverses while dislodging structures, and which scrambles the principles of communicative language. The deformation of words, glossolalia, differentiated repetitions, grammatical mistakes, the fluidity in intertextual space—all involve the pulsional mobility that overruns the heterogeneous place of the text. The text's functioning articulates itself as a practice of unlimited generation, as a perpetual transgression of resistances, inertias and stagnations.[9]

Certainly, in many respects, these formulations do little more than establish the fact that Stoïanova has indeed read her Kristeva. What is nevertheless important is that Stoïanova here grafts the Kristevean discussion of textuality directly onto music. In the process of doing so, she reconceptualizes the object of musicology while also submitting Kristeva's own rather rudimentary discussion of music to a gentle but telling critique.

Kristeva first discusses music at any length in *Language—The Unknown*.[10] Situated in the context of a general survey of how the emergence of language as an object for the human sciences altered the study of various signifying practices, Kristeva's presentation of music stresses the way it resists semiotic reduction while nevertheless embodying the possibility of a pure formalism (not unlike the one yearned for by Lévi-

Strauss). As one would expect from a survey (particularly one written primarily to secure one's advancement through the French educational bureaucracy), little more of interest is said about music. In fact, it is not until *Revolution in Poetic Language* that music reappears as a vital concern for Kristeva. Even in this work however, the musical work itself is not discussed much. Instead, Kristeva focuses on what she takes to be the musical aspects (rhythm, tonality, timbre) of modernist poetic verse. Perhaps the most significant development of her thinking on music is the relation she constructs here between it and what she calls *signifiance*. As she writes: "[l]anguage thus tends to be drawn out of its symbolic function (sign-syntax) and is opened out within a semiotic articulation; with a material support such as the voice, this semiotic network gives 'music' to literature."[11] Thus, music for Kristeva becomes virtually synonymous with the disruption of symbolic meaning—as though music's lack of semantic precision and its dependence on time separate it utterly from the preeminently social domain of meaning.

Stoïanova essentially accepts everything in Kristeva's discussion of music that links it to textuality, but when Stoïanova comes to elaborate her conception of musical textuality an important difference between the two women's positions emerges. Consider the following formulation: "The text and the musical statement transpose energetic charges, pulsional tensions, perceptual ensembles, pluralities as well as totalities, a mass of codified elements at the heart of an individual history inscribed within social life."[12] Here the heterogenity that Kristeva typically associates with the dynamics of the semiotic is linked both to textuality and music, but music now understood as an ensemble of bodies and institutions that is profoundly social. Instead, therefore, of textuality and music being equated in order to show how music's ineffability might be understood to designate that which outdistances the social, Stoïanova elaborates this equation in order to show how music, approached textually, reveals itself to be a system articulating the precarious heterogeneity of the social. On her account music is not synonymous with textuality understood as the *signifiance* erupting within a literary text otherwise dominated by the symbolic register. For how could that be so in music where the "symbolic" plays a rather muted role? But by the same token her discussion does not reduce music to the semantic conventions that prevail within either musicology or the institutions of nonacademic listening. In fact Stoïanova explicitly moves to dissociate music from the object it has become within musicology, arguing that semiological musicology in particular "studies that which is not musical in music" (p. 19).

Thus, textuality is used by her to situate the production of musical meaning in opposition to the disciplinary account of it offered within musicology. In this way Stoïanova brings her reflections on the text's relation to music to bear on the disciplinary object that organizes musicology, affirming once again the profound relation between the text and academic disciplines.

Practitioners of musicology would no doubt refuse Stoïanova's characterization of the limits of their discipline. Behind such a refusal might well be the collective conviction of musicologists that they do indeed study what is musical in music. The question we must pose is: what is that? what does musicology comprehend as its object? If we restrict ourselves to French musicology during the sixties and seventies when the textual paradigm emerged, one sees that its object was defined by the predominantly synthetic methods used to study the musical work.[13] In effect music was made into the sort of thing that invited the discovery of those general codes which enabled musicologists to explain all the various permutations of the musical message—permutations such as pitches, beats, compositional procedures, etc. What then is musical in music is the system of phenomena that is realized in what even today we would call a "piece" of music.

By contrast Stoïanova locates the specifically musical in a much wider field, and it is of crucial importance that, in order to do this, she has recourse to the model of textuality. Seen from a textual perspective, music has as its foundation the socially mediated relationship between three positions: the composer/author, the performer, and the listener—all of which can be distributed along both synchronic and diachronic axes. That is, a composer obviously can inhabit all three positions at once, just as a listener, especially in relation to certain avant-garde compositions, can participate in the composition of a piece through the exertions of an active interpretation. Of course, it is equally true that in a concert, for example, the three positions can be carefully, if not consistently, distinguished.

Traversing these fundamental positions are the varying signifying practices that will provide them with sociocultural definition. A composer, for example, must weave together the drives and fantasies that constitute his/her personal history and the various strata of the musical idiom: the graphic notation, the sonorities, the gestural practices, and the historical traditions binding them together. A listener, on the other hand, begins from the same subjective place, but s/he has to negotiate the point of intersection between the musical idiom and the institutions of reception—institutions which encompass the technologies of listening as well as the critical discourses that dictate taste categories. Necessarily, the musical analyst is confronted with this multiplicity and must decide either to reduce it by designating a specific practice as the properly musical or affirm the textual character of music and attempt to comprehend each practice and position as part of what Stoïanova calls "the musical apparatus."

In her own analyses Stoïanova tends to shift her focus among practices and positions in order to demonstrate how musical textuality reveals interesting things about various intersections within the reticulated system. Nevertheless, what consistently motivates her analyses is a preoccupation with the musical positioning of the subject. As one senses from her insistence upon the positions that constitute the sociopsychological basis of the musical apparatus, the production of music goes hand in hand with the production of multiple subject positions, some of which are sufficiently incompatible with one another to destabilize both the listening and the composing subjects. In fact, following Kristeva, Stoïanova designates as the musical avant-garde works which most systematically effect the destabilization of such subjects. Obviously, against the avant-garde stand the various elite and popular musics that mobilize the resources of the musical apparatus in order to subordinate the play of subject positions to a dominant position whose coordinates fall well within the interpellative mechanisms of society. Though this point is touched upon many times in *Geste, Texte, Musique*, its implications are perhaps best spelled out in a slightly earlier piece which discusses the nonnarrative aspects of musical minimalism. Stoïanova writes,

> The non-directional statement requires a new perception of musical time: the listener is no longer forced to follow the story of a narrative development, but can wander, as he [sic] wishes, abandoned to his phantasms within the enveloping space of the minimalist statement. . . . The minimalist statement renounces the idea of communication which asks the listener to follow a determined path. Conceived as a superimpostion of "geological strata" (P. Glass) the non-directional minimalist statement offers up *instances of undirected and uncontrollable identification*.[14] (my emphasis)

Foregrounded here is the connection between narrativity and subject positioning. What makes minimalism interesting for Stoïanova is the way it essentially disperses the interpellative mechanisms of traditional tonal music, hence the stress placed on the *plurality* of identifications. Of course behind this evaluation stands her commitment to textuality—a commitment which refuses to separate signifying practices from the constitution (or subversion) of subjects. Though undeveloped even in this essay, the line of inquiry opened here has been pursued in extremely fecund directions by a number of writers.[15] For my purposes it suffices to stress that tonality, as a sonoric dialect, presupposes features that have direct implications for the subjectivities of performers and listeners. Tonality accedes to narrativity through its obedience to a harmonic syntax developed in the seventeenth century, where the establishment of a tonic key and the introduction of specific thematic materials carried with them the implicit map of a compositional adventure organized around the topos of a homecoming: the seemingly "natural" return to tonic as the sign of an inevitably rational achievement. Listeners have learned to respond to this tonal dialect by accepting the terrain of this adventure as second nature, that is, as so normal as to be essentially synonymous with sentient existence as such. A "good listener" is therefore a particular kind of subject, not simply a subject exemplifying certain kinds of listening skills.

What nevertheless may be misleading about this discussion of minimalism is that it creates the impression that only within this particular idiom is a genuine heterogeneity of subject positions made accessible. This is not the case, and though it is important to stress that Stoïanova's reading of minimalism conditions her critique of the interpellative reductivism of the traditional musicological repertoire, it is equally important to recognize that her commitment to the textual paradigm is meant to authorize her insistence upon the interpellative heterogenity of music when the latter is comprehended as a social apparatus. When, for example, in chapter seven Stoïanova discusses the role of gesture in music, she makes this point explicitly arguing that, "[i]f the barrier between gesture and music is razed, the musical work inevitably becomes a *multiplicity,* a space open to multiple, plurivalent inscriptions" (p. 202). As she goes on to enumerate, one of the inscriptions music becomes open to is that of the cinema.

This observation raises several issues, only two of which I want to address here. First, it is important to note that Stoïanova is not immediately referring here to film music. While it is likely that this material interests her, a different connection among these signifying practices is being underscored. By stressing the notion of a cinematic inscription within or upon music, Stoïanova draws out the idea that musical meaning is constructed within a heterogeneous cultural field where materials that we might not immediately associate with "music" in fact operate within our experience of the musical apparatus. Thus, it is apparent that the textual model is meant to encompass the transactions that take place within such an apparatus. Secondly, what is certainly implicit within Stoïanova's discussion of gesture is the idea that because the musical apparatus encompasses a multiplicity of inscriptions, music activates a heterogeneity of subject positions. In other words, even as we are positioned as the competent listener for a specific piece of music, we encounter in this process what might be termed a microhistory of positions—a history comprised of the other inscriptions (visual or kinetic associations etc.) that function to make the piece "mean" for us. It is precisely through this idea of the multiplicity of inscriptions that Stoïanova's commitment to music's ability to proliferate positions regardless of whether or not it communicates "minimalistically" becomes undeniable. Moreover, insofar as this commitment motivates her critique of traditional musicology, it is obviously linked to what for her constitutes the urgency of the textual paradigm.

However, despite the challenge represented by Stoïanova's discussion of gesture and music, it does not yet explicitly broach the issue of what I have called intratextuality, and this may well have to do with the implicit literary quality of her textual model. To speak of a theatrical or cinematic inscription within music does not, in and of itself, address the question of the different disciplinary systems that may be informing one another in our experience of a piece of music or, for that matter, in a film where those of us who can typically expect to hear voices and music while seeing images. In other words, while it is clear that Stoïanova's perspective is certainly interdisciplinary, it is not clear that the notion of textuality which supports it is capable of serving antidisciplinary aims. Nevertheless, her work provides us with a sufficiently ambitious notion of the musical text to lay out and explore the notion of intratextuality, particularly as it might be shown to manifest itself through a specific artifact. Perhaps only through analysis can we discover what, within the very concept of the text, contributes to its musicological latency.

## II

Sergei Eisenstein's *Alexander Nevsky* recommends itself for the analysis I am proposing on several grounds. First, Eisenstein's work (specifically *October*) has already been the object of one of the exemplary instances of "textual analysis" and thus has a decisive relation to the traditions I have been examining.[16] In fact, as we saw in the presentation of Ropars's notion of the text, Eisenstein's theoretical work has served as a virtual condition of possibility for the textual analysis of film. Secondly, *Alexander Nevsky* is a rigorously collaborative work, bringing together the talents of Eisenstein and Sergei Prokofiev. One extended sequence of the film, "The Battle on the Ice," invites our particular attention because Eisenstein himself has discussed the relation between the image and the music as it operates there. And lastly, because Eisenstein's work is so fundamental to the discipline of film study, a challenging example of it may well serve to illustrate what is at stake in the effort to bring textual analysis and antidisciplinarity into alignment. Let us then turn directly to the discussion of the film.

At the most general level *Alexander Nevsky* is an allegorically structured propaganda film. Released in November 1938, *Alexander Nevsky* was financed by the Soviet state, and in many ways it represented Eisenstein's return to favor in the Soviet Union. There, his career had been damaged by his long absence and his many incomplete projects. What constitutes *Alexander Nevsky* as a propaganda film—aside from the fact that it was financed by the state and that a newly elected member of the Supreme Soviet (Nikolai Cherkassov) played the title role—was its designated task of mobilizing the Russian people in the wake of recent signs of belligerent Nazi expansionism. The closing sequence of the film contains the warning, "Let people come to us a guest without fear, [b]ut he who comes with a sword shall die by the sword," followed by the phrase, "Arise, people of Rus!" inscribed in graphically dramatic rolling titles.

What makes the film allegorical is the split staging that organizes the narrative material. Eisenstein and Pyotr Pavlenko (who helped write the shooting script) decided to forge a link between the anticipated struggle against the Nazis and a medieval conflict (thirteenth-century) between Nevsky and the "Teutonic knights." In a manner that is reminiscent of the way French republican artists like to drape the revolution in classical Roman motifs, the mise-en-scène of the film situates the diegesis in the medieval period. As with many allegories, this one makes its status as allegory function within the ideological statement of the film. Specifically, Eisenstein is able to link the temporality of the allegory to the narrative issue of whether or not one sees him/herself in terms of a nationalist interpellation, as a subject of Russia's past.

Despite the fact that the overt propagandistic aim of the film conflicts with certain of Eisenstein's political convictions, it does nevertheless inflect the network of antagonisms that structures the film. The effect of this inflection is that the entire network, including those aspects of it which address the film's relation to its own historical moment, is slanted toward the national antagonism. As I have already suggested, this is by no means a simple antagonism, involving as it does not only the allegorical staging of the narrative (that is, a past and present version of both Russia and Germany), but also the triadic conflict between Mongolia, Russia, and Germany that is introduced within the medieval setting.[17] Nevertheless, the propagandistic effect of the film rests upon the narrative privileging of the national conflict, which in turn gives priority within the film to the "Battle on the Ice" where the articulation of the national conflict culminates. Since my aim is to explore the iconic and sonoric relation as it operates within and around the confines of this sequence, it is necessary to situate the sequence fairly precisely within the narrative presentation of the network of antagonisms.

Traversing and defining the national antagonism within the film are the two additional antagonisms of class and gender. In order, ultimately, for the propagandistic aims of the film to be fully realized these antagonisms must be subsumed under the national one. Subsumption, particularly for Eisenstein, is a difficult process. What makes it difficult are the two requirements that subsumption must meet: (1) that the intensities giving urgency to the antagonisms of gender and class be "transferred" to the national conflict and (2) that the resolution of the national antagonism be effected through a "sublation" where the antagonisms of gender and class are simultaneously canceled and preserved, that is, expressed at a "higher" level. It is indispensable to this process that one of the ultimately sublated antagonisms serve as a "conversion table" where other antagonistic intensities can be exchanged without slackening, where defeating the Teutonic knights can be made the equivalent of another conquest. Significantly, it is the gender antagonism that serves in this capacity, functioning first to subsume the class antagonism and then providing the national struggle with a surplus charge, a surplus desire. Let us tease out the threads of this process within the film.

Immediately after the opening sequence in which we witness the encounter between Alexander and the Mongolian envoy, there is a cut to a title, "Novgorod," which effects our entry into the city of that name. As with so many transitional cuts in this film, there has been a rotation of the compositional axes, where the previously horizontal plane of the white lake has, in effect, been lifted into a vertical position to serve as the backdrop for the title lettering. As if to underscore the gesture of "entry," we are positioned outside the city below a bridge where our two "protagonists," Vasili Buslai and Gavrilo Oleksich, are standing. It is spring.

Framed in a medium shot from the back, we watch as their eyes catch sight of what turns out to be a young woman, Olga Danilovna, who is on her way to an open-air market situated not far from the riverbank. As they crane to follow her, the camera cuts to Olga as seen from their point of view, instituting the convention of the cinematic gaze where women appear as sights and men act as seers. In the ensuing action, essentially the collaborative "courting" of Olga, we come to recognize that Gavrilo and Vasili are soldiers whose desire for fighting (they fought with Alexander in his commemorated defeat of the Swedes) has yielded to a desire for women. As Vasili says, "We've had our fill of fighting. It's time to think of other things."

The enunciation of this segment is textually decisive.[18] Through a series of seven shots the two men are transported from the bridge to the market where they are positioned in front of the armorer's stall. As they continue looking at Olga, they are joined from behind by Ignat, the armorer, who observes in a highly marked "folk" discourse, "The bulls are lowing, spring's in the air!" Their conversation is presented in a medium shot which constitutes them as a triad, with the armorer pinned behind the two soldiers (figure 2). As they talk, shots alternate between Olga,

**Figure 2**

the implict "subject" of their conversation, and the triad. This arrangement and articulation of bodies is important because of the way it is used both graphically and thematically to effect the conversion of intensities referred to above. In fact, as we shall see, this material functions as a proairetic code throughout the film. As an initial step in the direction of this conversion, the arrangement of the male bodies is quickly displaced onto the relationship between the two men and the woman, when Gavrilo breaks away and approaches Olga. Quickly, Vasili follows and the triadic relation is reconstituted with the two men on either side of the woman, Olga thus substituting for Ignat (figure 3). Though initially in front of her, Olga walks between them, and they close ranks behind her.

Figure 3

She is pinned between them and their boastful proposals, each promising to make her more happy if she would permit him to send a matchmaker to her home (figure 4). Thus, the tension between the two men and Olga is not only split so that the two men are caught in an antagonism be-

Figure 4

tween themselves and her, but the entire antagonism of gender, and now sexuality as well, is explicitly presented as an obstruction to the national antagonism: Gavrilo and Vasili would rather fornicate than fight. Obviously, if *Alexander Nevsky* is to be an effective propaganda film, this will have to be contained.

At this point the gender antagonism is abruptly displaced by the class antagonism. As Olga insists that she be given an opportunity to reflect upon the two competing offers, the peal of the *veche* bell is heard on the soundtrack calling the citizens of Novgorod to an urgent meeting. The triad disperses as Gavrilo, Vasili, and Olga join the crowd surrounding a wounded Pskovian soldier who informs those assembled that the "Germans" have plundered Pskov and are on their way to Novgorod. After a few supporting cries from the crowd, a city official interrupts from a podium to insist that a peace treaty has been signed with the Germans and that the wounded soldier is needlessly agitating the crowd. Thus, an opening is created for a second refusal of the urge to fight—a refusal which aligns this moment thematically with the exchange between the lusty soldiers, Vasili and Gavrilo. What gives this moment its specifically class character is the fact that immediately following the official's declamation on behalf of the peace treaty, a merchant joins him on the podium to say, "What if they have taken Pskov, and if it comes to that, we can buy our way out. It wouldn't be the first time! We've no use for war, brother." As he speaks, other merchants gather around the podium to express their solidarity with the speaker. Significantly, this development is interrupted with a cut away to Olga in close up who cries, "Would you barter the Russian land for merchandise!" She is shouted down, but her position is taken up by the male figure whom she had replaced in the triad detailed above—Ignat. His speech, delivered from the podium, makes the class antagonism obvious. He says, "To you rich it's all one, who's your mother and who's your mother-in-law. Where there's profit that's where your native land is. But for us common people, falling to the Germans means real death."

This is a crucial intervention, not only because it stems the tide undermining Russian national resolve, but also because it links the contradictory interests of the merchants to the kinship system which is implicitly at stake in the courting of Olga by Vasili and Gavrilo. The enabling trope for such a linkage is, of course, the imaginary maternal body of Mother Russia. The point Ignat makes against the merchants is that the economic interests of their class contradict the national interests, and while this is not yet Marxian class analysis, it does nevertheless disclose that a class antagonism traverses and obstructs the crowd's perception of the national antagonism. Moreover, this moment in the film not only links the obstructions of class and gender, it subordinates the former to the latter.

Though Alexander is not yet summoned to lead the Russians into battle, ultimately Ignat's intervention prevails. By linking the class antagonism to the kinship exchange that founds the social construction of gender, Ignat is able to bring the crowd around to the patriotic position, that is, to the position where the national antagonism subordinates all others. Apparently necessary to this maneuver is the suggestion that those who cynically pursue profit do not distinguish between a bond of blood (the mother) and a bond of convention (the mother-in-law). It is as though anyone who cannot tell such a difference is to be suspected of treason against, presumably, the "motherland." Because the allusion to kinship resonates with nationalist themes, it not only works to eliminate the class-based opposition to the national struggle, it also effectively serves up the antagonism of gender as the conversion table channeling all intensities into the patriotic struggle. As we shall see, the eventual sublation of gender requires cunning and delicacy.

After three intervening sequences—the extended presentation of German atrocities in Pskov (a plot development that, in effect, assumes that the spectators have accepted Ignat's reasoning and are in this respect "ahead" of the Russian people); a missing sequence (actually no longer in the film) which repeats the scene of the assembly in Novgorod only focusing this time on Vasili's reluctance to fight and his encounter with the Pskovian refugee, Vasilisa (their ultimate pairing orthographically stages the fantasy of sexual relating/differing); and the actual summoning of Alexander—we return again to the scene of Novgorodian assembly where Alexander finally calls the people to arms. In the pandemonium that ensues the penultimate step in the conversion process is taken. Just prior to the end of this sequence Vasili and Gavrilo once again trap Olga. The triadic arrangement is reconstituted, and the men implore her to choose one of them as her suitor (figure 5). She responds, "Let fate decide

**Figure 5**

how it is to be. The braver of the two in battle may send the matchmaker." In saying this Olga fuses the antagonism of gender to the national struggle, allowing the competitive desire for her (between the two men and between each of the men and her) to energize the patriotic fight against the Germans. Once this is in place, the only remaining step in the transfer of antagonistic energies is the one that involves the open appropriation of the sexual energy latent within the gender antagonism by the army.

This step is taken in a brief segment that directly precedes the "Battle on the Ice." Interestingly, the genesis of this segment is described in great detail by Eisenstein in "True Ways of Invention."[19] What is striking about this discussion is that Eisenstein presents what I have been calling the last step as *the* crucial problem for the cortical sequence of the film, in fact, the sequence which Eisenstein actually filmed first. In the decisive battle Alexander again emerges as a military hero, but Eisenstein also wanted him to emerge as a "genius." It is the achievement of the latter effect that so preoccupied Eisenstein. In "True Ways of Invention," Eisenstein characterizes a genius as someone who recognizes the universal implications of a chance observation or event. What frustrated him (and Pavlenko) for so long was the discovery of a narrative means to motivate the presentation of Alexander's genius. The solution to this dilemma came during a period of insomnia. Apparently, Eisenstein (who, of course, is implicitly being presented as a genius filmmaker) discovered the motivating element in a book of risqué folktales which he happened to have by his bedside. In thumbing through the book, he came upon the story of "The Hare and the Vixen" and realized instantaneously that it was the perfect way to motivate the presentation of Alexander's genius. By having Ignat, whose discourse was already conspicuously marked with the appropriate signs of folk identity, present the tale in Alexander's presence, and by having Alexander recognize its universal implications, Eisenstein was able to realize the effect he was seeking. What is decisive about this for our purposes lies in the content of the folktale.

Setting aside for the moment the fact that Alexander's genius is bound up with his ability to perform a spontaneous Proppian analysis, let us consider the presentation of the folktale in the film. Ignat, who delivers the tale, is seated amidst a group of soldiers, and he says:

> A hare leaps into a ravine with a vixen on his tail. He makes for the forest, the vixen after him. So the hare hops between a pair of birch trees. The vixen springs after him—and sticks. Pinned between the two birches, she wriggles and she struggles, but there is no getting free. Calamity! Meanwhile the hare stands alongside her and says in a serious voice: "If your agreeable," he says, "I'll now put paid to your virginity, all of it. . . ." "Oh, how can you, good neighbor, it isn't done. How can you serve me such a shameful trick. Have pity!" she says. "This is no time for pity," the hare tells her. And he pounces.[20]

When Ignat concludes, Alexander asks two questions which indicate that he is savoring the tale for its strategic elements. Moments later when Alexander formulates his battle plan, it is clear that he has appropriated the ribald folktale, which resonates with precisely the gender antagonisms established in the opening of the film, for the greater purpose of saving the Russian nation—hence his "genius." The plan involves using a group of soldiers led by Vasili to serve as the hare who lures the German vixen in between the groups led by Alexander and Gavrilo who together serve as the white limbs of the birch trees. Once the vixen is pinned, she is to be pounced upon by the Muzhiks—a peasant militia. As if to be sure that the spectators have grasped the parallels, the strategy discussion concludes with Gavrilo reminding Vasili about their competition for Olga.

In essence then, a male fantasy of violent defloration not only serves to motivate the battle plan that resolves the national antagonism, but it provides a context wherein all obstructive antagonisms can ultimately be converted into the fight for the nation. The presentation of the folktale and its appropriation by Alexander is the final step in this transfer of intensities. Significantly, not even the triadic structure is sacrificed since Olga and the Teutonic vixen are both to be pinned and violated by bodies on either side of and behind them. And though there is a vital homosocial subtext here, it is not permitted to flourish. In fact, this triadic structure, which extends to embrace both the conflict with the Mongolian hordes (Russia wedged between Germany and Mongolia) and the allegorical structure of the film itself (the present wedged between the medieval past and the future of a possible Nazi conquest), reaches into the relations between the image and soundtrack.[21] This is perhaps best demonstrated by considering the "Battle on the Ice" sequence.

Up to this point I have refrained from discussing the soundtrack, not because it has been irrelevant, but because Eisenstein himself invites us to. In his own analysis of the soundtrack he privileges the sequence of the battle, and while I will have occasion to refer both to other moments in the film and to other essays of his, I want to follow his lead, precisely in order to appreciate fully the limits of his discussion.

*Alexander Nevsky* is the first of two films Eisenstein worked on with the composer Sergei Prokofiev (the other being *Ivan the Terrrible*). Eisenstein discusses this collaboration, of which he was tremendously proud, in the third section from his extended essay entitled, "Vertical Montage."[22] It was written three years after the completion of the film and just prior to the beginning of the work on *Ivan the Terrible*. Since the notion of intratextuality which concerns me bears on the theoretical modeling latent within Eisenstein's discussion, I will focus initially on his comments concerning the general relation between Prokofiev's score and the imagetrack.

As with any competent theoretical writer, Eisenstein begins by trying to establish the general categories that allow him to speak coherently about a profound connection between two otherwise distinct modes of signification. He writes,

> Musical and visual imagery are actually not commensurable through narrowly "representational" elements. If one speak of genuine and profound relations and proportions between the music and the picture, it can only be in reference to the relations between the *funda-mental movements* of the music and the picture. . . . We can speak only of what is actually "commensurable," i.e., the movement lying at the base of both the structural law of the given piece of music and the structural law of a given pictorial representation. Here an understanding of the structural laws of the process and rhythm underlying the stabilization and development of both provides the only firm foundation for establishing a unity between the two.[23] (Eisenstein's emphasis)

The category introduced here is that of "movement," specifically, a movement that is common to both the structure of the image and of the music. In an effort to actually locate this movement, Eisenstein appeals to the notion of rhythm. This appeal makes a certain amount of sense given that rhythm involves temporally structured movement, and it applies, fairly commonsensically, to the pace and design of the horizontal montage within a film. As the essay continues, Eisenstein elaborates these basic ideas by treating rhythm as a process which manifests itself in the creation of a "line," and when he turns to demonstrate how his own work in *Alexander Nevsky* has adhered to these principles, he attempts to illustrate the "correspondences" that occur between the musical line and the pictorial line.

It is worth pointing out, before turning to the actual analysis, certain unusual and ultimately problematic aspects of this discussion. First of all, Eisenstein never manages to distinguish clearly between two very different things: (1) the material conditions of commensurability between sounds and images and (2) the methodological aims that should follow from the existence of such material conditions. What comes up over and over in Eisenstein's analysis is the term "unity" which conveniently blurs the distinction by implying that there is something about both music and pictures that *obliges* us to relate them by unifying them. In their trenchant discussion of Eisenstein's self-analysis, Hans Eisler and Theodor Adorno rightly insist that in spite of Eisenstein's critique of formalism (i.e., Hector Berlioz's notion of the equivalences between chords and colors), he sinks back into formalism precisely in the insistence upon

unifying two practices which ought more properly be related by articulating that which divides them.[24] It is as though Eisenstein has permitted
his approach to be literally dictated by what he takes to be the material
"nature" of the object.

Secondly, this approach would appear to contradict the one sketched
out in Eisenstein's, Alexandrov's, and Pudovkin's early "Statement" on
the soundfilm, where it is argued that "every ADHESION of sound to a
visual montage piece increases its inertia as a montage piece" and that as
a consequence "ONLY A COUNTERPUNTAL USE of sound in relation to the
visual montage piece" is appropriate (their emphases).[25] Though it is true
they are not speaking here directly of music, the choice of an explicitly
musical category, counterpoint, would suggest that this is not because it
slipped their minds. In short, what is peculiar about this entire discussion
of "vertical montage" is the fact that montage has been eliminated from
it. In effect, when Eisenstein realizes his dream of the soundfilm, not
only has he forgotten it, but in his characterization of his achievement
he refuses to dialecticize the category of unity and develop a properly
montage-oriented discussion of the music/image relation.[26] This outcome
was perhaps anticipated in his reference to "musical *imagery*" where
sonoric signification is already being sacrificed to an iconic paradigm,
but let us first explore the terms of Eisenstein's analysis. We can then
proceed to connect these to the narrative logic of antagonisms already
sketched out and then raise the question of how this all stands in relation
to textuality and antidisciplinarity.

Eisenstein focuses almost his entire analysis on the twelve shots that
comprise the segment he refers to as "the dawn of anxious waiting."
These are the opening twelve shots of the "Battle on the Ice" sequence. As
one can see from the printed diagrams (figure 6), he correlates seventeen
bars of music to these shots, and while one might well wonder whether
this gives him access to the structural laws underlying either the music or
the image, it is perhaps best to begin by taking him at his word. Accord-
ingly, what Eisenstein sets up are two gestures or patterns that indicate
how the music and the image "correspond." In the first we see a correspondence between the compositional properties of shots one and three
(where figures fill the lower left foreground of the frame and are opposed
on the right by sky and cloud formations) and the musical movement of
bars one and two, and five and six (where a C minor chord is followed
by five quarter notes: G, A, B, C, E-flat). In the second gesture we see a
correspondence between the compositional properties of the transition
between shots three and four (where the shot with figures in the left

**Figure 6**

AUDIO-VISUAL CORRESPONDENCES

(A Sequence from *Alexander Nevsky*)

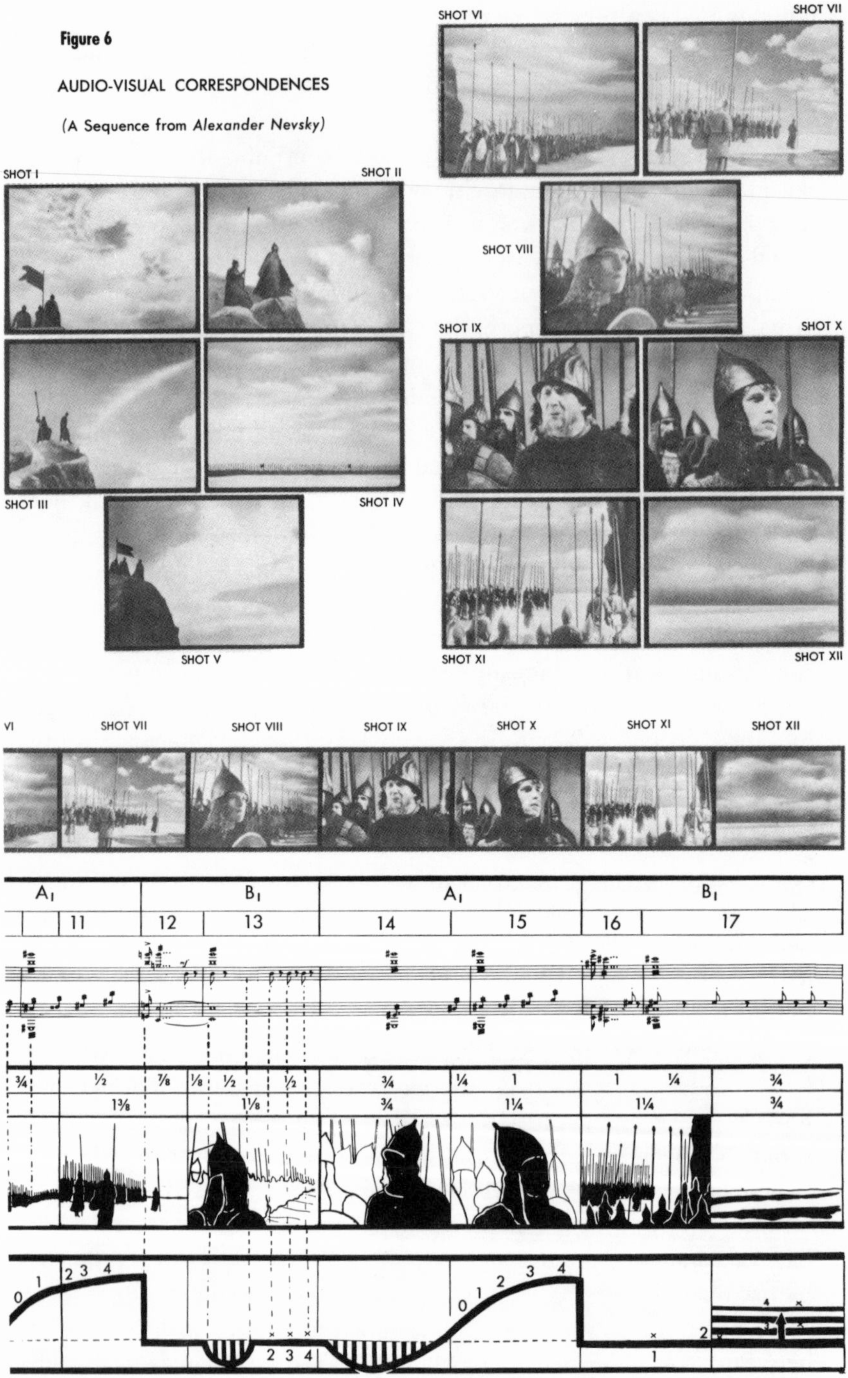

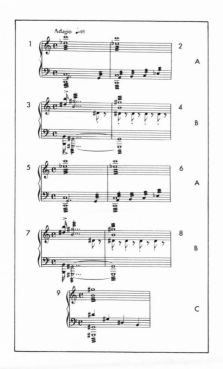

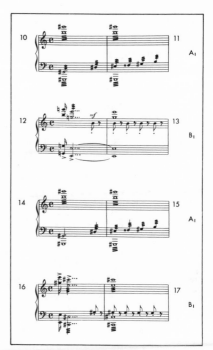

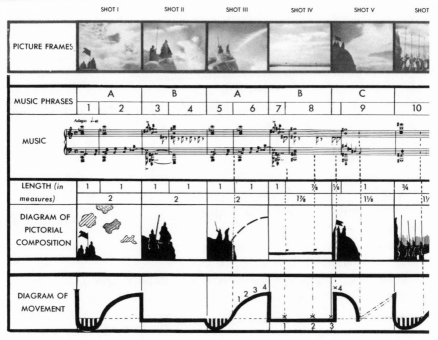

foreground is followed by a shot of the horizon in the middleground of the image) and the musical movement of bars seven and eight (where a C-sharp minor chord is followed by five eighth notes [separated by eighth-note rests]: two D-sharps/E-flats and three Ds). Together, these gestures are taken to establish the linear code of movement that organizes this segment of the film. One can consult the "diagram of movement" stratum (see figure 6) to have before him/her a representation of this code. Eisenstein is exceedingly cunning in his effort to make this code apply to each of the twelve shots in the segment.

But actually his persuasiveness may ultimately work against him. So eager is he to establish the didactic merits of his analysis, he permits the tendency to confuse the enabling conditions of commensurability with methodology to lead him to extrapolate this segment as a "master code" for the entire film. As he says, "The method used in it [the "Battle on the Ice" sequence] of audio-visual correspondence is that used for any sequence in the film" (p. 174). While anyone is likely to be impressed by the subtlety with which the correspondences between image and music have been worked out, one is entitled to wonder whether this really meets the condition of constructing a dialogue between the structural laws at the base of both signifying practices. Here, it seems to me, we encounter issues that are crucial to the notion of intratextuality.

Let's come back to the narrative materials sketched out above. Since the "Battle on the Ice" sequence embodies the culmination of those antagonisms set in place prior to it, shouldn't we expect to find within it a form of vertical montage that engages this placement? If it is possible to argue that the structural law informing the imagetrack has something to do with the obsessively triadic organization of the narrative material, then wouldn't it make more sense to seek the structural law, the fundamental movement, of the music in the music's articulation of the antagonisms that constitute the narrative dimension of the imagetrack? To do so requires a shift of focus. Instead of concentrating on the "dawn of anxious waiting" segment, it is necessary to (1) examine closely the actual musical articulation of the national antagonism and the "pinning" of the Teutonic wedge and (2) situate this musical material in the context of the piece as a whole. Only then can we even begin to talk about the rather dubious notion of structural laws.

A conflict, for Eisenstein the dialectician, ought to require a treatment that brings out its status as a conflict. Which may very well imply that unity requires disunity if it is to express a whole which is about discord. Strangely enough, this is exactly what seems to be going on in the actual attack of the Teutonic knights—a segment that Eisenstein chooses to ignore or, to put a slightly more flattering light on the matter, chooses to subsume beneath his discussion of the "dawn of anxious waiting" segment. The musical material that executes this attack is quite different from the material in the opening segment. From the point of view of the music alone, it repeats, not surprisingly, two separate moments in the score: (1) the orchestral and harmonic elements that were introduced in the sequence dramatizing the plunder of Pskov (referred to in Prokofiev's cantata as "The Crusaders in Pskov") and (2) the orchestral and harmonic material introduced in "Arise, ye Russian People" which accompanies the final moments of the Novogorod assembly sequence. As the score section titles suggest, the music here not only accompanies a conflict, it articulates a musical conflict which is inscribed in the structure of the cantata. Since this material would seem to be pertinent to the structural law of movement defining the music, it is worth considering more carefully.

Once the German cavalry appears, a brass motif is introduced which simulates diegetically a bugle call while also introducing a rather unstable harmonic package and a disorganized rhythmic pulse. The motif oscillates wildly between tight, whole step movements and jumps which, while only five steps apart, ultimately combine to create a melodic span of twelve steps within the motif. This material is repeated, and much like the "dawn of anxious waiting" segment, it is rhythmically synchronized with the gestures of the German bishop as he makes the sign of the (iron) cross while blessing the knights. Abruptly, this motif is given rhythmic foundation in the strings and percussion. I say "rhythmic foundation" because the pulsation of running eighth notes hammered out by the snares and tom-toms provides a diegetically serviceable "gallop" for the German cavalry charge which functions to support the brass motif. But melodically, the gallop is organized around a half-step oscillation in the strings that is as ominous as it is indecisive. One might also say, and it would certainly be in keeping with the narrative themes, the gallop sounds vulnerable because practically any additional melodic content would suffice to reorient it. Just thirty bars into the attack and following upon some reiterated brass cascades, the harmonic material from "The Crusaders in Pskov" is introduced by the choir. Aside from the fact that the words sung here contain self-referential allusions to "cymbal shod" feet, this material provides an harmonic envelope for the brass motif and the gallop by moving purposefully in whole steps within the structure of a minor triad. The function of this triadic progression is to give the in-

decisive movement in the lower strings direction vis-à-vis the tonal flow
of the cantata. In effect these materials taken together form the musical
"wedge" that articulates the movement of the German troops.

The wedge, once formed, accelerates and reaches a crescendo where
everything explodes into percussive chaos. At this moment in the cantata
we encounter, of course, the Russian forces who are introduced musi-
cally with material repeated from the "Arise, Ye Russian People" section
(which itself repeats material from the "Song About Alexander Nevsky"
section). Specifically, the Russian presence is announced with an "an-
swering" brass motif which is as tightly constructed as the German motif
is loose. Stridently inflected with strong double snare beats on the downbeat, this material creates the impression of almost stubborn stability.
However, no sooner is the "Arise" theme established than it is interrupted
by a repetition of the percussive explosion. This interruption is in turn
followed by a resumption of the "Arise" theme. Slowly we realize that
we are hearing the "pinning" of the wedge formation as we move back
and forth between the Russian and German musical "signatures."

As my allusion to the narrative theme would lead one to expect, from
this point forward the Russian musical material essentially divides into
two. On the one hand, we hear a continual, though intermittent, elaboration of the "Arise" theme. On the other hand, we also are introduced to
some absolutely new material which bursts upon us as a Sousa-like fanfare. It is in double time, and its aggressively major, triadic organization
allows this new material to assume the identity of the roguish hare. In
fact this material is first exploited in the attack upon the German wedge
from the rear by the Mikula (leader of the Muzhik militia), and it is used
to accompany the images of the rout. As "The Battle on the Ice" concludes, we hear a virtuosic exchange of themes where the brass motif that
inaugurated the German cavalry charge is ineluctably drowned out (in
the film the German soldiers literally fall through the ice on Lake Chud-
skoye) by the fanfare. When the last German soldier slips into the icy
water, the trapped middle note (G sharp) of the motif bends and slides
down after his vanishing cape.

On the basis of this, by no means exhaustive, description of the musical material, it can nevertheless be argued that Eisenstein has not accurately identified the structural commensurability of the imagetrack and
the soundtrack. What is clearly important in the structure of the cantata
is the harmonic and rhythmic articulation of the national antagonism. As
we watch the film of this antagonism, we actually hear what sounds like
the violation and displacement of neo-Gregorian church music by eth-

nically inflected Sousa-like marching music (setting aside for a moment the secular and conspicuously Western repertory music that concludes the film). It is this relation that, even in Eisenstein's terms, should dictate the discussion of the "dawn of anxious waiting" segment. If, as Stoïanova might argue, the music is constructing multiple and in this case clearly antagonistic subject positions, one would have to consider how these interact with the positions constituted by the images. Granted, there would appear to remain a high level of "correspondence" between the structural movement of both signifying practices, but this may have more to do with the specific intratextual field they define than with the gestures the sonoric and iconic signifiers allegedly share. As we shall see, there is a certain ominous quality to this correspondence.

Insofar as Eisenstein approaches filmmaking from within an hieroglyphic and therefore textual paradigm, he does so by taking literary and art historical disciplines as his points of departure. This is why, in his characterization of the affinity between music and pictures, he has immediate recourse to the clearly problematic category of "musical *imagery*." This is problematic because it situates reflection on music within a pictorial framework, where, in effect, what Eisenstein is seeking to demonstrate has already been smuggled into his descriptive terms. While it is certainly true that Eisenstein did not invent the notion of "musical imagery," this does not vitiate the fact that his explicit attempt to theorize the relation between music and image begins by accepting from disciplinary history the legacy of assuming the priority of iconicity. Though this places Eisenstein into rather close proximity to Ropars, he at least refuses to treat music as essentially *beyond* meaning.

No doubt what is odd about such a claim, even at this rudimentary level of elaboration, is that, as I have acknowledged, *Alexander Nevsky* was a genuinely collaborative effort. Sometimes footage was shot to follow musical material; other times footage dictated the preparation of the music.[27] The possibility of such cooperation would seem to require that Eisenstein be receptive to the specificity of the musical medium, and in fact he was. In Prokofiev's own essay about their collaboration, he stresses how Eisenstein's "respect for music was so great that at times he was prepared to cut or add to his sequences so as not to upset the balance of a musical episode."[28] Eisenstein repaid this compliment when he referred to Prokofiev as precisely the ally he and Eduard Tisse had been looking for in their "campaign of conquest of the sound film."[29] With so much goodwill, one wonders what could have led to the state of affairs I have outlined above. Yet, if we consider carefully the way Eisenstein actually discusses Prokofiev's talent as a composer and the specific nature of his achievement in scoring the film, then a plausible answer emerges.

In Eisenstein's homage to Prokofiev, "P-R-K-F-V" from 1946, he begins by characterizing the precision that defines the composer's magic as an "absolute exactitude in transposing musical imagery into a mathematically exact means of expression, which Prokofiev has harnassed with a bridle of steel."[30] The immediate context of Eisenstein's remarks was the tight production schedule imposed upon the Nevsky film project by the Soviet state, but their semantic texture says more than that Prokofiev simply was capable of working both quickly and reliably. Specifically, we see not just an insistence on the notion of musical imagery, but a characterization of the composer's labor that associates it with both mathematics and equestrianism. This association is not accidental. Later in the essay Eisenstein, in attempting to fathom the secret of Prokofiev's scoring technique, describes his "enormous, strong hands with steel fingers which force the keyboard to groan when he attacks it with all the elemental impetuosity of his temperament."[31] Or again later, as Prokofiev sits in the preview room watching the "rushes" his hands tap on the arms of his chair. What Eisenstein sees is "[h]is moving fingers grasp the structural canons governing the lengths of time and tempo in the edited pieces."[32] Two things are striking about these passages: (1) we see, particularly in relation to the earlier image of the "bridle," a metonymic displacement wherein the hands of the composer are understood to be "grasping" the presumably mathematical proportions of the film image, and (2) we recognize in the appeal to "structural canons" a reference to the laws of movement that Eisenstein believes to be the enabling conditions for the commensurability of image and music. There is an unmistakable preoccupation here with violence and with formal structure, both of which are thought to belong properly to musical composition.

Perhaps this is the time to recall Eisler's and Adorno's assessment of Eisenstein's discussion and underscore the irreducibly formal approach to music that characterizes it. So striking is this to Eisler and Adorno, that they are moved to compare the approach taken in Walt Disney's *Birds of a Feather* favorably to the one proposed by Eisenstein—a polemical barb if there ever was one since Adorno, in particular, was no friend of the "culture industry" and since Eisenstein often wrote patronizingly of Disney.[33] Extrapolating from their observations in the present context, I would argue that Eisenstein's formalism derives from his unexamined conviction that meaningful expression *requires* linguistic mediation. While it is certainly true that music can channel energy and give shape to aesthetic experience, Eisenstein apparently believes it must bond with pictures and or words to become articulate. Significantly, music bonds with images only at a level which is devoid of sense, that is, "pure" structure, and instead of gaining access to the formation of linguistic meaning, music is thus ravaged by the contents which it has helped to organize. What impressed Eisler and Adorno about Disney's approach is that it recognized that "musical associations" are effects of the way *both* images and sounds are intertextually inflected. By seeking to build up a direct correspondence between musical and pictorial movement, Eisenstein essentially forgets this insight. Only by assuming that meaning is somehow already secured in the pictorial or linguistic spheres can music be treated as possessing a mathematical profile that is to be "broken" by a Prokofievian rider. What permits there to be correspondences of the sort detailed by Eisenstein in "the dawn of anxious waiting" segment is the fact that Prokofiev accepts the fiction of "musical imagery," that is, sounds which have been ravished by iconic maps indicating the meaning value they can be given. No wonder the two men spoke so highly of their collaboration—it merely confirmed the disciplinary intercourse that defined their relations.

Recognizing this invites us to return to the film and pay particular attention to the diegetic presentation of musical performance or, put differently, the filmic articulation of images of music. The one moment to which I have already referred (cf., fn. 27) is interesting because of the way it heralds the Sousa-like fanfare that bursts in upon the film from nowhere, at least from the standpoint of the harmonic logic of the cantata. But two other moments might even more amply reward further scrutiny. I am thinking of the two presentations of the organist who is accompanying the German invaders as part of the bishop's entourage.

The first of these occurs in a comparatively brief (twenty-five shots) sequence that links the rally in Novgorod to the initial skirmish in the forest between Alexander's forces and the Germans. Thematically, the sequence is staged as a benediction of the German army and its leaders. As it opens, we see the backs of the bishop and his assistants framed before their field tent. The cut inaugurating the sequence serves as a downbeat, and the neo-Gregorian chant, "A foreigner, I expected by feet to be cymbal shod/ Victory to the arms of the cross bearers! Let the foe perish!" (in Latin), begins with bellow-driven pipe organ accompaniment and remains almost constant throughout the sequence—the moment of its brief interruption is very important. The harmonic properties of this material were first introduced in the "Crusaders in Pskov" sequence, and they have been described carefully above. In the sixth shot of this sequence, we are shown the organist and his organ framed against the sky as he plays in diegetic synchronization with the ritual of benediction (figure 7). Though we are not shown his fingers of steel, as a keyboardist who quite literally makes his instrument groan, he is certainly the closest thing to an inscription of Eisenstein's fantasy of the composer contained in the film. It is therefore important that the music in this sequence is strictly marked as diegetic in that the film here figures into its own iconic texture the very production of the musical soundtrack. Let us therefore scrutinize this moment carefully.

Figure 7

In shot seven we see the two hooded figures who are working the bellows that drive the organ (figure 8). Significantly, these embodiments of the enabling conditions of the music are shot so as to form a triad with the organist at the apex. As they open and close the "legs" of the bellows (derived, of course, from belly) not only do they keep time to the music, but they appear to wrestle with the apparatus that is "wedged" into the organ. Thus, the image of the music is staged in a way that graphically associates it with the battle strategy derived from Ignat's folktale. The otherwise fortuitous aspects of this association are systematically dispelled as the sequence unfolds. In shot ten we see the entire retinue

Figure 8

**Figure 9**

with the organist framed in the upper-right-hand corner of the image (figure 9). Tverdilo, the traitorous mayor of Pskov who is kneeling among the "blessed," is soon approached by his confederate, Ananias, who informs him that Alexander has decided to lead the Russians into battle. Tverdilo immediately crosses the frame to share this with the Grand Master (leader of the Teutonic knights). The benediction is abruptly halted as the Grand Master turns to address the soldiers. Perhaps the most dramatic sign of the termination of the ceremony is the cessation of the organ music and singing in midphrase. While it is certainly true that this development marks the hypocrisy of the knights, it is equally important that the Grand Master's desire to speak of the impending battle decisively interrupts the music.

As if to underscore the association between the music and the folktale, the Grand Master uses the space created by his silencing of the music to say, "Brother knights, King Alexander has dared to rise up against us, but God has punished him. His advance army is snowed up in the forest like a bear. We must make haste to hunt down the Russian beast." During his remarks we are shown, in shot sixteen, the organist listening to this characterization of the strategic situation of the Russian forces (figure 10). As the Grand Master's remarks conclude, the organist resumes the

**Figure 10**

neo-Gregorian theme. Thus an association is made within the film between the voice (which identifies the Russians as an animal trapped in the
forest—the "narrateme" of the folktale), the image (which straddles the
organist over the secular and sacred divisions that constitute the German
forces), and the music (which in its harmonic properties—a crowded
progression that inches repetitively through the steps of a minor triad—
loops the listener through a confident though curiously static phrase).
What is so suggestive about this association is that it stages the relation between the imagetrack and the soundtrack in a way that begins
to position the music as the mediation between them. The voice, which
seems fastened to the image, appears to control the music, even providing
it with a narrative meaning. But as this sequence concludes, the music
escapes this arrangement in a suggestive way.

In shot twenty-three we return to the setup of shot ten with the organist playing in the upper-right-hand corner of the frame as the knights
rush off to the ambush. The music remains diegetic. In shot twenty-four
we see the organist in close-up as he turns to stare into the camera and
then gaze offscreen to the left (figure 11). This is a gesture which falls into

**Figure 11**

the general filmic code of "transition" or "transfer," and sure enough,
in what presents itself as a point-of-view shot, we see in the subsequent
shot the trunks of two trees framed against the sky—the organist's gaze
positioned essentially between them.[34] (See figure 12.) Though the music
continues, it begins to become ambiguous. For one thing, we are not *certain* that what we are seeing in shot twenty-four is the view from the
organist's organ. Since the music continues, this conclusion does recom-
mend itself. However, because this shot is immediately followed by one
which, while still of the forest, is clearly not in the same space and time of
the preceding shot and because the music continues on into it, the music
sacrifices its ability to anchor the immediately preceding shot of the two
trees. In fact the music begins to wander away from the image, becoming

**Figure 12**

strangely nondiegetic and thus somewhat detached from the image and the voice. Significantly, this nondiegetic wandering is surrounded with specific iconic cues. The peculiar way in which this development is thus made to resonate with the specific terms of the folktale (not only do we have the narrateme of the trapped animal, but we also have the organist positioned between the trunks of two trees) remains nearly indeciperable until we come to the second, very brief, segment depicting the performing organist.

In this segment of only fourteen shots, we witness the turning of the tide in the battle. It begins with the piercing of the Russian defenses, which is witnessed in horror by the bishop who is positioned, as he was earlier, just outside his tent. The music is identical to that in the benediction sequence, and it is again marked as diegetic. Since the musical material that accompanied the charge of the German wedge included this music, its recurrence here has the effect of a reprise. In shot six of this segment we see the organist performing as he is suddenly set upon from behind by Vasilisa and—all importantly—Ignat (figure 13). He, and his organ, are trapped between the two, and he is thrown to the ground. As he falls and drags his hands across the keys, the neo-Gregorian theme degenerates into a row of desperately ascending notes. This is the last

**Figure 13**

time we hear this music. In the remaining eight shots of the segment, we witness the conspicuously symbolic collapse of the bishop's field tent. Significantly, its fall is perpetrated by Ignat who is shown in two separate shots energetically "wedging" his axe blade into the central pole of the tent (figure 14). As the tent falls, there is a distinctly nonvocal, nonmusical crash which immediately gives way to the Sousa-like fanfare that announces the Russian rout. As a consequence, this segment "rhymes" with the earlier one where the delirious pipe music announces the entry of the fanfare.

**Figure 14**

What we have been shown here is the "fate" of the musical soundtrack. Because the organist functions to inscribe the presence (both diegetic and nondiegetic) of musical composition, the sonoric and iconic details of his inscription work to give this presence meaning. It is a presence that extends beyond the music on the soundtrack to include the very fact of the musical soundtrack—something which Eisenstein was deeply involved in. When we see and hear the organist's diegetic performance choked off, we are invited to recognize this as an answer to the ambiguity opened in the earlier sequence where the organist's music wandered off into a space that reached beneath, or beyond, the voice and the image. Significantly, this wandering was visually channeled between the two tree trunks. As if to bridle this movement, and the entire possibility of the music's refusal of the guardianship of the voice and the image, the organist is later assaulted from behind by a woman warrior (Vasilisa, who becomes the "consolation prize" for Vasili when it is clear that Gavrilo's greater valor has won him Olga) and Ignat—the bearer of the strategic folktale. Literally, the musical soundtrack is violated by the image, or more specifically, by an image from a literary text—"The Hare and the Vixen." Moreover, this violation is coded in such a way that the musical inscription of the national antagonism is turned against the musical signifier so that, in effect, musical composition as a whole is cast into the role of the German vixen who is pinned and ravished by the voice and the image, that is, the presumably more reliable bearers of meaning. Consider, in this light, the inverted visual doubling of Olga and the organist (figures 15 and 16). Perhaps this is why the folktale, and Alexander's spontaneous Proppian analysis of it, became so central to the very core of *Alexander Nevsky*— the core is defined by an antagonism that formalism both instigates and vanquishes. Prokofiev has not been enlisted in the campaign to conquer the sound film; he has been made complicit with the conquering of sound within film.

**Figure 15**

**Figure 16**

It is in this sense, I would argue, that Eisenstein's insistence upon the strict linear commensurability of the music and the picture is a sham. What motivates it is not ill will, but inattention to the heterogeneous models of textuality that could be made to operate within a sound film. In spite of everything Eisenstein (and Prokofiev, for that matter) says about the specificity of the music as a montage element, it is clear that, as he says in another context, "the image remains the decisive factor of the audio-visual combination."[35] What makes the image decisive is not the rather obvious fact that we are discussing film, though this is certainly pertinent. Rather, what makes the image decisive is its relation to meaning, and specifically linguistic meaning. Though this is not the context in which to engage the vexed disciplinary matter of the relation between pictures and words, in his essay on "Imagery" Eisenstein does nevertheless make his dependency on literary materials—not just for images, but for his *notion* of the image—quite explicit.[36] Thus, the image remains "decisive" to the audio-visual combination because the image provides music with an iconic map that latently organizes the sonoric sign.

If at this point we begin guiding this discussion back in the direction of the text, then I would argue that Eisenstein effectively subordinates the textuality of music to a literary paradigm. He does this naively because neither he nor Prokofiev give any thought—as far as I know—to the paradigms of interdisciplinarity that already structure their collaboration. My operating assumption is, of course, that the "subtext" of the violation of music's hermeneutical virginity is the result of the unconscious functioning of an interdisciplinary paradigm—a paradigm that comprehends textuality, insofar as it does so at all, as a framework whose vertical dimension is defined by a profoundly antitextual reductionism. In other words, while the very concept of a rigorously articulated sound film would appear to embrace the necessary heterogeneity of the textual paradigm, the actual articulation of signifying practices is carried out in a manner that undermines textuality by subjecting it to the discipline of literary study. This is what was meant when earlier I argued that Eisenstein never managed to distinguish his analysis of the object (in this case, music and images) from the methodology he believed could properly articulate it aesthetically. His method, because of its disciplinary derivation, was already obscuring itself in the object constructed by a discipline Eisenstein was in no position to interrogate.[37] Were this not the case, perhaps he would not have gravitated immediately to that part of *Alexander Nevsky* which, while impressive, abandons the counterpuntal hopes that animated his earlier discussion of the sound film. These hopes would be better realized by beginning with the assumption elaborated by Stoïanova, namely, that music is organized by an indigenous, disciplinarily inflected model of textuality.

My own reading of *Alexander Nevsky* and Eisenstein's commentary upon it proceeds on the basis of Stoïanova's insight. In fact, I would argue that unless one accepts the framework of a textual perspective within music itself, it is impossible to experience the film in the way presented here. In this respect I have certainly fabricated a reading of the film that proposes to interfere in the "reality" of the work. Cortical to the framework of my analysis is the notion of intratextuality which seeks to gauge the effects of different disciplinary projects as they encounter one another in the heterogeneous space of the text. What enables one to "hear" the violation of the musical soundtrack is a form of attention that leads him/her to expect some kind of interpellative solicitation within the music. When this interpellative activity is subordinated to the image, that is, when the various subject positions constructed by the clash between secular art music and neo-Gregorian hymns are blended unnoticeably into the positions constructed by the imagetrack, then the textuality of music is essentially sacrificed to literature. If *Alexander Nevsky* was indeed "counterpuntal," that is, organized even *vertically* by the principle of montage, then these positions would be permitted to circulate and contend with those constituted by the image. In a most peculiar way Eisenstein fails to hear what, from the standpoint of the narrative, ought to be a rather noisy silence, the violation of the music. But, as I am clearly suggesting here, unless one is prepared to explore the dynamics of intratextuality, vertical montage will be consistently misrecognized because it is far too easy to fall victim to the disciplinary constraints that already operate in the hierarchized commerce among disciplines. As a consequence, instead of seeking points of expressive antagonism, one sets out in search of "correspondences." That this fate befell even Eisenstein, who had an ear and an eye for such antagonisms, testifies to the far-reaching power of disciplinary reason.

# 8

## * Conclusion: Textual Politics

The reader is now aware of the arguments advanced which illustrate that the textual analysis of film requires one to take stock of the peculiar coincidence between the film and the conditions of its study. Perhaps by turning our attention to how this issue arises within the preceding analysis of *Alexander Nevsky*, it will become possible to spell out the relation between intratextuality and the aims of antidisciplinary research in terms that will facilitate a more synthetic and retrospective discussion of the political stakes raised by the argument animating this book.

In chapter one it was argued that antidisciplinarity sought to oppose disciplinary reason by linking the texture of an artifact to the institutionally mediated social forces that set its limits as a particular embodiment of textuality. The establishment of such a linkage presupposes the ability to gauge how social forces operate in the constitution of borders which, by definition, bring different practices and agendas into relation with one another. In the final analysis this is what is decisive about the notion of intratextuality. Without it we gain access only to the comparatively homogeneous tissue of intertextual references that constitutes the hermeneutical field of a particular textual example. With it one can pose questions that bear on the institutional maintenance of the hermeneutical field as such—questions which quickly center upon the political problems of how institutions are constituted, reproduced, and transformed. These are not concerns which come *after* the particular text in question or which are properly "extrinsic" to it—they are concerns which address the very definition of the textual artifact as an artifact. Insofar as the artifact is meaningful to a particular social group, it is because its members continue to support the disciplinary structures (many of which are not "merely" academic) which read the artifact on their terms. "Intrinsic value" is, in fact, one such term and not simply because it alludes to something valuable that is realized within a particular text, but because, on top of that, it necessarily implies that texts have, presumably by virtue of their "natures," clear and distinct insides. In cases where the particular text in question is "mixed media," this is a tremendously difficult position to sustain. If media genuinely are different from one another (and thus indeed can be *mixed* ), then we are obliged to think about the forces which operate both to preserve and to alter the relevant differences among the various media as they come to be constituted as objects of research. Obviously, this has a special pertinence for sound films. But I would also argue, following Stoïanova, that even music (and not even necessarily vocal music) is constituted at the point where several different, institutionally regulated, "gestural" practices converge. This is precisely what the textual model is meant to affirm, which is no doubt why the discipline of musicology remains so resistant to the paradigm shift advocated by Stoïanova. Positivism within the field of cultural studies typically falters when confronted with the tenacious heterogeneity of social practices and struggles. Perhaps it is only because positivism has promised so much that such moments of hesitation are so energetically denied by its proponents.

However, it is one thing to insist upon the irreducibly interdisciplinary character of aesthetic phenomena; it is quite another to direct this insistence against disciplinary reason itself. The question that needs to be posed is: what is to be done with the intratextual evidence a particular reading produces? With regard to a film like *Alexander Nevsky* it is important that such evidence be used to dislodge the film from the disciplinary sites where it has traditionally been held. In effect this means producing readings of the film that seek to make it unmanageable, not so that it becomes meaningless, but so that the difficulties it can be made to pose appear resolvable only in relation to the disciplinary framework that otherwise organizes the reception of the film.[1] With Eisenstein's sound films in particular this requires us to examine the status of the music (as well as the other elements on the soundtrack) both intertextually (how *Alexander Nevsky* stands in relation to *Ivan the Terrible* or other professionally scored films of the period whether Soviet or not) and intratextually. Pursuing the latter would mean exploring how the soundtrack participates in the construction of the social parameters of the musical signifier, as well as how a filmicly inflected analysis of the *Alexander Nevsky* cantata might open up a way to challenge musicology's evaluation of Prokofiev's oeuvre. Of particular interest might well be those moments in the score where Prokofiev, in developing musical passages from film props, created musical gestures which would stand in a suggestively peculiar relation to both the classical repertory and Prokofiev's "own" style—his penchant for ingenius modulations.[2]

Obviously, the crucial point is not to challenge disciplinary readings simply by replacing them. Antidisciplinary research requires that readings reach from within artifacts to the paradigms that govern their interpretation and beyond these paradigms to the structures of disciplinary power that support them. In extending across this heterogeneous expanse, reading must submit to the transformations wrought upon it by the media through which it is conducted—I am thinking here of the way Kuntzel (at least on Bellour's interpretation) "reads" films by making videos. Practically, this means that part of a contemporary analysis of *Alexander Nevsky* might well include institutional militancy aimed at resisting the location of film studies within a literature department (where the traditional emphasis on narrative might make the symbolic "violation" of music harder to avoid). Here, reading becomes the interventions one might make in a faculty meeting designed to settle the question of where film studies ought to be institutionally housed. Instead, however, of merely invoking the fate of music in Eisenstein's film as a telling example, one might usefully see his/her vote as an effort to elaborate and prolong a reading of the film by altering the future history of the institutional boundaries where such a reading is to occur.

But why stop there? A reading of Eisenstein's film that seeks to pressure the limits of disciplinary power might well articulate itself as social insurgency aimed at supporting the refusal of "docility" imposed upon women within what has been called "rape culture." Here reading manifests itself in much the same "language" as a strike or a work stoppage, where the mute or boisterous defiance of the body becomes a group's "response" to an intransigent position at the bargaining table. As anyone who has ever participated in one knows, a strike is a move, a statement articulated in a different symbolic medium which nevertheless seeks to shift the balance of power—a balance that teeters on the edge of a *written* contract. When men and women act to "take back the night," they are contesting disciplinary power from within its sphere of influence. This struggle finds its echo in a reading of *Alexander Nevsky* that seeks to capture what within its intratextual dynamic can be made to provoke our participation in the dismantling of the disciplinary machinery that obscures the film's violence against women.

If we embrace the textual paradigm and seek to finish it, then such gestures as these ought not be seen as extrinsic to the reading of the film because ultimately they engage critically the very conditions of reading themselves. "Our" *Alexander Nevsky* thus *means* the transformations our readings engender regardless of at what level of the social they are located. Once we acknowledge that what enables a reading to "make sense" reaches well into the institutional field of the social, then it becomes possible to extend the range of what a reading ought to concern itself with. By refusing the antidisciplinary scope of the textual model, we implicitly condone critical readings that exhaust their oppositionality without seeking to transform the institutional conditions of their own authority. Of course, such a transformation cannot be achieved simply by adopting a paradigm that invites one to reflect upon its enabling conditions. But by the same token it just as surely cannot be achieved by endorsing a paradigm that insists that "mere readings" must give way to action when "real" social issues are at stake. This perspective has already produced enough intellectual paralysis within the academic Left, and it is no more worthy of perpetuation than is the self-indulgent complacency that leads academic intellectuals to think that simply writing a textual analysis of a Hitchcock film is tantamount to the articulation of an oppositional politics. The text, as a methodological field fraught with ambivalence and antagonisms, is divided against itself. To model analyses around it is to commit oneself to a process wherein the elaboration of a reading leads to those points where, at times, the reading must reconfigure itself in another mode of symbolic production. At other times, the reading must simply break off, inviting what has been excluded by it to pirate the reading and thus "pluralize" it. Here too the elaboration of a textual interpretation encounters what contests disciplinary power, but in a manner that refuses to speak for what our immediate social context is not yet prepared to integrate while nevertheless refusing to be silent about it. The point is to develop the institutional means whereby this insight is not exhausted in isolated moments of interpretation, and this implies inscribing such an insight in the paradigm that organizes the production of interpretive statements.

What antidisciplinarity thus depends upon is a notion of reading that understands how its specificity as a practice derives from the institutional field which surrounds it. Since this means that all readings have institutional implications, isn't it time that we began reading so as to undermine the institutions of disciplinary power at the very points where they have typically reproduced themselves with the greatest efficiency? Those who insist that such an aim is better realized by mobilizing the disenfranchised fail to see that "we" (Left academics) are to be counted among the disenfranchised—even if, by virtue of our professional status, "we" stand further away from the centers of misery and suffering. Why not labor to make education into an openly insurgent practice and break the hold that the vocational or professionally oriented disciplines have had on the commerce between the university and society? In this way we "redeem" (as Benjamin liked to say) the text, and we make its emergence worthwhile.

The present configuration of intellectual power in the "advanced" countries has given this labor a special urgency. Certainly, few within the teaching profession have failed to notice the journalistic attention currently being lavished upon academic politics. No less a mainstream public institution than the *New York Times* has taken to regularly devoting space to "trendy" academic conferences where academic intellectuals gather to debate questions of theory, power, and interpretation.[3] While it is true that the analytical perspective taken on such events is as shallow as it is patronizing, it is important not to overlook what journalistic coverage implies, namely, that the struggle over the humanities curriculum has become a public and therefore undeniably social issue. I would argue that textuality has a potentially vital role to play in such a context.

In scrutinizing the various analyses (both journalistic and scholarly) of academic politics, one is struck by the convergence of two lines of hostile argumentation. On the one hand, in a gesture that harks back to William Bennett's castigation of the sixties in his NEH report, "To Reclaim a Legacy,"[4] one finds the argument advanced that the so-called curriculum wars (among other like phenomena) at Stanford and elsewhere are due primarily to the smoldering *ressentiment* of sixties radicals who, when unable to win in the streets, were forced to retreat into the institutions of postsecondary learning. Of course, the very existence of such a concern belies the traditional conservative denial of education's role in the formation of cultural hegemony—one rarely protests the *loss* of something deemed insignificant. On the other hand, this perspective is often complemented by one that, in echoing the logic of the critique of "reverse discrimination," advances the argument that the recent push toward multiculturalism (hence the "crisis" in *the* humanities curriculum) is producing a new form of authoritarianism, no longer driven by the essentialism of "unity," but by the essentialism of "diversity." Here one encounters the hotly debated problem of "political correctness." These positions interact by demonstrating that, insofar as the radical politics of the sixties have had any practical consequences for American education whatsoever, they have degenerated into intolerant, dogmatic assertions of incommensurable differences. While it is certainly true that the new social movements organized around "identity politics" must guard against the xenophobia or racism that an obsession with political correctness can generate within them, their members need be no more vigilant than the adherents of liberal or conservative humanism who for centuries have confused "tolerance" with affirmation and empowerment—and have done so at tremendous costs.

How then does the text figure in such a debate? When we quarrel over a university curriculum we are, whether intentionally or not, engaging the problematic of disciplinary reason. Disciplines, after all, still form the organizing intellectual hubs of a curriculum. Moreover, when debating the contents of a humanities curriculum, a certain vision of interdisciplinary support and solidarity is *necessarily* presupposed. For D'Souza this vision exhausts itself in the talismanic phrase, "liberal education," but more typically it is rarely given explicit articulation, and this despite "the education President's" embrace of James Pinkerton's openly Kuhnian rhetoric of the "new paradigm." Instead, discussion often focuses on which cultural traditions (and their "textual" representatives) ought to be included in order to "diversify" the curriculum without, of course, compromising either the integrity of Western values or the clear conscience of those who want to "reason" through stereotypes. What consistently seems to elude serious discussion is the issue of the model of the disciplinary object that serves to coordinate the various components of the curriculum. In a country otherwise so preoccupied with democracy, it seems strange indeed that we have not yet attempted to generate a radically democratic paradigm for curricula in the humanities. To avoid this task in the name of making sure that Americans know what "they" ought to know is paradoxical to say the least. The Eurocentric notion of a Western core is no more satisfying than the "melting pot" ideology which it parrots. The point is to democratize the production of the pot, and it is not surprising that cultural conservatives have, of late, begun to call for an attenuation of democracy in post-secondary education.[5]

This is more than a question of structure, it is a question of aims. If one were to introduce here the antidisciplinary paradigm of textuality,

then it would become possible to insist that curricular revision ought not
be restricted to a prudent shuffling of contents, but that it ought to be
forced to confront the problem of disciplinary power as such. Curricular
expansionism, after all, is perfectly consistent with disciplinarity, unless
the model of what organizes this expansion is designed to interrogate
the sociopolitical relations that made the expansion so urgent in the first
place. Let us not forget that the war over the humanities curriculum is, in
fact, being waged, on one side, by partisans of the new social movements
who want to carry the radicalization of democracy into one of the centers
of its traditional legitimation—educational institutions. This is what empowerment is all about. Those who bemoan "political correctness" are
often those who prefer to reduce democracy to a topic of debate, rather
than actually participate in a debate where what, for them, passes as
"common sense" is no more essentially empowered than, say, euthanasia.

The text is useful here precisely because its ambivalent character gives
conceptual shape to this kind of interrogation. Why restrict the debates
over curricula to arguments about whether the Platonic dialogues ought
to be taught in conjunction with historical studies of slavery in Athens
(of course they should), when it is equally urgent to sort out what kind
of paradigm might support and legitimate the conjunction of these texts?
Including the previously excluded is politically neutralized when doing
so is carried out in the orbit of a paradigm which closes back in around
itself as soon as the credentials of its "initiates" have been verified. What
is distinctive about an antidisciplinary object or methodological field is
its aim to institutionalize a form of inclusivity that actually encourages
curricula to undergo legitimation crises—and not simply at the local level
of a particular institution, but at the level of the borders that distinguish
the local from the global. I would argue that the text gives academic intellectuals on the Left a way to conceptualize the link between the struggle
to make sense of a particular artifact, and the struggle to transform the
general conditions under which that construction takes on its cultural
value. Forging such a link might well create the conditions under which
the institutional quarantine imposed upon intellectuals of the so-called
sixties generation could be broken, without lapsing into a new essentialist authoritarianism—after all the model of textuality does not seek
to reify differences, but rather to put them in contact in a way that em-
powers those differences to engage and alter one another. The models
that have heretofore served to undergird the movement toward curricular
revision, have sought to prevent just such a development. Moreover, the
mass-mediated public sphere in this country has operated in a manner

that obscures, without resolving, this fact. Thus, there is an opportunity here for what I am calling textual politics.

This opportunity ought not be missed. In an intellectual context where D'Souza and others argue that the chief deleterious consequence of politicized scholarship is its censorious impact on public discourse, it is insufficient to argue that public discourse is already founded on political exclusions of specific discourses. Such a claim has the impact of implicitly validating D'Souza's position: obviously (he might argue) the reason that he cannot adequately articulate and defend his position is because "politically correct" discourse has so contaminated public discourse as to make a convincing articulation of his position impossible. Thus, the absence of debate stands forth as a resounding confirmation of the analysis, and D'Souza is invited to do what the "politically correct" are accused of doing, namely, silence others beginning, of course, with himself. Refusal parades as victimization. In order to locate this absence in such a refusal, it is necessary to move beyond the model of antinomous discourses struggling to occupy the same space. Textuality, by insisting upon the subversive pressure of the "not yet," provides a way of grasping what D'Souza most fundamentally refuses, namely, the necessity of articulating within one's own position the ambivalence that enables those in whose name the debate over "political correctness" is waged to appropriate it and, conceivably, even reject the antinomy this (non)debate tends to project into the discursive firmament itself. This is much more than a matter of anticipating, and to that extent identifying with, the others' position. It is a matter of inscribing within one's own position the possibility and necessity of a position which is obscured by what one opposes. Radical democracy ought to involve listening to those whose voices have been drowned out by the very voice of advocacy. Textual politics seek to frame the conditions under which this would be possible, and if the articulation of this politics requires that we hesitate suspiciously before the category of discourse, I believe the stakes warrant doing so.

The history I have fabricated here thus seeks to associate two moments: one in which certain systemic transformations in the structure of French intellectual power precipitated in the model of textuality; the other, now, when academic intellectuals are struggling to redefine the political parameters of the institutions in which, and against which, they work. My aim has been to' argue that the sociohistorical developments (the political birth of the new social movements, the *rapprochement* between mass culture and the academy, the institutional reconfiguration of disciplinary knowledge, etc.) inscribed in the emergence of textuality have acquired a new pertinence in the context of our present struggles over the humanities curriculum in postsecondary education and the political status of cultural interpretation within daily life. True to the paradigm argued for here, the two moments I have freely associated have been altered by the relation I have fabricated between them. This is no doubt more apparent in the case of the collective memory constructed here for the emergence of the text, since several before me have constructed this narrative rather differently. But perhaps the degree to which this relation alters the present is obscure primarily because we remain unsure as to the limits and range of our own readings, not because—as some would have it—text acts do not matter. Where, after all, is the historicity of the present to be located if not in the practices devoted to grasping it?

Of course, the paradigm used to associate these two historical moments also requires that one not treat them as components of a monadic crystallization that verges on blasting apart the historical continuum, as Benjamin would have it.[6] This is not because textuality refuses to accommodate the utopic, the not yet integrated, but because the movements pressuring us to finish the text and thereby associate these moments may very well not be interested in speaking from the space opened by Benjamin's ejaculations. Thus, the historical juncture fabricated here seeks to assume responsibility for the way it inevitably extends the reach of disciplinary power—Western knowledge really does alter what it knows—while also embracing the possibility that what resists such power, both from within and without, will, if given the room to speak, tell us something "we" are in no position to hear. About this, of course, we can *know* very little. Nevertheless, we must still do everything in our power to listen.

# ✳ Notes

*Introduction: The Two Texts*

1    Most immediately I am evoking the discussion of the book that takes place in the opening section of Jacques Derrida's *Of Grammatology*, trans. Gayatri Spivak (Baltimore: Johns Hopkins UP, 1978), 6–18, but in point of fact the effort to grasp the significance of printing as a psychosocial technology goes back quite a long way even within the modern period. Some relevant sources include: El Lissitzky's discussion of the "new book" in *El Lissitzky: Life, Letters, Texts*, ed. Sophie Lissitzky-Küppers (London: 1968 [original 1923]), 355–360; Lucien Febvre and Henri-Jean Martin, *The Coming of the Book: The Impact of Printing 1450–1800*, eds. Geoffrey Nowell-Smith and David Wootton, trans. David Gerard (London: New Left Books, 1976 [original, 1958]); Marshall McLuhan, *The Gutenburg Galaxy* (New York: New American Library, 1962); Elizabeth Eisenstein, *The Printing Press as Agent of Social Change* (Cambridge, Mass.: Cambridge UP, 1979); Hans Magnus Enzensburger, "The Virtues of the Needle and the Other Book," trans. Ingrid Eggers, *Discourse* 2 (Summer 1980): 53–59; Donald Lowe, *The History of Bourgeois Perception* (Chicago: U Chicago P, 1982), passim; Paul Hirst and Penny Wooley, *Social Relations and Human Attributes* (London: Tavistock Publications, 1982), 31–43; Walter Ong, *Orality and Literacy: The Technologizing of the Word* (London: Routledge, Chapman, and Hall, 1982); and Michel de Certeau, *The Practice of Everyday Life*, trans. Steven Rendall (Berkeley: U California P, 1984), 131–153. If one resituates Derrida's argument in the context established by these works, then it would appear he is arguing that the formation of subjectivity that accompanied the emergence of the book is being transformed by the social developments registered in the emergence of the text. The book is thus thought to be following the way of the subject who read it.

2    There are two other important traditions of reflection on "the text" that will no doubt come to mind for many readers. I am thinking, of course, of the enduring philological

tradition of "textual criticism" that is lucidly discussed in E. J. Kenney, *The Classical Text: Aspects of Editing in the Age of the Printed Book* (Berkeley: U California P, 1974), as well as the phenomenological text developed in the work of Wolfgang Iser and Paul Ricoeur. See in particular Wolfgang Iser, *The Implied Reader: Patterns of Communication in Prose Fiction from Bunyan to Beckett*, (Baltimore: Johns Hopkins UP, 1974), and Wolfgang Iser, *Prospecting: From Reader Response to Literary Anthropology* (Baltimore: Johns Hopkins UP, 1989), 258. For Ricoeur's perspective see Paul Ricoeur, *Hermeneutics and the Human Sciences*, ed. and trans. John B. Thompson (Cambridge, Mass.: Cambridge UP, 1981). Two aspects of the semiological text, which is the focus of this book, derive from these traditions and deserve some comment. From the philological tradition the text has retained the notion of material boundaries, or what within the tradition of textual criticism was understood as the definitive edition or version. Though philology tended to pose this issue in terms of the original, and therefore definitive, inscription of the writer's intentions, it nevertheless insisted upon the material force of what the text "said." Semiology appropriated the notion of material force while stripping it of its idealist account of a fixed meaning. From the phenomenological tradition the semiological text has retained the notion of the constitutive force of interpretation. Both Iser and Ricoeur emphasize the way the reader's engagement with what should properly be called the text functions as a context where the subjectivity of the reader is at stake in his/her production of meaning. Despite the fact that this tradition emphasizes the ethical problem of becoming the bearer of the writer's meaning, it foregrounds the problem of the subject's relation to a symbolic system which addresses him/her from afar. Obviously, these inheritances undergo profound change in the elaboration of textuality during the sixties and seventies in France.

3   Oswald Ducrot and Tzvetan Todorov, *Encyclopedic Dictionary of the Sciences of Language*, trans. Catherine Porter (Baltimore: Johns Hopkins UP, 1979 [original 1972]).

4   Robert Darnton, *The Business of the Enlightenment: A Publishing History of L'Encyclopédie* (Cambridge, Mass.: Cambridge UP, 1979), 522.

5   Jean-René Ladmiral, "La vocabulaire de la linguistique," *Quinzaine Littéraire* 145 (July 16–31, 1972): 22–23.

6   See the discussion of the relation between language and cultural creativity that transpires in the opening chapter of Wilhelm von Humboldt's *Linguistic Variability and Intellectual Development*, trans. George Buck and Frithjof Raven (Philadelphia: U Pennsylvania P, 1972).

7   It should be pointed out at this juncture that several commentaries on deconstructive criticism have had recourse to the model of the dictionary as a way to explain the logic of supplementation that is important to the notion of textuality I am seeking to elaborate in this book. See Roger Laporte's "Une double stratégie," *Ecarts* (Paris: Editions Galilée, 1976), 144–145, and Josué Harari's introduction to *Textual Strategies: Perspectives in Post-Structuralist Criticism* (Ithaca: Cornell UP, 1979), 17–72.

8   In addition to the essay of Jameson discussed below, one can find versions of this criticism in Edward Said, "Criticism Between Culture and System," in *The World, The Text, and the Critic* (Cambridge, Mass.: Harvard UP, 1983), 179–225; Richard Rorty, "Nineteenth-Century Idealism and Twentieth-Century Textualism" in *The Consequences of Pragmatism* (Minneapolis: U Minnesota P, 1982), 139–159; and Henri Meschonnic, "Politique, théorie et pratique de *Tel Quel*," *Cahiers du chemin* 15 (avril

1972), 57–101. Strictly speaking, Meschonnic emphasizes less the problem of referentiality than the more Gramscian problem of "organicity," but many of the political conclusions drawn are strikingly similar.

9   Fredric Jameson, "The Ideology of the Text," in *The Ideologies of Theory*, vol. 1 (Minneapolis: U Minnesota P, 1988), 17–71.

10  See Ernesto Laclau and Chantal Mouffe, *Hegemony and Socialist Strategy*, trans. W. Moore and P. Commack (London: New Left Books, 1985). Also Ernesto Laclau, *New Reflections on the Revolution of Our Times* (London: Verso, 1990).

11  Ernesto Laclau, "Populist Rupture and Discourse," *Screen Education* 34 (1980), 87.

12  For numerous suggestive formulations on the concept of utopia, see Ernst Bloch, *The Utopian Function of Art and Literature*, trans. Jack Zipes and Frank Mecklenburg (Cambridge, Mass.: Massachusetts Institute of Technology UP, 1988).

13  A particularly rich and terse formulation of the "reading formation" position is contained in Tony Bennett, "Texts, Readers, and Reading Formations," *The Bulletin of the Midwest Modern Language Association* 16, no. 1 (Spring 1983): 3–17. To be sure, Bennett's thinking has developed a great deal since this early formulation. Needless to say, it is this essay which I am taking to be illustrative of the position I am criticizing.

14  Julia Kristeva, "Problèmes de la Structuration du Texte," *Théorie d'ensemble* (Paris: Editions du Seuil, 1968), 297–299.

## 1    Textuality and the Critique of Disciplinary Reason

1   Roland Barthes, "From Work to Text," in *Image, Music, Text*, trans. Stephen Heath (New York: Hill and Wang, 1977), 155–164. Also Roland Barthes, "De l'oeuvre au texte," in *Revue d'esthétique* 3 (1971): 225–232. In addition there is a very interesting discussion of the text's relation to the structures and dynamics of disciplinarity in Barthes's "Research: The Young," *The Rustle of Language*, trans. Richard Howard (New York: Hill and Wang, 1986), 69–75. Originally published as an introduction to a special issue of *Communications* on textual theory as a research tool, this piece confirms and extends a number of the theses that often seem only implicit in "From Work to Text."

2   Two representative statements on this issue in addition to Jameson's are those of Alex Callinicos, *Against Postmodernism: A Marxist Critique* (New York: St. Martins P, 1990), 68–73 passim, and Andreas Huyssen, "Mapping the Postmodern" in *New German Critique*, no. 33 (1984), 5–52.

3   There is a tradition of this reflection within the French "history of science" that reaches back at least to Koyré and perhaps even to Comte, but which for my purposes can be documented by referring the reader to Georges Canguilhem, *On the Normal and the Pathological*, trans. Carolyn Fawcett (Dordrecht and Boston: D. Reidel Publishing, 1978); Louis Althusser, *For Marx*, trans. Ben Brewster (New York: Vintage Books, 1970); Louis Althusser and Etienne Balibar, *Reading Capital*, trans. Ben Brewster (London: Verso, 1979); Michel Foucault, *The Order of Things* (New York: Vintage Books, 1973); and Pierre Macherey, *A Theory of Literary Production*, trans. Geoffrey Wall (London: Routledge and Kegan Paul, 1978).

4   The tradition I am evoking here is an enduring and diversified one. Within the late modern period it is most immediately associated with the works of Hans-Georg Gadamer, *Truth and Method*, trans. Garrett Barden and John Cumming (New York:

Continuum Books, 1982); Karl Otto Appel, "Communication and the Foundation
of the Humanities" in *Man and World* 5 (1972), 3–37; and Paul Ricoeur, *Hermeneutics and the Human Sciences*, ed. John B. Thompson, trans. John B. Thompson
(Cambridge, UK: Cambridge UP, 1981).

5    The number of interesting works on May 1968 in Paris continues to grow. For a sense
of the contextual dynamics I am evoking, see at least the following sources. Henri
Lefebvre, *The Explosion*, trans. Alfred Ehrenfeld (New York: Monthly Review P,
1969); Daniel Singer, *Prelude to the Revolution* (New York: Hill and Wang, 1970);
*Reflections on the Revolution in France: 1968*, ed. Charles Posner (New York: Pen-
guin Books, 1970); *Mai 1968 en France*, Jean Thibaudeau (Paris: Editions du Seuil,
1970) for the "friends of the text" version (Sollers has an introduction to this volume,
"Printemps Rouge"); and if one wants a more "immediate" sense of the institutional
implications, it is worth consulting either the columns written by Alain Touraine for
*Le Monde* during the spring and summer of 1972 when the "reforms" provoked by the
events of May were being instituted or the later book by Jean-Louis Schefer, *L'Espèce
de chose melancholie* (Paris: Flammarion, 1978).

6    See the papers collected in *Interdisciplinarity*, eds. Léo Apostel, Guy Berger, Asa
Briggs, and Guy Michaud (Paris: Organization for Economic Cooperation and Development, 1972).

7    I am thinking here in particular of the work being conducted by the scholars associated
with the organization called GRIP (Group for Research into the Institutionalization
and Professionalization of Literary Studies) much of which is, unfortunately, only
available in the organization's research reports and newsletters.

8    Thomas Kuhn, *The Structure of Scientific Revolutions* (Chicago: U Chicago P, 1969)
and "Second Thoughts on Paradigms" in *The Essential Tension* (Chicago: U Chicago P, 1977). My reading of these pieces has been much influenced by Gayatri Spivak's
discussion of discipline in her "Revolutions That As Yet Have No Model: Derrida's
*Limited Inc.*" in *Diacritics* 10, no. 4 (December 1980): 29–49.

9    Roland Barthes, "The Death of the Author" in *Image, Music, Text* 142–148.

10   Edward Said, "Criticism Between Culture and System," in *The World, The Text, and
the Critic* (Cambridge, Mass.: Harvard UP, 1983), 179–225.

11   Though it would take me too far afield to detail it here, there is an important—one
might even say, formative—"dialogue" between Barthes and Foucault on the notion
of the author. Introduced in the mid-fifties by Robert Mauyi, Foucault and Barthes
spent considerable time in each other's company while in Paris. As early as 1960, in
the essays later collected as *Critical Essays*, Barthes identifies the author as a polemical
target. In the piece "Authors and Writers," he establishes an opposition that situates the author as a historical precipitate aligned functionally with the priesthood. In
*Criticism and Truth*, written only six years later, Barthes first associates the author
and death by indicating the conservative morbidity underlying Picard's defense of the
institutional reading of the French canon. By 1968, of course, Barthes has refigured the
author's relation to death in order to argue that this means of conceptually policing
the act of reading has been outdistanced by both contemporary literary production
and theory. One year later Foucault enters the fray with *The Archaeology of Knowledge* (where the author is attacked as a symptom of our methodological investment
in continuity) and "What is an Author?" In the latter piece Foucault openly engages

Barthes project by attempting to specify its historical coordinates. There is, however, both here and in "The Order of Discourse" (Foucault's inaugural lecture) a gentle rebuke aimed in Barthes's direction, one designed to caution Barthes about the excesses of historicist projection. Moreover, in "What is an Author?" Foucault increases the polemical force of his rebuke by pointedly attacking a position Barthes was increasingly to align himself with, namely, that of Derrida's. What is assailed here is the risk of transcendentalizing the absent origin of writing in dancing on the grave of the author. Clearly, despite these differences the rethinking of the relation between agency and subjectivity that was to characterize the work of both writers is what is at issue in their "dialogue." Interestingly, just before they died both Barthes and Foucault were involved in recasting the transcendental horizon as "power" in order both to avoid and register it. See, in particular, Barthes's "Inaugural Lecture," *A Barthes Reader*, ed. Susan Sontag (New York: Hill and Wang, 1982), 457–478.

12   The term "sciences humaines" confronts the translator with a difficult task. Taking it literally reduces it to nonsense because Americans (in particular) do not typically refer to something called the "human sciences" as an academic category. Translating it as "the social sciences" restricts its scope because the French use the term to include those aspects of the "humanities" Americans typically oppose to the social sciences. I have kept the phrase "human sciences" because, with these qualifications, I hope to signal that Foucault is referring to all the disciplines that engage in scientific or aesthetic reflection on the human subject.

13   There is an important discussion of the dynamics of institutionalization that has inspired my own analysis here in Samuel Weber's *Institutions of Interpretation* (Minneapolis: U Minnesota P, 1987).

14   One of the most interesting and fruitful attempts to demonstrate the social character of even "hard" scientific facts has been Bruno Latour's and Steve Woolgar's *Laboratory Life* (Beverly Hills: Sage Publications, 1979). Though they make little effort to detail the disciplinary aspects of their analysis, it would not be difficult to do so, particularly once the notion of discipline is extended beyond the domain of academic specializations.

15   René Girard, "From Mimetic Desire to the Monstrous Double," *Violence and the Sacred*, trans. Paul Gregory (Baltimore: Johns Hopkins UP, 1977), 143–168. A surprising corroboration of Girard's perspective is contained in Laurence Veysey's *The Emergence of the American University* (Chicago: U Chicago P, 1965) where academic disciplines, which figure prominently in Veysey's account, are linked to the dynamics of a secularized and thus displaced piety.

16   Frank Kermode, "The Institutional Control of Interpretation," *Salmagundi* 43 (1979), 72–86.

17   Paul de Man, "Resistance to Theory," *The Resistance to Theory* (Minneapolis: U Minnesota P, 1986), 15.

18   Though it would take me too far afield to elaborate it, a case could be made for seeing Foucault's substitution of "genealogy" for history (and "archeaology," for that matter) as an attempt to register the impact of textuality on the discipline of history. This seems particularly plausible when one compares the descriptive tropes used to characterize the genealogical enterprise—moments of emergence, intersections of developmental lines, permeation of boundaries, etc.—with those used by Barthes and

others to evoke the text. As such, I would argue that this is further evidence of the, albeit unthematized, solidarity between the theory of textuality and the analysis of disciplinary power.

19 Michel Foucault, "What is an Author?" *The Foucault Reader*, ed. Paul Rabinow (New York: Pantheon Books, 1984), 113–117 in particular.

**2** *The Text Goes Pop*

1 Portions of this chapter were first presented at the conference "Turning Points in History" in Amsterdam, September 26–30, 1988 in the workshop "Aspects of Popular Culture." This is a revised version of what appeared in the conference proceedings published through the *History of European Ideas* by Pergamon Press. See John Mowitt, "The Coming of the Text: The Text of Publicity," *HEI* 11 (1989): 573–582. I kindly thank Pergamon Press for permission to reproduce these materials here.

2 Roland Barthes, *The Fashion System*, trans. Matthew Ward and Richard Howard (New York: Hill and Wang, 1983), 295–299.

3 Louis Althusser and Etienne Balibar, *Reading Capital*, trans. Ben Brewster (London: Verso Books, 1979), part 2 passim. For the reading I am giving to this important analytic concept, see the book cited earlier, *Hegemony and Socialist Strategy* by Ernesto Laclau and Chantal Mouffe.

4 Roland Barthes, "Literature Today," *Critical Essays*, trans. Richard Howard (Northwestern: Northwestern UP, 1972), 152–153. This extrapolation of fashion recurs in Barthes's work from the period. See also Barthes, "Literature and Signification," *Critical Essays*, 265. Significantly, both of these "responses" were solicited by *Tel Quel*.

5 Roland Barthes, "Historical Discourse," *Introduction to Structuralism*, trans. Peter Wexler, ed. Michael Lane (New York: Harper Torchbooks, 1970), 145–155.

6 Barthes's relation to the events of May 1968 is discussed in precisely the terms I am proposing in his "Writing the Event," *The Rustle of Language*, trans. Richard Howard (New York: Hill and Wang, 1986), 149–154.

7 Walter Benjamin, *Charles Baudelaire: A Lyric Poet in the Era of Late Capitalism*, trans. Harry Zohn (London: New Left Books, 1973), 113–138. For Barthes's own gloss on the notion of shock as it is utilized within the German Marxist tradition, see his "Brecht and Discourse: A Contribution to the Study of Discursivity," *The Rustle of Language*, 212–222.

8 This concept is derived from the work of Theodor Adorno where it has been lucidly discussed in the following two pieces: *Aesthetic Theory*, trans. Christopher Lenhardt, eds. Gretel Adorno and Rolf Tiedemann (London: Routledge, Kegan Paul, 1984), 257–259, and "Lyric Poetry and Society," *Telos* 20 (Summer 1974): 56–71.

9 *Théorie d'ensemble*, eds. Philippe Sollers et al. (Paris: Editions du Seuil, 1968).

10 Jacques Derrida, *Positions*, trans. Alan Bass (Chicago: U Chicago P, 1981), 37–96.

11 *La Nouvelle Critique's* solicitation of *Tel Quel* extended well beyond the offer to open its pages to the debate under discussion here. In fact, this debate was exploited by the magazine to promote a colloquium devoted to the theme "Littérature et idéologies" that transpired in the provincial town of Cluny between April 2 and 4, 1970. The proceedings of this conference were then published in a special issue of the magazine, *La Nouvelle Critique*, "La colloque de Cluny II, Littérature et idéologies," spécial 39 bis (Paris: 1970). Most of the writers affiliated with *Tel Quel* were present, and even when

they were not delivering papers, their concerns set the terms of most of the debates. In light of this it may seem strange to present *LNC* as an embodiment of the logic of mass culture, but actually I think there are two good reasons for doing so. On the one hand, *LNC* was certainly not alone in its solicitation of the *Tel Quel* intellectuals. Sollers, Barthes, Kristeva, and others were frequently being invited to contribute, in one forum or another (interview, written commentary, or a simple statement of opinion either in print or on television) to a number of unquestionably "popular" venues. For example, Sollers gave an important early interview to *France Nouvelle* in the spring of 1967, and several of the *Tel Quel* writers appeared on Bernard Pivot's celebrated talk show *Apostrophe* throughout the late sixties and early seventies (for an illuminating discussion of the cultural function played by Pivot's program, see Steven Heath, "Friday Night Books" in *A New History of French Literature*, ed. Denis Hollier [Cambridge Mass.: Harvard UP, 1989] 1054–1060). *LNC* was thus not only following suit, it was actively (as is clear in the editorial statement) entering into the spiral of mass cultural practices, and even if it managed to keep its distance from that which we would unhesitatingly designate as the worst of mass culture, it is clear that the text whose theory it sought to engage was undeniably woven into the fabric of commodity discourse. On the other hand, precisely because *LNC* was (and remains) comparatively unmarked or uncompromised by the demands of mass culture, its demonstrative value in the present context is particularly high. That is, if it is possible to show that *even* in a venue like *LNC* the text is indissociable from the logic of mass culture, then the general claim concerning the text's relation to the cultural dynamics of fashion is all the more secure.

12    The most systematic attempt to situate *La Nouvelle Critique* (as well as other periodicals associated with the PCF) in this moment of French political history remains George Lichtheim's in *Marxism in Modern France* (New York: Columbia UP, 1966). In tracing what he calls the "transformation of Marxist theory" during the sixties, Lichtheim argues that communist intellectuals were faced with two decisive developments: one, the definitive waning of the political meaning of the Resistance which had been key to communist electoral strength since the war; and two, the impact of modernization, particularly of the media, on national political discourse. Concerning the first issue, one has only to acknowledge the fact that during the sixties the PCF was actively seeking to form coalitions with the various socialist and liberal factions of the noncommunist Left to recognize that this might well have implications for an opinion magazine like *La Nouvelle Critique*. Since the issue of technological innovation and its implications for the formation of readership are explicitly addressed in the editorial statement, it is clear that something like modernization is indeed prompting such local concerns. Specifically though, Lichtheim argues that confronted with this situation Left intellectuals split into two camps, those who stayed within the party and consequently lapsed into the pessimism of defensive orthodoxy and those who were primarily active as academics and who seized this opportunity to begin renovating Marxist theory from the outside. Clearly, this might well explain what is happening at the offices of *La Nouvelle Critique*. For another discussion of these same issues that centers on the impact of Althusser's work, see Mark Poster, *Existential Marxism in Postwar France* (Princeton: Princeton UP, 1975), chap. 8.

13    Though some may feel that I am placing undue emphasis on the history of a single periodical, it is worth pointing out that *La Nouvelle Critique* was not alone in its

mid-decade crisis. In fact, the issue of *Revue d'ésthétique* in which Barthes published "From Work to Text" is part of a new series begun by that periodical in the early seventies.

14  Régis Debray, *Teachers, Writers, Celebrities*, trans. David Macey (London: Verso Books, 1981), part 2 passim.

15  The tradition that has defined itself by defending "civilization" from the ravages of mass culture dates from the very inception of the latter. This suggests what a painstaking analysis would no doubt bear out, namely, that "mass culture," as a diagnostic category, is an effect of the effort to obscure the contradictions of what Norbert Elias called "the civilizing process," as they manifest themselves within the discourses of cultural criticism. Perhaps the most recent contribution to this tradition, Allan Bloom's *The Closing of the American Mind* (New York: Simon and Schuster, 1987), not only confirms the extent to which this discussion has come to focus on the institutional organization of knowledge, but it reveals the extent to which this tradition is willing to compromise its universalist pretensions by blithely equating America with the position held by "civilization" in the older agonistic formula: mass culture vs. civilization. Though Bloom distinguishes himself from a precursor like Matthew Arnold by attempting to ground his diatribe in the specific practices of the university, his ideological aims cannot bear such particularization without sacrificing the transcendental stature that gives them what critical punch they have. To this extent even his work respects the limits of this tradition.

16  See in particular, Régis Debray, op. cit., and Pierre Bourdieu, *Homo Academicus*, trans. Peter Collier (Stanford: Stanford UP, 1988). Two of Bourdieu's earlier essays on education have been influential for Debray and thus deserve citation. "Intellectual Field and Creative Project" and "Systems of Education and Systems of Thought" in *Knowledge and Control*, ed. M. F. D. Young (London: Macmillan, 1971), 161–207.

17  Foucault makes this remark at the close of his introduction to *Discipline and Punish*, trans. Alan Sheridan (New York: Pantheon Books, 1978), 31. More than a simple rejection of traditional historicism, this point resonates with Benjamin's strategy of "backing into the future," that is, reading the historical record with an eye toward enabling those in the present to redeem the irreversible loss of the past by producing a future without precedent. Though Foucault demurs on Benjamin's messianism, both writers succeed in drawing our attention to that which in the present will come to animate the historical struggle for a different future.

18  Jürgen Habermas, *The Structural Transformation of the Public Sphere*, (Cambridge, Mass.: Massachusetts Institute of Technology P, 1990). Also, one should consult his encyclopedia entry "The Public Sphere," trans. Frank and Sarah Lennox, in *New German Critique* 3 (1974): 49–55. As I make plain in the body of the text, Habermas's work on the public sphere has not terminated with these pieces. Some of the relevant elaborations include: *Towards a Rational Society*, trans. Jeremy Shapiro (Boston: Beacon Press, 1968), particularly chaps. 1, 5, and 6; *Theory and Practice*, trans. John Viertel (Boston: Beacon Press, 1973), particularly the introduction and chap. 4; *Legitimation Crisis*, trans. Thomas McCarthy (Boston: Beacon Press, 1975), passim; and *Communication and the Evolution of Society*, trans. Thomas McCarthy (Boston: Beacon Press, 1979), particularly chaps. 3, 4, and 5.

19  Jürgen Habermas, "The University in a Democracy: Democratization of the University" *Towards a Rational Society*, 1–12.

20   Terry Eagleton, *The Function of Criticism* (London: Verso Books, 1984), 87.

21   Jean-François Lyotard, *The Postmodern Condition*, trans. Brian Massumi (Minneapolis: U Minnesota P, 1985), 60–67.

22   *Change*, under the editorship of Jean-Pierre Faye (previously a member of the *Tel Quel* editorial board), emerged as a splinter journal within du Seuil toward the end of the sixties. Though initially this split seemed motivated by a professional conflict between Sollers and Faye, its nasty ad hominem character might, in light of Debray's analysis (a writer who, perhaps ironically, figures in the rivalry between Sollers and Faye), be read as a desperate attempt by Faye to avoid the inevitable, namely, the depoliticization of the intellectual public sphere. For Faye's position in this debate, see the interview with him in *La Gazette de Lausanne* (October 10–11, 1970), or his interview with Bettina Knapp in *L'ésprit créateur* 13, no. 1 (1973): 71–83. For Sollers's position see "Vérité d'une marchandise: le bluff *Change*" *Tel Quel* 43 (Autumn 1970): 71–96.

23   This is a concept I am borrowing from Mikhail Bakhtin. See in particular his, *The Dialogic Imagination*, trans. Caryl Emerson (Austin: U Texas P, 1984), 272–274, and *Problems of Dostoevsky's Poetics*, trans. Caryl Emerson (Minneapolis: U Minnesota P, 1984), 182–185. By evoking it here I mean to suggest that the discursively embodied interests defining the social field of Parisian intellectuals toward the end of the sixties were not simply diverse or contradictory, but intensely interactive. One's "own" words were indelibly marked by the roar of the discursive crowd.

24   Gilles Deleuze, "A propos des nouveaux philosophes et d'un probléme plus général," a supplement to *Minuit* 24 (May 1977).

25   Michel Foucault, "What is an Author" *The Foucault Reader*, ed. Paul Rabinow (New York: Pantheon Books, 1984), 101–120.

26   Raymond Bellour, *Le Livre des autres* (Paris: Union Générale d'Editions, 1973), 207.

27   Surprisingly, even in Jacques Derrida's otherwise probing and at moments tormented discussion of the "de Man affair," there is an unhinged assault on journalism and the discourses of publicity. The tenor of Derrida's comments might lead one to conclude that up until the moment when the de Man story broke academia had been untouched by such practices. His assault effectively eliminates the distinction between the words "bad" and "publicity" as they appear in the expression "bad publicity." Actually, de Man's tragedy only makes explicit what is obvious, namely, that professors often write or have written journalism and that the discourse of publicity has always already mediated the reception of such writing. See Jacques Derrida, "Like the Sound of the Sea Deep within a Shell: Paul de Man's War," trans. Peggy Kamuf, *Critical Inquiry* 14 (Spring 1988): 590–652. I return to the theme of "political correctness" in my concluding chapter.

**3**   *The Text* tel quel: *Derrida's Play*

1   Julia Kristeva makes this point explicitly in her autobiographical essay, "My Memory's Hyperbole," trans. Athena Viscusi, *The Female Autograph* eds. Domna Stanton and Jeanine Plottel (New York: New York Literary Forum, 1984), 268. It is also worth noting here that not long after the journal's inception, Editions du Seuil inaugurated the prestigious "Collection 'Tel Quel' "; a press series under various editorships that did much to disseminate the academic influence of *Tel Quel*.

2   Two other writers who worked in affiliation with *Tel Quel* during the sixties and

seventies, and who helped to elaborate the specifically interdisciplinary character of textuality, were Marcelin Pleynet and Jean-Joseph Goux. Though neither Pleynet nor Goux wrote extended theoretical essays on the text, their work in the fields of art history, anthropology, political economy, and psychology drew extensively on the textual model. In his discussion of Mondrian's use of color, for example, Pleynet explicitly sought to illustrate how the Derridean notion of the "trace" could be utilized to delineate how Mondrian's canvases contested the paradigms undergirding the "system of painting." His work, nevertheless, anticipates some of the issues explored in Derrida's *The Truth in Painting* by nine years. Goux, whose fusion (or confrontation) of Marx and Freud was one of the most fruitful of the period, drew on the Kristevean discussion of textuality in order to radicalize Marx's insight into the status of money as a "general equivalent." Though less a theoretical interrogation of the paradigms of political economy than a revision and intensification of the Marxian breakthrough, Goux's work established a synthetic framework against which Kristeva's feminism was forged, while also anticipating some of the theoretical innovations we currently associate with post-Marxism. For examples of their work in English, see Marcelin Pleynet, *Painting and System*, trans. Sima Godfrey (Chicago: U of Chicago P, 1984), and Jean-Joseph Goux, *Symbolic Economies: After Marx and Freud*, trans. Jennifer Gage (Ithaca: Cornell UP, 1990).

3    Paul Valéry, *Tel Quel*, vols. 1 and 2 (Paris: Editions Gallimard, 1941–1943). Though in the first issue of *Tel Quel* (the quarterly) the name is presented as though it derived from a translation of Nietzsche (typically undocumented), in the "Declaration" it is Valéry's work that is cited, and the obvious titular precedence is undeniable.

4    Philippe Sollers (though unsigned), "Déclaration," *Tel Quel* 1 (1960), 3–4.

5    There are a number of useful discussions of this debate now in print. Two of the most pertinent for my purposes are Serge Doubrovsky, *The New Criticism in France*, trans. Derek Coltman (Chicago: U of Chicago P, 1973); and Philip Thody's introduction to Roland Barthes, *Criticism and Truth*, trans. Katrine Pilcher Keuneman (Minneapolis: U of Minnesota P, 1987).

6    Terry Eagleton, *The Function of Criticism* (London: Verso Editions, 1984), 107–108.

7    Jacques Derrida, "The Law of Genre," trans. Avital Ronell, *Glyph* 7 (1980): 202–229. Though the reading of Blanchot that defines this essay never explicitly broaches the issue of the generic problems posed by Derrida's own text, it is easy to see how the general propositions would apply.

8    Philippe Lacoue-Labarthe, "Typographie," *Mimesis des Articulations* (Paris: Editions Aubier Flammarion, 1975), 165–224. In this connection, and especially since I have made an issue of the debt owed to *Tel Quel* by the theorists of textuality, it is worth mentioning Paul Valéry's discussion of the relation between philosophy and writing which is spread throughout his *Cahiers*. Derrida makes much of this in his discussion of Valéry in "Qual Quelle: Valéry's Sources," trans. Alan Bass, *Margins of Philosophy* (Chicago: U of Chicago P, 1982), 273–306. Though the words of Derrida's title derive from the *Cahiers* and have little explicitly to do with *Tel Quel*, they do plainly evoke the journal's title and *its* "source."

9    Jacques Derrida, *Edmund Husserl's "Origin of Geometry": An Introduction*, trans. John P. Leavey (Stony Brook: Nicholas Hays, 1978), 88.

10   Jacques Derrida, "Force and Signification," *Writing and Difference*, trans. Alan Bass (Chicago: U of Chicago P, 1978), 3–30.

11   Derrida, "Force and Signification," 8.

12   Jacques Derrida, *Of Grammatology*, trans. Gayatri Chakravorty Spivak (Baltimore: Johns Hopkins UP, 1976). See also "De la grammatologie," *Critique* 21, no. 223 (December 1965): 1016–1042 and 22, no. 224 (January 1966): 23–53.

13   Derrida, *Of Grammatology*, 65.

14   Derrida, *Of Grammatology*, 149 and 158.

15   In the "letter" Derrida appends to the edition of *Limited Inc.* edited by Gerald Graff, he returns to this question and develops it in ways that resonate strongly with the argument advanced here. Specifically, Derrida rewrites the phrase, "there is nothing outside the text," as "there is only context," picking up on a homonymic pun he had introduced elsewhere in the phrase, "*ce q'on texte*," as a way to gloss the notion of practice. Rather than develop the notion of "contextuality" that erupts here, Derrida simply stresses that he found the "initial" phrase more provocative. See *Limited Inc.*, ed. Gerald Graff (Evanston: Northwestern UP, 1988), 136.

16   Derrida, *Writing and Difference*, 199.

17   Derrida in recent years has made several attempts to connect his grammatological critique to a more institutionally focused critique of knowledge. See in particular, "The Principle of Reason: The University in the Eyes of its Pupils," *Diacritics* 13, no. 3 (1983): 3–20; "On Colleges and Philosophy," *Institute of Contemporary Arts Documents* 5 (1986); "The Age of Hegel," *Demarcating the Disciplines* (Minneapolis: U of Minnesota P, 1987), 3–43; and "Où commence et comment finit un corps enseignant," *Politiques de la philosophie*, ed. Dominique Grisoni (Paris: Editions Grasset et Fasquelle, 1976), 57–97.

18   Jacques Derrida, *Speech and Phenomenon*, trans. David B. Allison (Northwestern UP: Evanston, 1973), 112–113.

19   The recent scandal erupting around the discovery of Paul de Man's early critical essays, essays in which de Man appears to align himself with the fascist Right in prewar Belgium, has obliged Derrida (among others) to address seriously the political implications of deconstructive criticism. Though much has been said on both sides of this issue (see *Critical Inquiry* 14, no. 3 (Spring 1988) and 15, no. 4 (Summer 1989) in particular), the best way to assess Derrida's reading of fascism in relation to his own project is to consult his recent *Of Spirit: Heidegger and the Question*. Trans. Geoffrey Bennington and Rachel Bowlby (Chicago: U of Chicago P, 1989) where, through a reading of his own prior readings of Heidegger (among other things), this aspect of his project is addressed at length.

20   Derrida, *Of Grammatology*, 18.

21   Jacques Derrida, *The Truth in Painting*, trans. Geoffrey Bennington and Ian McLeod (Chicago: U of Chicago P, 1987), 175–181.

22   Jacques Derrida, *Positions*, trans. Alan Bass (Chicago: U of Chicago P, 1981), 90–91.

23   Mikhail Bakhtin, *Rabelais and His World*, trans. Helene Iswolsky (Cambridge: Massachusetts Institute of Technology P, 1968), 1–58.

**4**   *The Text* tel quel: *Kristeva's Productivity*

1   Julia Kristeva, *The Kristeva Reader*, ed. and trans. Toril Moi (New York: Columbia UP, 1986), 74–88.

2   Julia Kristeva, *Le Texte du roman* (The Hague: Mouton, 1976), 12. As my analysis

of this passage unfolds, the reader may feel that I am placing undue emphasis on this particular formulation concerning textuality. Allow me to point out, however, that Kristeva would appear to encourage such emphasis since she publishes this formulation four different times, repeating it nearly verbatim and following a generative procedure that is comparable to that of Raymond Roussel, the writer she discusses at length in "La productivité dite texte." See the following additional sources: Kristeva, "The Bounded Text," in *Desire and Language*, ed. Leon Roudiez (New York: Columbia UP, 1980), 36; Kristeva, "Problèmes de la stucturation du texte," *Théorie d'ensemble* (Paris: Editions du Seuil, 1968), 299; Kristeva, "Prolegomenon," *Revolution in Poetic Language*, trans. Margaret Waller (New York: Columbia UP, 1984), 16.

3   On this issue see the just cited essay of Kristeva's, "Problèmes de la structuration du texte," where in its opening pages she draws upon Louis Althusser's distinction between "real objects" (empirical) and "objects of knowledge" (theoretical) in order to designate *the text* as the "object of knowledge" that should organize the analysis of literary discourse.

4   Karl Marx and Frederick Engels, *The German Ideology*, ed. C. J. Arthur (New York: International Publishers, 1973), 50–51.

5   Julia Kristeva, *Revolution in Poetic Language*, trans. Margaret Waller (New York: Columbia UP, 1984), 16–17.

6   Jean Baudrillard, *The Mirror of Production*, trans. Mark Poster (St. Louis: Telos P, 1975). It is worth pointing out in the present context that in this book Baudrillard attacks Kristeva for at once acknowledging that Marx's notion of production is limited, while remaining faithful to the problematic it enabled Marx to delineate, namely, the critique of the political economy of capitalism. The pertinence of Baudrillard's critique is vitiated by the fact, made abundantly clear in his more recent work, that his rejection of Marx's problematic has led to an utter depoliticization of cultural criticism. See in particular Baudrillard's interview, in *Thesis Eleven* (1984), 166–70.

7   Some of the more interesting recent commentaries are Kaja Silverman, *The Acoustic Mirror* (Bloomington: Indiana UP, 1988); Toril Moi, *Sexual/Textual Politics* (London: Metheun, 1985); Alice Jardine, *Gynesis* (Ithaca: Cornell UP, 1985); and Teresa de Lauretis, *Alice Doesn't* (Bloomington: Indiana UP, 1984).

8   Kristeva, *Revolution in Poetic Language*, 30.

9   Kristeva, *Revolution in Poetic Language*, 105.

10   Kristeva, *Revolution in Poetic Language*, 59–60.

11   Kristeva, *Revolution in Poetic Language*, 186.

12   Kristeva, *Revolution in Poetic Language*, 87.

13   Kristeva, *Revolution in Poetic Language*, 26.

## 5   *The Text* tel quel: *Barthes's Pleasure*

1   Roland Barthes, *Critical Essays*, trans. Richard Howard (Evanston: Northwestern UP, 1972), 214.

2   Roland Barthes, *Sade/Fourier/Loyola*, trans. Richard Miller (New York: Hill and Wang, 1976), 3.

3   Perhaps the most obvious indication of Kristeva's direct influence on Barthes is his "Theory of the Text" from the *Encyclopaedia Universalis*, translated by Ian McLeod in Robert Young, *Untying the Text* (London: Routledge, Kegan Paul, 1981), 31–

47. There, in "defining" (strictly speaking) the notion of the text, Barthes presents Kristeva's innovations as virtually synonymous with textuality—even to the point of utterly subordinating his own. There are numerous examples, of course, where Barthes openly borrows from Kristeva in the elaboration of his "own" analyses. See Roland Barthes, "The Grain of the Voice," *Image, Music, Text*, ed. and trans. Stephen Heath (New York: Hill and Wang, 1977), 179–189. In addition, Barthes's review of Kristeva's *Semeiotiké* in *The Rustle of Language*, trans. Richard Howard (New York: Hill and Wang, 1986), 168–171, is also revealing. Barthes's relation to Derrida is more oblique. Nevertheless, Derrida's influence is legible in the texture of an essay like "Mythology Today," where Barthes deconstructs the object of semiology in a way that mimicks Derrida's critique of Saussure in *Of Grammatology*. Moreover, Barthes explicitly refers to Derrida as one of his "creditors" in an early interview with Raymond Bellour. See Raymond Bellour, *Le Livre des autres* (Paris: Union Générale d'Editions, 1978), 222.

4    Barthes, *Image, Music, Text*, 164.

5    Roland Barthes, *Roland Barthes by Roland Barthes*, trans. Richard Howard (New York: Hill and Wang, 1977), 51. The reader might also fruitfully consult pages 127–129, where Barthes characterizes his predilection for words that fit into binary oppositions.

6    Barthes, *Image, Music, Text*, 163–164.

7    See, as a later formulation of this pleasure, Roland Barthes, *The Rustle of Language*, 38–41.

8    Barthes, *The Rustle of Language*, 100–105.

9    Young, *Untying the Text*, 38.

10   Barthes, *Sade/Fourier/Loyola*, 7–8.

11   Barthes, *Sade/Fourier/Loyola*, 8–9.

12   Roland Barthes, *The Pleasure of the Text*, trans. Richard Miller (New York: Hill and Wang, 1975), 59.

13   Barthes, *The Pleasure of the Text*, 62.

14   Barthes, *The Rustle of Language*, 348–349.

15   Barthes, *The Pleasure of the Text*, 60.

16   Barthes, *The Pleasure of the Text*, 30–31.

17   Barthes, *Roland Barthes by Roland Barthes*, 79.

18   Guy Hocquenghem, *Homosexual Desire*, trans. Daniella Dangoor (London: Allison and Busby, 1978). See chapter 4, "Capitalism, the Family, and the Anus," in particular.

19   Barthes, *Roland Barthes by Roland Barthes*, 69.

20   Alice Jardine has attempted to theorize these issues by drawing on the notion of "gynesis." Though it is much too rigorous a contribution to sort through in detail here, Jardine's term seeks explicitly to capture the heterotopic space of gender formation in a manner that outdistances many of the current discourse-oriented accounts. Specifically, Jardine tries to grasp how gender identity develops without presupposing the sexed (and presumably precultural) body as the organizational index. Her debt to Kristeva is enormous. See *Gynesis*, 114–116.

21   Laclau and Mouffe, *Hegemony and Socialist Strategy*, 134–148.

22   This characterization of Derrida's early work may strike the reader as odd, but I remind him/her of Derrida's formulation in "Structure, Sign, and Play in the Discourse of the Human Sciences," where he explicitly argues that the grammatological decen-

tering of Western ethnography carried out implicitly by Claude Levi-Strauss (and explicitly by him) was conditioned by the anticolonial struggles that have contested and reversed European hegemony throughout the twentieth century. See Derrida, *Writing and Difference*, 282. Homi Bhabha's critique of this material in "The Other Question: Difference, Discrimination, and the Discourse of Colonialism," *Literature, Politics and Theory*, ed. Francis Barker et al. (London: Methuen and Co., 1986), 148–172, while forceful, is also flawed. In showing that cultural difference has become a "presence" within deconstruction, Bhabha seems more interested in locating a disabling contradiction in Derrida's project, than in telling us what a cultural hermeneutics that is in deep dialogue with Western critical theory ought to look like in order to "know" the specificity of non-Western others. Also in this regard consider the way Derrida aligns his project with the anticolonial struggles of the people of Vietnam in the opening of his paper, "The Ends of Man." Derrida, *Margins of Philosophy*, 111–114. See as well, "Racism's Last Word," *Critical Inquiry* 12, no. 1 (1985): 290–299. Though one might always wish to accuse Derrida of "opportunism" for such gestures, doing so should not be used as an alibi for refusing to confront his work. What I have sketched here is a perspective that allows us to examine how, to use the vocabulary of "dependency theory," crises at the periphery might articulate themselves in their nonindigenous specificity within the core. In this sense the text as an antidisciplinary field is no less a modality of anticolonialism than is Frantz Fanon's francophone (published by Editions Maspero in Paris) *A Dying Colonialism*. See my "Algerian Nation: Fanon's Fetish," *Cultural Critique* (forthcoming). Whatever the failings of such an endeavor, I think it better to avoid overlooking the historical specificity that Derrida and others are continually accused of denying, than to rely on such oversight in order better to enumerate the errors of an opportunism that applies just as readily, though in another register, to the tabulators themselves.

### 6 The Textual Analysis of Film

1 This movement and its relation to the work of Christian Metz in particular has been carefully documented in Edward Lowry, *The Filmology Movement and Film Study in France* (Ann Arbor: UMI Research P, 1985).

2 Some of the foundational statements on "auteur theory" are contained in *Movies and Methods I*, ed. Bill Nichols (Berkeley: U California P, 1976), 224–250. Bazin's relation to this position is thoroughly discussed in Dudley Andrew, *André Bazin* (New York: Oxford UP, 1978), 187–93. For a discussion of the model of subjectivity latent within the notion of an auteur, see Jean-Louis Baudry, "Author and Analyzable Subject," *Apparatus*, ed. Theresa Hak Kyung Cha (New York: Tanam P, 1980), 67–84.

3 Christian Metz, *Language and Cinema*, trans. Donna Jean Umiker-Sebeok (The Hague: Mouton, 1974), 88.

4 Thierry Kuntzel, "Le Défilement: A View in Closeup," *Apparatus*, 233–248.

5 Metz, *Language and Cinema*, 101–103.

6 Christian Metz, *The Imaginary Signifier*, trans. Celia Britton, Annwyl Williams, Ben Brewster, and Alfred Guzzetti (Bloomington: Indiana UP, 1982), 29–31.

7 Metz, *The Imaginary Signifier*, 191–93. Here Metz criticizes Marie-Claire Ropars's discussion of metaphor in *October* by arguing that a "textual" reading which problematizes the opposition between metaphor and metonymy undermines the category

of the diegetic. Underlying what turns out to be a relatively gentle criticism, is Metz's concern that analysts know when and where to draw the line between what is germaine to the fictive space of the narrative and what is germaine to the discourse of the film. Of course, with such knowledge secured one can also better preserve the distinction between a film and its reading—a distinction Metz knows that Ropars's version of textual analysis is explicitly seeking to challenge.

8   Raymond Bellour, *Le livre des autres* (Paris: Union Générale d'Editions, 1978), 239–287.

9   Raymond Bellour and Janet Bergstrom, "Alternation, Segmentation, Hypnosis: An Interview with Raymond Bellour," *Camera Obscura* 3–4 (1979): 84–85.

10  Raymond Bellour, "The Unattainable Text," *Screen* 16 3 (1975): 19–20. Also, "Le texte introuvable," *L'analyse du film* (Paris: Editions Albatros, 1979), 35–36.

11  Raymond Bellour, *L'Analyse du film*, 124–125.

12  Roland Barthes, "The Third Meaning," *Image, Music, Text*, trans. Stephen Heath (New York: Hill and Wang, 1977), 56–65. Incidentally, in this essay Barthes underscores the importance of the relation between textuality and citation in a way that would appear to invite Bellour's reading. See page 67 in particular.

13  Raymond Bellour, "Thierry Kuntzel and the Return of Writing," trans. Annwyl Williams, *Camera Obscura* 11 (1983): 29–59. Significantly, this essay first appeared in *Cahiers du cinéma*.

14  Bellour, *L'Analyse du film*, 29–30.

15  Jacques Lacan, *Ecrits: A Selection*, trans. Alan Sheridan (New York: W. W. Norton, 1977), 250–256. Also, see Jacques Lacan, *The Four Fundamental Concepts of Psychoanalysis*, trans. Alan Sheridan (New York: W. W. Norton, 1982).

16  For an excellent example of this scholarship, see Nancy K. Miller, "Arachnologies: The Woman, the Text, the Critic," *The Poetics of Gender*, ed. Nancy K. Miller (New York: Cornell UP, 1986), 270–295.

17  Jean-Louis Baudry, "The Apparatus," *Apparatus*, 41–66.

18  Dana Polan, " 'Desire Shifts the Differance': Figural Poetics and Figural Politics in the Film Theory of Marie-Claire Ropars," *Camera Obscura* 12 (1984): 67–85.

19  Marie-Claire Ropars, *L'Ecran de la mémoire* (Paris: Editions du Seuil, 1970), 224. Unless otherwise noted, this and all other translations from Ropars's work are my own.

20  Marie-Claire Ropars, *De la littérature au cinéma* (Paris: Librairie Armand Colin, 1970). See chapter 4 in its entirety.

21  This point is clarified by Lowry's discussion of Ayfre in *The Filmology Movement and Film Study in France*, 69–70.

22  Marie-Claire Ropars, "The Graphic in Filmic Writing: *A bout de souffle* or the Erratic Alphabet," *enclitic* 5:2/6:1 (1982): 149. In analyzing Godard's film, Ropars feels authorized to read the mere appearance of a copy of *Cahiers du cinéma* as a metonymic figure for auteur theory.

23  Claude Bailblé, Michel Marie, and Marie-Claire Ropars, *Muriel: histoire d'une recherche* (Paris: Editions Galilée, 1974), 321–322.

24  Marie-Claire Ropars, "*Muriel* as Text," *Film Reader* 3 (1978): 262. I have only slightly modified this translation of the lecture in the interest of legibility.

25  Ropars, "*Muriel* as Text," 262.

26  Marie-Claire Ropars, *Le texte divisé* (Paris: Presses Universitaires de France, 1981), 9.

27  Ropars, *Le texte divisé*, 73.

28   Ropars, *Le texte divisé*, 150–154. Also see, Ropars, "The Graphic in Film Writing," 147–161.

29   Ropars, *Le texte divisé*, 122.

30   Marie-Claire Ropars, "Film Reader of the Text," trans. Kimball Lockheart, *Diacritics* 14, no. 2 (1984): 18.

31   Marie-Claire Ropars, "The Disembodied Voice (*India Song*)," *Yale French Studies* 60 (1980): 249.

**7**   *Toward the Textual Analysis of Music*

1    Claude Lévi-Strauss, *The Raw and the Cooked*, trans. John and Doreen Weightman (New York: Harper Torchbooks, 1970), v. See also, Claude Lévi-Strauss, *Myth and Meaning* (New York: Schocken Books, 1979), 44–54. Here Lévi-Strauss discusses at some length the points about musical meaning I am presenting.

2    The scandalousness of such an assertion concerning serial music is spelled out convincingly by Susan McClary in "Terminal Prestige: The Case of Avant-Garde Musical Composition," *Cultural Critique* 12 (1989): 57–81.

3    Célestin Deliège, "La Musicologie devant le structuralisme," *L'Arc* 26 (1965): 50–59.

4    Only a few of the book-length studies of either Jean-Jacques Nattiez or Nicolas Ruwet have been translated into English. See Jean-Jacques Nattiez, *Fondements d'une sémiologie de la musique* (Paris: Union Générale d'Editions, 1975); *Music and Discourse: Toward a Semiology of Music*, trans. Carolyn Abbate (Princeton: Princeton UP, 1990); and *Proust as Musician*, trans. Derrick Puffett (Cambridge: Cambridge UP, 1989), as well as his articles: "Is a Descriptive Semiotics of Music Possible? *Language Sciences* 23 (1972): 1–7; "The Concepts of Plot and Seriation Process in Musical Analysis," *Music Analysis* 4, no. 1/2 (1985): 107–118; and "Varèse's *Density 21.5*: A Study in Semiological Analysis," *Music Analysis* 1, no. 3 (1982): 243–340. Also see Nicolas Ruwet, *Langage, musique, poésie* (Paris: Editions du Seuil, 1972), as well as his articles: "Musicology and linguistics," *International Social Science Journal* 19, no. 1 (1967): 79–87, and "Methods of Analysis in Musicology," *Music Analysis* 6, no. 1/2 (1987): 11–36.

5    See, for example, Nattiez's discussion in *Fondements*, 38–44.

6    Daniel Charles, "L'écriture et le silence," *Musique en jeu* 11 (1973): 99–108, and "La musique et l'écriture," *Musique en jeu* 13 (1973): 3–13. Surprisingly, Attali makes no mention of this material in his book.

7    Charles, "La musique et l'écriture," 13.

8    Charles, "L'écriture et le silence," 106.

9    Ivanka Stoïanova, *Geste, Texte, Musique* (Paris: Union Générale d'Editions, 1978), 10.

10   Julia Kristeva, *Language the Unknown: An Initiation into Linguistics*, trans. Anne Menke (New York: Columbia UP, 1989), 308–311.

11   Julia Kristeva, *Revolution in Poetic Language*, trans. Margaret Waller (New York: Columbia UP, 1984), 63.

12   Stoïanova, *Geste, Texte, Musique*, 24.

13   See Ruwet, "Methods of Analysis in Musicology," passim.

14   Ivanka Stoïanova, "La musique répétitive." *Musique en jeu* 26 (1977): 71.

15   For a sampling of work in both the popular and the repertory traditions, see Richard Leppert and Susan McClary, *Music and Society: The Politics of Composition, Per-*

*formance and Reception* (Cambridge: Cambridge UP, 1987), as well as Simon Frith and Andrew Goodwin, *On Record: Rock, Pop and the Written Word* (New York: Pantheon Books, 1990). For a relatively recent book that somewhat cautiously makes reference to the notion of musical textuality, see Alan Durant, *Conditions of Music* (Albany: State University of New York P, 1986).

16  See Marie-Claire Ropars-Wuilleumier, Pierre Sorlin, and Michèle Lagny, *Octobre: Ecriture et Idéologie* (Paris: Editions Albatros, 1976). It is also worth noting here that in the most systematic attempt in recent years to theorize narrative film music, the score for *Alexander Nevsky* is mentioned only in passing. See Claudia Gorbman, *Unheard Melodies: Narrative Film Music* (Bloomington: Indiana UP, 1987), 117. This is particularly surprising because Gorbman is not only acutely aware of the discussion around filmic textuality, but she devotes an entire chapter to Eisler and Adorno's discussion of film music, a discussion which addresses Eisenstein's "self-analysis" at some length and which raises criticisms that resonate with my own. Also, in the only other sustained analysis of the Eisenstein/Prokofiev collaboration (specifically on *Ivan the Terrible*), though a great deal is said of the music/image relation, too much energy is spent demonstrating that Prokofiev was not the "Russian Max Steiner," rather than examining the cultural work performed through the semiotic emplacement of the musical soundtrack as such. See the otherwise excellent study of Kristin Thompson, *Eisenstein's Ivan the Terrible: A Neoformalist Analysis* (Princeton: Princeton UP, 1981), 203–260.

17  The film opens with an encounter between what is called the "Mongolian Host" and a group of Russian fisherpeople which includes Alexander. The Mongolian leader is seeking to enlist Alexander's help in the former's campaign against enemies at home and abroad. Alexander declines, and though this possible future threat is mentioned again later in the dialogue, Alexander's decision effectively seals the film around the binary antagonism between Russia and the Teutonic knights. An alternative ending to the film which reintroduced this material, complete with a supplemental rout of the Mongols, was dropped. See *Eisenstein: Three Films*, ed. Jay Leyda (New York: Harper and Row, 1974), 182–186.

18  "Enunciation" is a linguistic term borrowed by film analysis, particularly in France, where it refers to the production of the relation between form and content at the level of the shots comprising any specific film. This level of analysis is precisely what is underdeveloped in a reading of *Nevsky* that otherwise shares much with my own. See Leon Balter, M.D., "*Alexander Nevsky*," *Film Culture* 70–71 (1983): 43–87.

19  Sergei Eisenstein, *Notes of a Film Director*, trans. X. Danko (New York: Dover Publications, 1970), 43–52.

20  Leyda, *Eisenstein: Three Films*, 121. There is a variant version of the folktale that appears in the script, but the one that actually appears in the film is the one quoted here. In any case the proairetic structure of entrapment remains constant.

21  It is worth noting here that Eisenstein was quite taken with this figure of the entrapped wedge. In "Alexander Nevsky" (*Notes of a Film Director*, 32–43) where Eisenstein lays out the historical details motivating his script, he refers, in a confidently objective tone, to the "terrible, invincible wedge formation," in which the Teutons "actually" attacked. Moreover, in response to the agreement in 1944 between the U.S.S.R. and Great Britain to oppose Germany, Eisenstein wrote an article for *Kino* entitled, "Hitler Squeezed in the Pincers," making explicit the articulation of the allegory organizing

*Alexander Nevsky*. This evocation of the "pincer" also appeared in "Ways of True Invention," where it is openly associated with the battle on the lake (*Notes of a Film Director*, 44).

22   See, "Form and Content: Practice" in Sergei Esenstein, *Film Sense*, trans. Jay Leyda (New York: Harcourt, Brace Jovanovich, 1970), 155–216. The other two pieces of this essay are also included in this volume: part 1, "The Synchronization of the Senses" (67–109), and part 2, "Color and Meaning" (111–153).

23   Eisenstein, *Film Sense*, 163–64.

24   Hans Eisler and Theodor Adorno, *Composing for the Films* (New York: Oxford UP, 1947), 62–88.

25   Sergei Eisenstein, *Film Form*, trans. Jay Leyda (New York: Harcourt, Brace, Jovanovich, 1970), 258. This essay and its importance for Eisenstein's film practice is interestingly discussed in Kristin Thompson, "Early Sound Counterpoint," *Yale French Studies* 60 (1980): 115–140. Surprisingly, in spite of the obvious borrowing of "counterpoint" from musicology, Thompson says very little about the status of music in early sound films—not all of which lacked scores.

26   In responding to the early reviews of *Alexander Nevsky* sent to him by Leyda, Eisenstein complained that they did not emphasize strongly enough the way the "unity" of sound and image in the film represented a realization of his dreams. See, Jay Leyda, *Kino: A History of the Russian and Soviet Film* (Princeton: Princeton UP, 1973), 350.

27   Eisenstein, *Film Sense*, 158–159. Here Eisenstein describes how he was obliged to construct some prop instruments in order to provide Prokofiev with a cue for the introduction of the rout fanfare. The best general discussion of this collaboration appears in Douglas Gallez, "The Prokofiev-Eisenstein Collaboration: *Nevsky* and *Ivan* Revisited," *Cinema Journal* 17, no. 2 (1978), 13–35.

28   Sergei Prokofiev, *Prokofiev: Autobiography, Articles, Reminiscences*, ed. S. Shlifstein, trans. R. Prokofieva (Moscow, no date), 114.

29   Eisenstein, *Notes of a Film Director*, 148.

30   Eisenstein, *Notes of a Film Director*, 149.

31   Eisenstein, *Notes of a Film Director*, 158.

32   Eisenstein, *Notes of a Film Director*, 159.

33   Eisler and Adorno, *Composing for the Films*, 66–67. See also Sergei Eisenstein, *Eisenstein on Disney*, trans. Alan Y. Upchurch (London: Methuen Paperbacks, 1985), passim.

34   In this context it is important to direct readers to another extended discussion of Eisenstein's on music. See Sergei Eisenstein, *Non-Indifferent Nature*, trans. Herbert Marshall (Cambridge: Cambridge UP, 1987). Here, in the title essay, Eisenstein discusses the transition from silent to sound film, spelling out the way landscape was used in silent film as a "musical" signifier. This discussion has obvious resonances with this particular moment in the sequence where two different approaches to the relation between music and images are, in effect, superimposed.

35   Eisenstein, *Notes of a Film Director*, 118. It is worth pointing out here that Eisenstein makes this point in reference to his earlier "Statement" on sound film, which, I would argue, his current practice contradicted.

36   Sergei Eisenstein, *Eisenstein 2*, trans. Alan Y. Upchurch (London: Methuen Paperbacks, 1985), 14–20. The reader might also usefully consult "Lessons from Literature,"

in Sergei Eisenstein, *Film Essays and a Lecture*, trans. Jay Leyda (Princeton: Princeton UP, 1982), 77–83.

37    Though it may seem anachronistic to speak of a "discipline" of film studies in this context, it is important to remember that Eisenstein actually taught film theory and production at the Soviet Cinema Institute throughout much of his career. For Eisenstein's observations about his activities as a teacher and Institute administrator, see Eisenstein, *Film Essays and a Lecture*, 66–77. There is no doubt that Eisenstein had "disciples" and that he was regarded as a master of a specific object of knowledge. One needs only to consult Samuel Beckett's application to the Institute to have this confirmed. See, Eisenstein, *Eisenstein 2*, 59. In addition, one might also usefully consult Vladimir Nizhny's *Lessons with Eisenstein* (New York: Da Capo Press, 1979), where the Eisensteinian approach is presented as virtually synonymous with filmmaking as such.

## 8    Conclusion: Textual Politics

1    Those troubled by the suggestion that disciplines reach even into the "popular" reception of films might usefully consult the entry on *Alexander Nevsky* in Leonard Maltin's bestselling, *TV Movies and Video Guide*: "Epic tale of Cherkassov and Russian army repelling German invasion during 13th century, a disturbing parallel to world situation at time of production. Magnificently visualized battle sequences, wonderful Prokofiev score. A masterpiece" (p. 14, 1988 edition). As a widely circulated encyclopedic extension of the weekly, *TV Guide*, Maltin's book generates an interpretive context ("epic," "disturbing parallel," "magnificently visualized," "wonderful . . . score," "masterpiece") that orients a private home screening of the film in much the same direction that does the "academic" literature on the film. One should not be surprised, however, since Maltin was a member of the faculty at the New School for Social Research (NYC) for nine years.

2    In fact the struggle over Prokofiev's status within musicology and the Western concert repertory has already begun. Writing in response to Kurt Masur's presentation of the Nevsky cantata in San Francisco last year, Richard Taruskin (a musicologist at the University of California-Berkeley) moved aggressively to bid farewell to Prokofiev, arguing that despite his mastery of modulation and other talents, his later work (including his collaborations with Eisenstein) was so tainted by Stalinism that it deserved to be forgotten. In the flurry of letters that followed, few readers chose to contest Taruskin's basic assumption, namely, that music carries a political charge. Instead, efforts were made to challenge his conclusions. What this implies, of course, is that music—even so-called serious music—is no longer understood to embody the quintessentially formalist traits of the still widely influential positivist musicological paradigm. Significantly though, none of the parties to this debate sought to advance their positions in these terms, and this despite the fact that one of the two images accompanying Taruskin's article was a photomontage worked up from a still from *Alexander Nevsky* where the "conquerors" of the sound film (Eisenstein, Tisse, and Prokofiev) are posed in a triadic grouping. The version of this image that appears in the film is one where the surviving hero, Vasili, is flanked by both his new warrior bride, Vasilisa, and his mother. In the still, Prokofiev's face is mounted over the mother's. All of which is to say that the interdisciplinary and intratextual tensions that inflect

the music and which ought therefore to be part of any careful political evaluation of the film score are systematically overlooked in this quarrel. Before we make any decisions about the cantata, it would seem prudent to develop some kind of framework within which the various political forces operating within and around the piece can be gauged. See Richard Taruskin, "Prokofiev, Hail . . . and Farewell," *New York Times* (Sunday, April 21, 1991), H25 and 32. The letters from readers (including John Simon) appeared in the *New York Times* (Sunday, May 12, 1991). Thanks to Susan McClary for sharing these materials with me.

3    As a typical example, one might consult Richard Bernstein's review, "Academic Left Finds the Far Reaches of Postmodernism," from the *New York Times* (April 8, 1990), E5. A considerably more articulate, though no less conservative, version of these issues appears in Roger Kimball, *Tenured Radicals: How Politics has Corrupted Higher Education* (New York: Harper and Row, 1990). The managing editor of Hilton Kramer's *New Criterion*, Kimball writes regular articles for the journal all of which repeat, with a certain amount of stylistic gusto, his basic claim that the cultural legitimations for American world hegemony are being undermined by academics who are too preoccupied with "political" issues and critical theory to do any effective teaching of America's young. For Kimball's perspective on academic conferences, see Roger Kimball, "The Periphery vs. the Center: The MLA in Chicago," *The New Criterion* 9, no. 6 (1991): 8–17. Of course, the most controversial analysis of the politics of postsecondary education is Dinesh D'Souza's *Illiberal Education: The Politics of Race and Sex on Campus* (New York: Free Press, 1991). Unlike Kimball, whose conservatism lacks color, D'Souza has toured widely on the campus lecture circuit and has appeared on the *MacNeil/Lehrer News Hour* to spread the word. His book, perhaps even more than the exertions of the National Association of Scholars, has functioned to strip the initials "p c" of their technological denotation, "personal computer," replacing it with the political denotation, "political correctness," which—as Barthes would have been among the first to point out—is shadowed by the mirrored connotation of "c p" or "communist party."

4    William Bennett, "To Reclaim a Legacy: Text of Report on Humanities in Education," *Chronicle of Higher Education* 29, no. 14 (November 1984), 16–21.

5    Harvey C. Mansfield, Jr., who replaced the highly controversial Carol Iannone as the administration's nominee for the advisory council of the NEH, is quoted in the *Chronicle of Higher Education* for October 16, 1991, as saying that the principles laid down in the Constitution have "lately come to be menaced by the increasing democratization of politics" (A5). His remedy is, presumably, to save America's constitutional soul by resorting to the sort of authoritarianism that Jeanne Kirkpatrick once vainly struggled to distinguish from the so-called totalitarian regimes that have, of late, discovered their Ego Ideals in us.

6    Walter Benjamin, "Theses on the Philosophy of History," *Illuminations*, trans. Harry Zohn (New York: Schocken Books, 1969), 262–263.

John Mowitt is Associate Professor of Cultural Studies and
Comparative Literature and English at the University of
Minnesota.

Library of Congress Cataloging-in-Publication Data
Mowitt, John, 1952–
Text : the genealogy of an antidisciplinary object / John
Mowitt.
p.   cm.—(Post-contemporary interventions)
Includes index.
ISBN 0-8223-1251-4 (alk. paper).—ISBN 0-8223-1273-5
(pbk. : alk. paper)
1. Criticism—History—20th century.   2. Criticism,
Textual.
I. Title. II. Series.
PN94.M68 1992
801.95'09045—dc20   92-11618 CIP